WILD HORSE COUNTRY

BY THE SAME AUTHOR

Lethal Warriors

WILD HORSE COUNTRY

THE HISTORY, MYTH, AND FUTURE

OF THE MUSTANG

DAVID PHILIPPS

W. W. NORTON & COMPANY

Independent Publishers Since 1923

New York | London

Copyright © 2017 by David Philipps

For information about permission to reproduce selections from this book, write to
Permissions, W. W. Norton & Company, Inc., 500 Fifth Avenue, New York, NY 10110

For information about special discounts for bulk purchases, please contact
W. W. Norton Special Sales at specialsales@wwnorton.com or 800-233-4830

Manufacturing by Quad Graphics, Fairfield
Book design by Chris Welch Design
Production manager: Julia Druskin

Library of Congress Cataloging-in-Publication Data

Names: Philipps, David, author.
Title: Wild horse country : the history, myth, and future of the mustang / David Philipps.
Description: First edition. | New York : W. W. Norton & Company, 2017. | Includes bibli-
ographical references and index.
Identifiers: LCCN 2017018261 | ISBN 9780393247138 (hardcover)
Subjects: LCSH: Mustang.
Classification: LCC SF293.M9 P45 2017 | DDC 636.1/3—dc23
LC record available at https://lccn.loc.gov/2017018261

ISBN 978-0-393-35622-9 pbk.

W. W. Norton & Company, Inc.
500 Fifth Avenue, New York, N.Y. 10110
www.wwnorton.com

W. W. Norton & Company Ltd.
15 Carlisle Street, London W1D 3BS

1 2 3 4 5 6 7 8 9 0

For Whitman and Frost, who were born wild and free

No one who conceives him only as a potential servant

to man can apprehend the mustang. The true conceiver

must be a lover of freedom—a person who yearns to extend

freedom to all life.

—J. FRANK DOBIE

Contents

Wild Horse Country

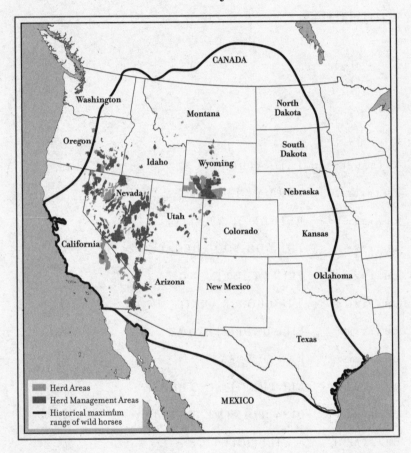

THE GATHER

Just after dawn on a frigid January morning, I clambered to the top of a coffee-colored rock spine rising a hundred feet above the gray floor of a broad bowl of sage and alkali dust called Sand Springs Valley and looked out across an unbroken expanse of nothing. Legions of gray brush spread out for miles toward dark mountains that against the brightening dawn looked like a dark tear across the winter sky. What was out here? Beyond the fog of my breath, not much.

Sand Springs is one of those rare scraps of American West that has changed little since the glaciers receded. There are no towns, no houses, not even a shack. I saw no fences, no power lines, no road signs, no roads. There were no blinking antenna spires, no cell towers, not even really a tree. All the bars on my cell phone had long since disappeared and the radio was static. Most of the mountains fencing in the valley were not just unvisited but nameless. I had bumped in on a dirt road that had turned to a gravelly track, then eventually shrunk to two ruts. Brush screeched along the belly of my truck and the smell of crushed sage under tires rose up as thick as incense. It was the kind of place where, if you broke down, you could wait days for help before deciding just to walk out on your own.

I was in the middle of Nevada, in the heart of a region known as the Great Basin—a vast accordion of long valleys and jagged mountain ranges that runs down the interior of the West, through Oregon, Idaho, Nevada, Utah, Arizona, and a sliver of eastern California. On a map, the long valleys look as if the center of the nation had been hastily ironed into pleats. The Great Basin is some of the driest country in North America, and the emptiest. It gets its name from the fact that creeks and rivers here never reach the sea. They either sink into the sandy sage or run out onto salt flats where the ever-present sun dries their modest flow into a shimmering white alkaline crust. Locals like to say that what the West once was, the Great Basin still is: open range, cattle rustlers, ghost towns, gold mines, and land so seamless you want to reach out and touch it to make sure it is not just a painted backdrop behind John Wayne.

When I reached the top of the rock outcrop, it was just after 7 a.m. and 19 degrees. The only man-made thing I could see in the vast sweep of hundreds of square miles of desert was some pink plastic tape—the type surveyors use. It had been stretched roughly into a rectangle the size of a walk-in closet along the uneven rocks on top of the spine. And I had been told to stand in it, and not to step out.

Standing next to me was a federal law enforcement agent with a pistol on his hip. He was tall, with thick forearms that he kept folded, and he wore inscrutable dark sunglasses even though the sun had not yet come up. Next to him was a public affairs officer from the Bureau of Land Management (BLM): a somewhat pudgy, smiling man with gray hair and what looked like a twenty-year-old Thermos that he kept constantly unscrewing to pour tiny cups of coffee for himself. The law enforcement agent's job was to make sure I stayed in the ribbon. The public affairs officer's job was to answer any questions about it.

As we waited for the sunrise to warm us, I asked him why, in such a remote place, we needed to stand within the ribbon.

For my safety, and the safety of the operation, he told me, never dimming his smile.

"What would happen if I stepped out of the ribbon?"

"The ribbon is here for you and you need to stay in it," he said.

"But couldn't we just move a little outside the ribbon, to a slightly better spot on the rock?" We were, after all, in the middle of nowhere. Who would know?

The law enforcement agent, who had not said more than a few words since I had met him a half hour earlier, slowly shook his head and said, "Just stay in the ribbon."

So we all stood inside the ribbon. I wiggled my toes in my boots to keep them warm and looked out at the sweep of the valley. I was there for one reason. I had always wanted to see wild horses. And this was the place to do it. As the first sunlight spilled into the valley, I raised my binoculars and peered out into the distance. Miles away, I saw them. A string of eight dots running. So small they looked like no more than ants in the vast valley, but so fast that they could be nothing else.

Wild horses! Just saying the words sets off a stampede of images: echoing box canyons and dusty blue mesas, hooves flying through golden grass, the defiant scream of a rearing stallion, heat waves rippling the distance, speed and strength and cliffs and cactus and dust and grit, lonely places where big empty skies define the day and coyote songs define the night, wild places forever beyond the grip of civilization.

Wild horses! Even if you have never seen one, chances are if you grew up in the United States you know what they mean. They are freedom. They are independence. They are the ragtag misfits defying incredible odds. They are the lowborn outsiders whose nobility springs from the adversity of living a simple life. In short, they are American. Or at least they are what we tell ourselves we are, and what we aspire to be. If you think I'm laying it on a little thick, consider this: There are only two animals for which the United States Congress has ever specifically passed laws to protect from harm. The first was the bald eagle. The second was the wild horse.

And yes, unusual as it sounds, the United States still has wild horses. Real wild horses. Not just a few relics carefully curated in a national park, but tens of thousands. They roam free, cared for by no one and controlled by no one, nearly as wild as the deer and the antelope. Even in the twenty-first century, when the wild is steadily disappearing, wild horses are not just surviving, but thriving. They are expanding. What a wonderful and strange thing.

Today wild horses still roam on more than thirty-one million acres in parts of ten western states. But few people will ever see one, because wild horses generally live where we do not—the empty spots on the map, remote scraps of the country too dry or rocky or hot or all-of-the-above to be of much use. They once roamed the whole West from the Great Plains to the Pacific, but they have been driven to the sharp angled remnants of the West where there is still room for things to be wild: Rimrock. Cedar breaks. Salt flats. Shale barrens. Almost any unwanted scrap where open space reigns and order and fences are scarce, you will find them. Badlands. Sage flats. Even nuclear test sites and bombing ranges. These are the parts of America most people only see from plastic airline portholes at thirty thousand feet, where gradually the land shrivels and the grid of roads breaks down until it is just mountains and canyons crossed by a few lonesome strands of highway. Almost all of it is located in the dry bowl of land between the Rocky Mountains and the Sierra Nevada. This collective group of relatively pristine remnants goes by many names. On my repeated visits I began to refer to it simply as Wild Horse Country.

Wild Horse Country is almost all desert. Distance and aridity rule. Little has fundamentally changed in the century since Mary Austin wrote in *The Land of Little Rain*, "There are hills, rounded, blunt, burned, squeezed up out of chaos, chrome and vermilion painted, aspiring to the snowline. Between the hills lie high level-looking plains full of intolerable sun glare, or narrow valleys drowned in a blue haze."

The official government names of designated wild horse ranges in Wild Horse Country give some taste of the landscape: Granite, Lava Beds, Slate Range, High Rock, Rocky Hills, Red Rocks, Sand Canyon, Sand Basin, Sand Springs, Black Mountain, Bald Mountain, Dead Mountain. Just reading them makes you thirsty. They are names that map the history of people who came looking for something and found only what a gray-haired curator with dirty bifocals at a one-room roadside Nevada history museum described to me as "nothing but miles and miles of miles and miles." They are names of want, failure, hideouts, last stands, and wind. Names of places that even the hardy homesteaders we learn about in school sized up and passed over: Stinking Water, Salt Wells, Rattlesnake, Dogskin. Cyclone Rim, Devil's Garden, Robbers Roost, Hard Trigger. Murderer's Creek, Deadman Valley, Confusion, Harvey's Fear.

It's not the land the horses chose. It is just the land that was left to choose. Hardscrabble islands of desiccated emptiness that herds were pushed into. Put together the patchwork where wild horses are found in the West and you have an area the size of Alabama. And a human population near zero.

Actual road signs I have seen on the way through:

NEXT GAS 167 MILES

DANGER CROSSWINDS 50 MPH +

CAUTION EAGLES ON HWY

That's Wild Horse Country. And yet, as Austin said of the desert, "Void of life it never is, however dry the air and villainous the soil."

The legend of the wild horse—all that stuff about freedom and toughness, which secured its place as an American icon? It is well deserved. Like nearly all Americans, the wild horse is an immigrant. And like many, it prospered through sheer grit. The herds on the land now are the descendants of the painted war ponies that allowed a few thousand native warriors to hold off the industrialized American army. They are also the descendants of the cavalry mounts that chased down Crazy Horse and cornered Geronimo. They are the descendants of the Pony Express runners that whisked messages from the Mississippi to San Francisco in ten days before the invention of the telegraph, and the cowboys' tireless sidekicks in the great cattle drives.

Somewhere back in time, they all descended from domestic horses, many of them of Spanish blood but likely as many or more from American stock. What you see on the range are ones that got away—the refugees, the outcasts, the fugitives. Their toughness is legend. One newspaper account from the early days of the California gold rush told of a mustang found trapped at the bottom of a dry well after twenty-two days—still doing fine. In San Francisco around the same time, a mustang rode five days straight during an endurance exhibition. In 1897, the United States Bureau of Animal Industry sponsored a 2,400-mile race from Sheridan, Wyoming, to Galena, Illinois. Any horse could enter. Two brothers caught wild mustangs, broke and saddled them, and, ninety-one days later— with no horseshoes and no grain—trotted across the finish line. The only survivor of Custer's Last Stand was a mustang named Comanche. He had been shot seven times, not counting an arrow wound from a previous battle. He lived for years afterward, developing a taste for whiskey in his old age.

"If I had my pick between a $1,000 Arabian steed and a common fuzztail," the cowboy and author Will James wrote a century ago,

"I'd much rather select the one with the snort and the buck, cause I know the trail between suns is never too long for him, no matter how scarce the feed and water may be."

Mustangs are the subject of hundreds of tales in pulp novels, movies, radio dramas, TV Westerns, and songs sung around the campfire. *Goodbye, old paint, I'm a-leavin' Cheyenne.* Sure, much of the history is just legend and myth, which has grown with the telling, but as I eventually learned in Wild Horse Country, legend and myth can have as much weight as fact.

Officially, the Sand Springs Valley, where I had gone to see wild horses, gets just over seven inches of rain a year. But on the ground, which is mostly rock and dust with low, thorny brush, it is hard to believe. There are no creeks or ponds. The terrain is so flinty and remote that NASA once tested a Mars Rover here. It is textbook Wild Horse Country. The Bureau of Land Management estimated that hundreds of horses roamed in the valley, but in the dawn light I saw nothing but a half-dozen distant dots. You would think a vast herd of horses would be easy to spot, especially with binoculars and a wide-open view of a treeless plain running for miles. But the West is not always what you think, especially when it comes to its wild horses.

Wild Horse Country is both harsh and intensely beautiful. The view can suddenly stop you in your tracks. The sun can flood an empty valley as clouds trail violet veils of rain that fall but never quite hit the ground. Canyons that feel like a tomb can, with one fresh mountain-lion print in the sand, seem suddenly alive and full of movement. The deserts of endless thorns and dust can suddenly break on a hidden spring where a quick step startles a whole congress of butterflies. The light can glint on rail-straight highways, making them shine like silver thread twenty miles long, connecting your boots to the distant horizon.

Like a lot of things that persist both in the present and in legend, Wild Horse Country is a heap of contradictions. The intermountain West is the emptiest part of the country and also the most urban. It is the most traditional and also the newest. Here ranches and strip malls are sometimes separated only by a few strands of barbed wire. The locals tend to see themselves as rugged individualists, and suspicion of the government runs deep, but no other place is under as much federal control or receives as much federal money. The situation with wild horses, too, is a contradiction. They are truly wild and directly descended from the herds of the old West. There is nothing phony about them. But they are tightly controlled by federal bureaucrats in Washington, DC, corralled by lawsuits and directed by sheafs of government impact statements. The riders that have the tightest hold on them are the riders in federal budget bills.

Wild Horse Country also occasionally contains rectangles of pink plastic tape. This is because nearly all wild horses—at least all those that are legally considered wild horses (I'll explain that part later)— are found on federal land and are controlled by the BLM, part of the Department of the Interior. Even though the BLM oversees 253 million acres of public land—roughly an eighth of the United States—I'm constantly running into people who don't know it exists. It is the agency that took control of the land no one had wanted after the federal government gave away land through the Homestead Act: valleys too dry to farm and mountains too scraggly to log. Almost all of the land is sandwiched between the Sierra Nevada and the Rockies. The harsher the climate, the more BLM land there is. Some desert counties in Nevada are 90 percent BLM land.

In 1971, Congress passed a law to protect wild horses. Since the BLM oversees so much unwanted land, and most wild horses live on the same unwanted land, it has fallen to the agency to oversee the horses, too. When I say "oversee," I mostly mean "remove." In an attempt to keep the horse population stable, the agency rounds up thousands of horses a year using helicopters that sweep across the desert and chase the herds into corrals, where they are trucked away and put in storage.

That is what I had come to see in the Sand Springs Valley. I wanted to know how it worked, why we do it, and how the horses fared. I also wanted to know what happened after the horses were trucked away. Helicopter roundups have been blasted by animal rights groups as cruel and unnecessary since they started in the 1970s. The BLM has continued, insisting it has little choice. I wanted to see firsthand if roundups were really so inhumane, and if there was any better way. That had brought me to this lonely rock spine where a roundup was about to begin.

Over the years, various animal rights groups have tried to shut down roundups. They have sued. They have blockaded. They have buzzed the area with an airplane. By the time I signed up to see the helicopters work in the Sand Springs Valley, roundups had grown so controversial that the agency had started limiting public viewing to a specific area. If I wanted to watch, I had to sign up to stand in the taped-off rectangle, presided over by an armed guard. I figured it was a small price to pay. But when I got there after driving about twelve hours, I realized the BLM had set up the rectangle in a place where part of the rock outcrop hid much of the roundup from view. I wouldn't be able to see the horses driven into the corral, or what happened afterward.

After spotting the first group of horses miles away through my binoculars, I lost them as they ran into a part of the valley hidden by the rock outcrop. I asked the public affairs officer if we could move out of the pink plastic tape again. He said no.

"Just a little, maybe up to the next rock?"

"No."

"Who is in charge? Maybe we could ask them?"

He explained that we had to stay where we were because if we moved closer to the corral, we would scare the horses.

"But aren't helicopters chasing the horses?" I asked. "And aren't they more likely to scare the horses than a guy crouched in the rocks?"

The public affairs officer shrugged. His job was not to engage in debate. We were staying where we were.

I was raised by parents with an orange VW bus and a sometimes-counterproductive resentment of authority—one I inherited and have nurtured through years as a newspaper journalist. I've learned that being gently defiant may not get you what you want, but it often gets you closer. I figured I could get the BLM to budge just a little by continuing to push, but it was no good. I argued for at least twenty minutes, but the pink tape never moved, and neither did I. It was a fitting introduction to Wild Horse Country. A lot of stuff the BLM does here makes little sense, and plenty of people have pointed that out for a time, but it hasn't kept the agency from doing it.

While I was still arguing, we heard the distant whine of helicopters. I lifted my binoculars and scanned over the miles of seamless sage. At first I saw nothing. Not even the black dots I had seen before. The helicopter echoed, and a sudden change in tone suggested it had veered hard and shot off in another direction. I pulled down the binoculars searching for some clue to focus on—a whirling blade, a flash of light on metal, a sudden dark movement, anything.

Suddenly I spotted them. A distant smudge of golden dust bloomed in the gray brush. Then, cutting in and out of the dawn light, glints from a helicopter rotor. Then it was gone back into the shadows. Then it returned. I thumbed the focus on the binoculars and saw the white bubble of the cockpit. It cut low over the ground, bent forward, tail up, like a patrolling dragonfly. It turned and dove and turned. In the jostling circle of the binoculars, I finally saw dark dots rise out of

A BLM HELICOPTER, MADE MINUSCULE BY THE VASTNESS OF THE GREAT BASIN,
CHASES WILD HORSES ACROSS THE SAND SPRINGS VALLEY IN NEVADA.

the sage. First one, then many. Horses! They were galloping across
the plain, flat out in a long line, kicking up a mane of sunlit dust! I
was thinking in exclamation points! *Here they are! Now run!*

From the rock, the distant chase unfolded, slow and silent. A file
of black dots stretched smoothly across the desert like a strand of
beads. But up close it must have been terrifying. In my mind, I heard
the throb of the helicopter beating down over the sage, the steel
scream of the engines, the blast of dust, the horses thundering over
hard, chalky earth. Hooves crashing through sage, legs cut by splintered branches.

I lowered my binoculars and saw that the band was still at least
two miles away, but the helicopter was tight on them, driving steadily
toward our rock spine. I glanced over at my partners on the outcrop,
hoping to share my excitement. But the law enforcement agent was

scraping at one of his nails with his car key. The public affairs officer sipped from his coffee cup. He was telling the law enforcement agent about how many years he had left until retirement.

This wasn't their first roundup. The BLM does dozens every year, annually removing about ten thousand horses. The agency doesn't call what it does "roundups." It calls them "gathers," which makes corralling galloping mustangs sound a bit like picking raspberries in the forest. People who oppose roundups—and there are many—call it "stampeding." They say the practice is needlessly traumatizing and ineffective. They sue every year to try to stop it. But by any name, the roundups go on. Since the 1970s, the BLM has corralled more than three hundred thousand wild horses and removed them from the West. Some of the big roundups last a month or more. The season essentially never stops. I guess after a few dozen gathers you can get kind of jaded and start inspecting your nails, but this was my first. And it was probably the first for these horses, too.

I went back to my binoculars.

The herd was close enough now to really see. I counted thirty-two, backs rippling with muscle, coats shining in the dawn light, stringy manes flapping like banners as they flew over the thorny brush. The BLM usually justifies roundups by saying horse herds have gotten too big and are eating the range down to nothing. It is a common refrain in the agency that there are too many horses and they have to be removed before they starve.

I expected to see bedraggled wraiths in my binoculars. I thought life on such a harsh range with so little feed would leave the horses as craggy as the desert, patchy with scars, ugly from neglect, with dull skin rippled over sharp ribs. But as the lead mare ran, I could see how sleek and glossy black she was. She had full muscles and deep, bright eyes. She looked like something out of a movie. Two horses behind her were dappled gray with long, light manes. They had no ribs or hips jutting from their hides. The group galloped with the grace of a herd you might see in an old Marlboro ad. Some were the color of old bourbon or chocolate. Some were like honey in the light. Others had white blazes. Horse people have names for all these horse colors, but, I should probably admit now, I am not a horse person. I have never owned any horses and only rode a dozen or so times long ago at summer camp. I never read *Black Beauty* or dreamed of riding away on a stallion. I don't know anything about conformation or breeding. I could not appreciate a fine, abundant cannon or prominent, capable withers. I wanted to learn about wild horses not because I love horses but because I love wildness. I always have. I love the wise and enduring simplicity of a life unbound. I have climbed hundreds of mountains, sometimes at night in the snow. I've explored canyons for days on end. Halfway through college, when I realized that much of what I was learning was of questionable worth, I withdrew for a semester, loaded a backpack, headed west, and walked and floated the length of the Colorado River. To this day, I love the parts of the West that remain untamed. And that is what brought me to Wild Horse Country. Mustangs embody the West that I love. Part of me just wanted to know that wild horses were still out there.

I also came to the roundup because I wanted to know how wildness on such a scale could persist at a time when everything seems increasingly penned in. How so many horses can live free when so much wildlife is threatened or disappearing. And I wanted to know what their existence said about the United States and the future of the West.

The horses galloped nearer. The shining white helicopter seemed to be right on top of them. It dodged left and right, low over the sage like a border collie, kicking up a halo of white dust. The horses thundered toward the outcrop where we stood. Right beside the outcrop, the BLM had set up a large, circular metal corral. The agency is an alphabet soup of acronyms. It calls the places where wild horses are found Herd Management Areas, or HMAs. It calls horse population goals for these areas the Appropriate Management Level, or AML. Before doing a roundup, it has to create an Environmental Impact Statement, EIS. It is common to hear BLM planners talk in a string of letters that makes no sense to outsiders. In a rare instance of clarity, it calls this corral simply, "the trap." The walls are usually six-foot-high steel fences, arranged in a circle about forty feet across. Plastic netting is strung along the fence so horses can't see through. A motivated mustang can clear a six-foot fence, and many would jump if they could spot their landing. The circular corral usually has a long V of fence angling out from a gate, like jaws. The walls of the V are called the wings. They are also six feet high, but they are made of feathery burlap strung between metal posts. The design makes the wings look solid to a galloping horse, but they give easily in case of a crash. The burlap is also light and easy to pack up for the drive to the next roundup. It's a design that's been used for a century, both by people trying to get rid of mustangs and by those charged with preserving them.

In the Sand Springs Valley, the wings spread out from the corral and around the corner of the outcrop where we stood, then opened wide into the sage, running at least two hundred yards. Now the whine of the helicopter had grown into a loud THWOP–THWOP–THWOP that I could feel against my chest. I put down my binoculars and watched the herd fleeing toward us. They crashed through the sage and jumped rocks. Their manes lashed their necks in the wind from the rotors. A mare stumbled and rolled head-over-tail before almost instantly rising into a run.

A lot of domestic horse lovers dismiss mustangs as ratty mongrels. A Thoroughbred breeder might look through the binoculars in this desert valley and see just stubby legs, short backs, and heads far too big for their necks. They might see horses too small for a respectable rider. Certainly they wouldn't fetch much of a price at the sale barn. But there is a chasm between what is attractive to breeders and what is attractive to life in the wild. Thousands of years of captive breeding have produced racehorses that run faster than wild horses, pedigreed Arabians with more desired lines, and draft horses with more bulk. But breeding has also brought problems. Today's domestic horses can struggle with bad teeth, rotten hooves, colic, joint trouble, jaw problems, parasites, and asthma. Many are wracked with anxiety disorders and bite themselves or pace endlessly. Several hallowed bloodlines are more inbred than a medieval monarchy. All Thoroughbreds today trace their lineage to just three stallions.

Domestic horses demand constant care: hoof trimming, shoeing, tooth filing, immunizations, worm medicine, mineral supplements. The only care wild horses get is natural selection. Parents are not chosen by studbooks but by the blows of competing stallions. The desert prunes any deficiencies. Wild horses may not look like much, but in many ways they are the best horses. The wild has given them no other choice. What emerged are animals that, according to their riders, have unparalleled intelligence, stamina, and overall resilience. Stories of their marathon runs are legend. One man on a mustang made the trailless, eight-hundred-mile ride from Santa Fe to Independence, Missouri, in fourteen days and said he could have done it faster if not for encounters with a blizzard and a group of banditos. To prove his point, the next time he and his mustang did the ride in eight.

Present-day owners of tamed wild horses joke that the animals can get fat eating tumbleweed and never need a vet. They are the choice of many modern riders in hundred-mile endurance races.

There is a well-known story in wild horse lore that was written down by a cavalry colonel in the 1860s on the Texas frontier. A band of Comanche warriors was visiting his fort and some of the officers goaded the braves into betting on a four-hundred-yard race between the two best horses. The soldiers wanted to test their prize Kentucky Thoroughbred, but when they saw a Comanche come to the starting line on a long-haired, spindly legged, "miserable sheep of a pony," they were so disgusted that they instead brought out their third-best horse. At the sound of a gun, the two took off. The brave swung a "ridiculously heavy" club and hollered madly, driving his pony. The mustang left the third-best cavalry horse in the dust.

The soldiers immediately demanded another race, double or nothing. They brought out their second-best racer. The Comanche on his miserable little mustang won again. Finally the soldiers brought out their prize Thoroughbred. Triple or nothing. At the sound of the gun, both horses took off at a full gallop. They were neck and neck when the Comanche threw away his club and gave a piercing scream. His mustang shot into the lead. About fifty yards from the finish, the Comanche flipped around on his pony so he could face the trailing American and, with "hideous grimaces," taunted him to catch up as he rode backward across the finish line

The helicopter banked from side to side, pushing the herd toward the rock outcrop, letting not a one escape. Down below, two cowboys in chaps and hats crouched in the brush near the wings of the trap. One held a tame horse by a halter.

"See that one there?" the public affairs officer said to me. "It is called the Judas horse."

"Why?" I asked.

"You'll see," he said.

The herd galloped within fifty yards of the wings, and the cowboy let go of the Judas horse. It bolted straight into the wings of the trap.

"She's trained to do that," the public affairs officer said. "And the other horses see her and follow her right in."

In the end, it seemed too easy. The helicopter brought the herd right up against the steep side of our rocky spine, then flared to scare the horses left into the wide wings of the trap. They saw the Judas horse leading the way and coursed smoothly into it. Maybe the horses saw the burlap walls as the banks of an arroyo that could lead to the way out. Maybe by the time they realized their mistake, it was too late. The cowboys jumped from the sage, hollering and waving their hats. The mustangs surged down the funnel of the wings and squeezed flank by flank into the trap. The chopper flared once more to scare them all the way into the corral and a cowboy ran in and slammed the gate.

Then it was over. The wild was gone. Only captives remained. I felt a deep sadness at the loss. But it wasn't quite over. In the chaos, a spindly black foal had fallen slightly behind the herd. Just at the mouth of the wings, the helicopter passed over it, chasing the adults. The foal bucked and jagged to the right, missing the wings of the trap. The helicopter could not swing back without losing the other horses now running down the mouth of the trap. The little foal galloped out into the sage with nothing but fenceless desert beyond.

To myself I shouted, "Go!"

But after a hundred meters, the foal's run slowed to a trot, then it stopped and turned. It could see its mother going into the trap. It watched, unsure what to do. Once the gate slammed closed, the helicopter whizzed off to find the next herd. In the quiet, the foal trotted to the corral and nuzzled the fence, smelling for its mother. I dropped my binoculars in surprise. I have always thought of horses as loners—solitary in a stall or under a rider. And in our world, that is how we tend to keep them. A horse is an individual piece of equipment. Little thought is given to their lives with other horses.

But out here the animals band together in families with complex social roles that have evolved over millions of years. They thrive on intimate relationships among mares, foals, and stallions. "The cruelest thing you can do to a horse is keep it by itself," one long-time wild horse watcher once told me. The words came back to me as I watched the foal pace back and forth along the fence, unwilling to run away, unsure what to do. After a few minutes, one of the cowboys walked slowly up and opened a small gate in the corral. The foal trotted right in.

"Can't be away from his mama, isn't that cute?" the public affairs officer said.

Once through the mouth of the trap, the horses swirled in confusion, turning and turning in the circular corral, looking for a way out before they finally came to a stop. I couldn't see this, because the BLM had put the pink-tape public viewing area in a place where I couldn't actually view much. But I could hear their hooves clomp, turning in the desert dust. Steam rose over the rocks from their hot, exhausted backs. The echoing shriek of a stallion cut the desert air. Then two more. The clang of a horse against the metal fence rang against the stones. Some were trying to escape. I watched the open desert beyond to see if any would clear the fence, but I saw only sage.

I heard the creak of the cowboys swinging open another gate and the horses cantered into a rear pen that I could mostly see from the pink-tape rectangle. The cowboys waved horsewhips topped with little white flags that I soon realized were actually plastic shopping bags. I looked over at the public affairs officer, who was pouring another cup of coffee, and asked why the bags were used.

"That way they don't have to whip 'em," he said. "For a wild horse, a plastic bag is scary enough to do the job."

The helicopter roared back over our heads and out into the desert for another round. I stayed and watched all day as it made trip after trip. In eight flights, the crew brought in 121 horses from a valley that had looked empty. One horse, trying to escape, rammed the corral fence and broke its neck, and the cowboys shot it. I couldn't see it, but when we heard the shot and I asked the public affairs officer what it was, he only said, "I'm not sure." I only found out later. Deaths from injuries in roundups, while not common, are a regular occurrence.

The other horses were sorted in the rear corrals and loaded six or eight at a time into gooseneck trailers. After driving an hour down a slow, twisting dirt track, the trucks reached the highway. I followed them to another corral at the roadside. There the horses were sorted by sex and age. The foal that came back for its mother was separated from her anyway. Those instinctive family bonds the bands had lived with in the wild were broken. I had come to the valley with the idea that roundups were necessary and as humane as possible. I had believed the agency when it said wild horses are overpopulated. I knew above all that the priority should be to protect the long-term health of the desert. But watching the families broken up was wrenching, and it made me wonder what kind of system we had created.

As the sun slid low over the far side of the valley, some of the horses were pushed up a ramp onto a waiting semi-trailer. The truck pulled away with a loud gasp and headed down one of those straight, empty Wild Horse Country highways.

"Where will they go?" I asked the public affairs officer.

"They go for adoption," he said.

"And what if no one adopts them?"

"Then they go to holding," he said. And knowing that my next question would be what "holding" was, he added, "It's basically pastures. Private ranches where they live out their lives, or at least stay until we figure out what to do with them."

"It's nice land, most of it in Oklahoma," he added. "They live way better there than they do here."

That day on the range, it became obvious to me that wild horses are like no other animal in America. I don't mean biologically, although horses have some fascinating adaptations to living in wide-open spaces (including the largest eyes of any land mammal). I mean culturally. And legally. The public imagination gives more meaning and respect to wild horses than to nearly any other wild animals. We have given wild horses their own law. That law has led to a system where we remove horses from the desert with helicopters and load them onto trucks so we can send them a thousand miles to ranches in the Midwest.

The fallout of all this is remarkably strange. When I visited Sand Springs, there were nearly fifty thousand horses in storage. The annual cost of caring for them was $50 million. We've spent a billion dollars rounding up horses since 1975. Just caring for the horses now in storage is expected to cost a billion more. If it had the money, the BLM would like to remove another fifty thousand horses, adding another billion in holding costs. But the money has pretty much run out.

Every year the BLM puts more horses in storage. The more horses it has in storage, the less money for other parts of the program. The storage system now eats up 66 percent of the wild horse program's budget, and it has pushed the program into a state of paralysis. Managers would like to improve grass and water on the land, but they have no money left for it. Managers would like to develop alternative population-control methods that avoid roundups, but they have no money left for it. In short, the BLM can't get out of its cycle of storing horses because it is too busy storing horses. So the roundups continue.

It's a practice no one much likes—not the bureau that devised it, not the ranchers whose cattle and sheep share the land with the horses, not the wild horse advocates sticking up for the rights of the herds. So how did it happen? And what, if anything, can we do about it? How did we get to a place where we spend $2 billion to gather and store animals that everyone agrees should be wild and free? I decided that afternoon, as I watched the truck full of mustangs pull away, that I would try to find the answers. I would scour the corners of Wild Horse Country to see if I could figure out how we got where we are, and where we should go.

Like the bald eagle, the wild horse was in pretty dire straits by the middle of the twentieth century. They had been hunted, killed, poisoned, rounded up, and sold for slaughter until there were only about seventeen thousand left. Then, in 1971, amid a raft of environmental protection laws, Congress passed the Wild Free-Roaming Horses and Burros Act, declaring that wild horses "are living symbols of the historic and pioneer spirit of the West" and "shall be protected from capture, branding, harassment, or death."

President Richard Nixon, who was never a big backer of environmental preservation but was a shrewd politician who knew good press when he saw it, paraphrased Henry David Thoreau at its signing, saying, "We need the tonic of wildness." He said wild horses "are a living link with the days of the conquistadors, through the heroic times of the Western Indians and the pioneers, to our own day when the tonic of wildness seems all too scarce."

The act protected the last remnants of the West's wild horses, putting them under the watchful guard of the government. (As the law's name suggests, burros are protected too, and though in many ways burros are even tougher and more independent than horses, they don't have the same prominence in the American imagination. Suffice to say, however, the issues affecting the two species are largely the same.) But the law unintentionally made wild horses into legal misfits. They are stuck in a world between wild animals and livestock. They are considered "wild" but not "wildlife." They are "fast disappearing" but don't count as an endangered species. They are American but not "native." And not all wild-born horses are protected under the law; only those that are born in designated areas of US Forest Service or Bureau of Land Management land count. These quirks can make for some confusing outcomes. For example, imagine a foal whose ancestors descended from escaped Spanish stock that has run loose in the West for four hundred years. Its parents are legally classified as wild horses. But if the mother wanders into a state park, national park, or Indian reservation to have her foal, the foal is not a wild horse. It is a feral stray and can be rounded up and sold to the slaughterhouse. Conversely, if another horse that is descended from captive domestic horses since the time of Homer gets free of the stable and has a foal on BLM land, that foal is legally a wild horse. In other words, the rights of a wild horse are a lot like the rights of citizenship. A lot of it depends only on where you were born.

That means not all horses that are wild are legally considered wild horses. Tens of thousands live on Indian reservations, state lands, and federal lands, including national parks and wildlife refuges, where protections don't apply. They can be trucked off to slaughterhouses, and often are. (In the Grand Canyon, rangers shot thousands of burros and eventually got rid of them entirely by relocating the few that remained.) To keep things simple, when I talk about wild horses, I'm referring only to the statutory wild horses. When referring to all wild-born, free-roaming horses and their descendants, I'll use the blanket term *mustang*.

The word *mustang* itself needs some explanation. In modern times among horse people, it has come to mean a horse of relatively pure Spanish blood—the horses that escaped from Spanish conquistadors centuries ago and still have the traits of Spanish Barb horses brought over by the first explorers. That definition is often used to devalue other wild horses. People—usually ranchers and government officials—will say that there are no true mustangs left, and that today's modern horses are just a degenerate muddle of domestic strays. Part of that is true. But it's also misleading. Almost all wild horses are a mix of different genetics, and some have little Spanish blood. But the Spanish, from whom the word *mustang* came, never used it to refer to their finest horses. Originally, *mustang* comes from the Spanish word *mesteña*—meaning stray livestock belonging to local herders, the *mesta*. Just like the wild horses of today, these stray *mesteña* were an outcast mix of high and low stock, some domestic and some that had been living free for generations. Sometime in the nineteenth century in Texas, the word *mesteña* jumped the fence to English, becoming *mustang*. And *mustang* became the preferred way to refer to the tough little wild-born, free-roaming horses, which often had Spanish blood, that populated the West.

The 1971 law was supposed to allow wild horses to roam the places where they existed at the time that the law was signed. The BLM was supposed to manage herds at levels that would maintain what the law calls a "thriving natural ecological balance and multiple-use relationship" with existing wildlife and cattle. Neither has happened.

Starting in 1971, the agency documented where horses were found and drew lines around the territory like so much pink plastic tape, designating 303 Herd Management Areas. Since then, it has administratively eliminated about a hundred areas, changing their designation from Herd Management Areas to Herd Areas. A Herd Management Area is where the primary use is supposed to be management of the horses. Herd Areas are where the BLM has decided horses are not supposed to be. The horses in those latter areas are slated for eventual elimination. Altogether, the areas that have been taken away from wild horses make up nearly thirteen million acres—a region about the size of West Virginia. Sometimes the agency said it was because of lack of forage or water. Sometimes the agency said it was because the horses would interfere with oil and natural-gas drilling. Sometimes, it appears, the agency did it just because locals asked them to.

Since taking control, the agency has struggled with the wild horse population. It set a goal for a total population in the West of about twenty-seven thousand horses, a number it felt could be sustainably managed on the land. The BLM has been rounding up horses continuously since 1977 but has never once met the goal. Over the years, under the guidance of a dozen different directors during both Republican and Democratic administrations, it has slipped farther and farther away. By the end of the Obama administration, there were seventy-seven thousand horses on the range—the largest population since the law was passed. The BLM says wild horses must be removed to avoid long-term damage to the land. Horse advocates have pushed back, saying the horse is a scapegoat for damage by cattle and sheep. The current system has led to both overpopulation and roundups, ensuring that no one wins.

The way we try to control wild horse populations only underlines their misfit status. With wildlife, federal and state governments either largely ignore populations, letting nature take its course, or set target populations and let hunters keep the numbers in check. Wild horses are the only species that the government captures in large numbers alive and then holds in storage. This is a stark departure from how we treat other Old World domestic animals that have gotten loose in America. Take feral hogs. The United States kills tens of thousands a year. Texas even has special helicopters specifically for gunning down hogs. It calls them "pork choppers." Sure, feral hogs aren't companion animals like horses. But consider our pets.

We euthanize millions of dogs and cats each year. We even have programs to electro-shock feral goldfish. Wild horses are different. We don't hunt them. We don't euthanize them. We don't eat them. More than perhaps any animal, we think wild horses deserve respect. The mustang is the closest thing in America to a folk hero of the animal kingdom.

This is not, by the way, a universal human instinct, or even one shared by modern, Western societies. It is uniquely American. In Canada, wild horses can be sold to slaughter. You can order horse steaks and burgers in some very nice restaurants in Montreal. In Western Europe, you can find frozen horse meatballs at the supermarket. The United States is even unique among nations that have large wild horse populations. Australia has a staggering half a million wild horses, which Australians call *brumbies*. (They also have about a million feral camels!) Law allows brumbies to be rounded up and exported as horsemeat, but Australian government scientists say the most efficient and humane "pest control" is to shoot them from helicopters.

The United States alone has chosen not to kill wild horses, even if that means warehousing the unwanted at a staggering expense. That has led to the bizarre situation in which we now find ourselves. When the BLM started rounding up horses in the 1970s, the plan was to find a home for every animal that came off the land. It never happened. While tens of thousands of people have adopted and trained mustangs, there have never been enough homes for all those that have been removed from the range. Several times, the BLM and lawmakers have proposed selling unadopted horses to slaughter buyers. That idea has provoked such outrage from the public that it has always been abandoned. Instead, the agency started storing surplus horses like the ones I saw in the Sand Springs Valley in a labyrinth of feedlots and pastures across thirteen states. It calls this labyrinth "the holding system." Every year the agency adds thousands of animals to the system. Our unique relationship with wild horses has led us to this stunning contradiction: The United States now has nearly as many wild horses in captivity as it has in the wild.

Anywhere you go in the West, you will see homages to the wild horse. Cars arriving at Denver International Airport are greeted by a thirty-two-foot stallion rearing in defiance. Statues of wild horses galloping in bands run along I-15 through Las Vegas. The mustang is the mascot of hundreds of schools across the West, including the Colorado elementary school I attended. Every Friday we would wear school shirts emblazoned with a running, snow-white stallion.

For us as kids, the mustang was a symbol of power and freedom. It is a stunning reversal that the wild horse can now be seen as a welfare case entangled in a federal bureaucracy. The animal that carried the explorers, lugged tools for prospectors, pulled the plows, powered the great cattle drives, and empowered the tribes of the plains now is a burden on the taxpayer, a ward of the state. This slow crumbling of a cultural icon is not the horses' fault, but ours. There is a fundamental conflict in how we approach wild horses that has gotten us into this mess. As one wild horse advocate said to me while we sat on rocks overlooking a roundup in Nevada's Stone Cabin Valley, "People don't have a wild horse problem. Wild horses have a people problem."

The night after the Sand Springs roundup, I camped out in the empty valley. The BLM staff had rolled up their pink plastic tape and gone home, so I was free to wander the plain below, where thousands of hoof prints from the roundup still dented the dirt. It was cold and I built a small fire with silver wood ripped from old sagebrush. I sat watching the stars over the flames and thinking about the horses out in the dark heading down the highway in dim trailers toward the holding system. I wondered how many horses were still roaming free in the valley under the stars, and what the future held for them. It seemed to me that they could not go on like this very much longer. Eventually Americans would get tired of spending so much on gathering and storing horses. Their image of wild horses would cease to be wild and free. Public opinion would turn against the mustang. And then what?

Maybe the public would demand that we start killing horses. Maybe Congress would loosen the protections of the law. Maybe mustangs, which were saved from the brink of extinction in 1971, would again face destruction. Wild horses have always been a bellwether for the West. If we could find ways to live in balance with them that are good for the long-term health of the land, the local people, and our stories of who we are, then it will go a long way toward preserving what we love about both the horses and the place.

That night as the campfire died, I felt like the long history of the wild horse was at a turning point, where people either had to find a way to live with mustangs, and the wildness they require, or forever lose one of the last untamed parts of the West. What was the proper place for the mustang in the West, if any? And how could we find it? I intended to travel Wild Horse Country until I found out.

WILD HORSE COUNTRY

CHAPTER 1

THE DAWN HORSE

I n a corner of northwestern Wyoming the long chain of the Rocky Mountains splits into two separate stands of peaks that corral a broad stretch of desert country called the Bighorn Basin. Almost no one lives there. The basin is roughly the size of West Virginia, but its sherbet-colored badlands have less than one percent of West Virginia's population. The land in most places looks like it always did: chalky, dry mesas fenced in by distant blue peaks. There are only two real breaks in the hills, cut by the deep, green Bighorn River, which flows in through a slot canyon in the south and out through another canyon in the north.

The Bighorn Basin exists in what people in the West call a "rain shadow"—a patch of perpetual drought cast by the mountains. It is created by prevailing winds pushing weather from west to east. Moist air cools as it rises over the twelve-thousand-foot peaks of the Absaroka Range before reaching the basin. The cold wrings out most of the moisture, which falls on the thick mountain forests as rain or snow. The air passing over the mountains and down into the basin warms and expands. Expanding air acts almost like a sponge that, once squeezed, absorbs more water. And so it almost never rains.

The basin receives only about six inches of rainfall a year—less than in the cactus-studded deserts of Arizona.

Where water flows out of the mountains in swift, emerald rivers, farmers have created a lush corridor of green. Waving fields of malt barley stretch out in neat irrigated rows above the muddy banks. Swallows cut through the moist air, snatching fat mayflies on the wing. Grebes and mergansers paddle the lazy currents. After a long, dry drive through the sage flats of Wyoming, the feel of water in the air along the river is so thick and abrupt that you can taste it. But walk away from the river, through the fields and across the two-lane highway that traces the Bighorn's banks through the basin, and your feet are soon kicking up chalky gray dust. The river and its irrigated fields on either side make only a thin line through the basin. Then bare shale terraces rise up and away from the fields, their red, gray, and green bands slumping together like slowly melting ice cream. The roads and farmhouses cease. On a map, the shale sometimes runs twenty miles without interruption in crumples and jags so erratic that it seems as if the contour lines were plugged into an electric socket.

The rain shadow has left the hills bare except for sparse polka dots of greasewood and black sage. There is no shade. It is boiling in the summer and arctic in the winter. There are creeks that were marked on the map long ago by cartographers with either a naive sense of hope or a cruel sense of humor, but there is almost never water. It is classic badlands: desiccated, defiant, devoid.

Naturally, it is Wild Horse Country.

I drove into the basin on a hot July afternoon to spend a few days out on the shale benches far from the paved road, looking for wild horses. I turned off the highway at the farming town of Worland (one of the biggest towns in the basin, population 5,487) and sped west, kicking up a plume of fine dust on a narrow dirt track.

As I drove, I scanned the empty horizon. I wasn't looking for mustangs—not live ones, at least. I was looking for the camp of Dr. Ken Rose, a longtime summer resident of the basin and professor of anatomy at Johns Hopkins University, who happened to be one of the leading experts on the first horses ever to walk the earth.

The Bighorn Basin may not be a very hospitable place for farming, or ranching, or really anything else, but it holds one of the greatest troves of early mammal fossils in the world. Scientists from around the globe, Rose included, have been making pilgrimages to the site for more than a century to search for old bones. I was making my own pilgrimage to the basin because it is one of the best places to study where the wild horse began. I wanted to see it because I had heard over and over from government employees, ranchers, big-game managers, and others who want to limit wild horse numbers, that wild horses aren't really wild—they are just escaped livestock that are now infesting the native ecosystem like so much kudzu. As a nonnative invader, the argument goes, mustangs represent an imbalance to the native ecosystem. They are a usurper, a contagion, and because of this, they must be rounded up to protect the natural balance.

The assertion that horses are not native made perfect sense to me at first. Europeans brought horses to the Americas. That is clear. There are a few fringe wild horse advocates who will argue that horses were actually here before Columbus arrived, but there is not good evidence. No explorers who made first contact with native tribes ever documented horses. If Europeans brought them, the argument goes, then they are an invasive species. If they are an invasive species, we must control them.

But as I kept turning the idea over in my mind, the main points started to dull by knocking into competing arguments. The first was that the wild horse is not invasive. I had some vague memory from a high school textbook of an illustration of prehistoric horses roaming North American among woolly mammoths and giant sloths millions of years before humans arrived. Second, I began to wonder what "native" really meant. Of course the definition seems obvious: A plant or animal is native when it exists in its natural range or ecosystem, as opposed to a species introduced by man. But it actually isn't so simple. That natural range of a species is often thought of as static. In North America, we generally define it as wherever it was found by the first European observers. Any subsequent changes often are portrayed as unnatural. But animals and ecosystems have migrated thousands of miles over the millennia, gaining new ground and losing old. Oceans have risen and fallen. Whole continents have been covered in ice. Landmasses have drifted from the equator to the poles, burying jungles in ice. Mountains have become seas and seas, mountains. Isolated continents have slammed into each other, unleashing their own invasive species like a geologic D-day landing. The writer John McPhee summed up the constant change on Earth with one observation: "The summit of Mt. Everest is marine limestone."

In North America, we generally use *native* to mean any critter that was here before Christopher Columbus hit land. In recent decades, we have given these native animals special rights, trying to protect them while working to eradicate the invaders. We spend millions of dollars trying to save a black-footed ferret or a sage hen in the West, and millions more building electric fences to keep the Asian carp out of the Great Lakes or kill Asian pythons in the Everglades. Wildlife laws protect the bobcat, but not the feral house cat. We want to preserve an old balance in a world where we have shifted the balance dramatically. I share this desire. I want protection for the natives. As I write this, a thumb-size broad-tailed hummingbird is hovering at a feeder in an old pine above my keyboard. I love seeing such a precise distillation of life so much that I would do nearly anything to protect its annual migration over hundreds of miles along the Rockies.

But what is really native? How long do migrants like the wild horse have to be here before they count? Certainly more than a hundred years, we would all likely agree. But what about a thousand? What about ten thousand? At some point, the label of being invasive must wear off. What is the process through which an animal becomes native? And how do we decide? Those were questions I wanted to start answering with a trip to Bighorn Basin.

As I looked for Professor Rose's camp, I drove through old beds of sandstone and shale laid down millions of years ago, when this part of Wyoming was a flat, muddy coast that alternated among thick jungle, tropical swamp, and shallow sea. A postcard sent during the era might have looked a lot like the coast of South Carolina. Over millions of years, the area was a depository for silt and muck washed down from the mountains to the west. The layers of sediment made a great Cenozoic layer cake, with bands of hard white sandstone and bands of crumbly shale in colors ranging from milk to gray to dusty mint to clay-pot red. They eventually piled up more than twenty-five hundred feet thick.

Then the whole area was slowly pushed up, between eighty million and thirty-five million years ago. The sea receded to the east. Layers of muck that had piled up and become stone were exposed to the elements as they rose. Eons of wind and rain have whittled them into buttes, mesas, and rumpled shale hills. This ancient, hardened layer cake of jungle muck is called the Willwood Formation. It makes up every hill and draw for miles around. Crush the shale between your fingers and it turns velvety smooth. Set a hard Wyoming wind on it and it fills the air, covering everything with fine dust. Get it wet and it turns into a slippery, sticky, shoe-sucking glop that the paleontologists who have been traipsing these hills for generations call gumbo.

I spotted Rose's camp about five miles from the highway. It was off in a low draw where occasional moisture in the sand had nurtured a few stunted cottonwoods, which offered a little shade and a buffer from the wind. It was near sunset when I parked on the edge of the camp, and I could see graduate students milling around a dozen tents tucked among giant sage bushes that grew five feet high. One big cooking tent stood in the middle.

The students—sunburned, weary, but otherwise cheerful—were splashing the dust off their faces and arms in plastic basins after a long day in the field. Most of them planned to spend the whole summer here, searching the hills for fossils by day and bringing back their finds at night.

When I got out of my car, Rose came out of the cook tent at a fast walk, hand extended to greet me. He wore a blue Oxford button-down shirt and wire-frame glasses, and had a distinguished gray professorial beard. But this East Coast University look was offset by a wildly battered cowboy hat crowned with a dark band of dirt and sweat and punctuated by a long magpie tail feather that poked from the band. It was a unique mix of starch and grit that only field paleontologists seem to have.

"To most people, this is badlands," he said, after shaking my hand and ushering me to the edge of the camp where we could see the bare shale hills beyond. "To paleontologists, it is the most valuable land in the world."

The Willwood has been a destination for researchers for more than a century because its many layers, gently laid down during a period between fifty-five and fifty-two million years ago, record a turning point in history, right after the dinosaurs disappeared, when mammals began to flourish. The period when it formed is called the Eocene Epoch, from the ancient Greek word *eos*, meaning dawn, because it was the dawn of the modern era. The Bighorn Basin is one of the few places in the world where a large slice of the Eocene is preserved. And it is perhaps the best place to see the beginning of horses.

"Everything is just right here for fossils," Rose said. Conditions were right millions of years ago to gently bury plants and animals in wet, flat, sediment-rich plains. After that, conditions were just right to bury those plains under more sediment so they could be pressed to make stone and be preserved. More recently, conditions were just right when the tectonic plate that makes up North America began to buckle, slowly uplifting the land. And conditions were just right when erosion removed thousands of feet of newer rock that covered the Willwood. On top of all that, the rain shadow was just right to keep almost all of the ground from being covered by grass and trees, letting wandering paleontologists find their quarry.

"You could not ask for better conditions," Rose said. Just then, a gust came up and took off his hat, which went bounding through the sage. He added, "Well, I guess a little less wind would be nice."

Rose grew up in New Jersey, far from the vast Eocene beds of the West. But, as a boy, he had developed an insatiable thirst for collecting—primarily trilobites, sharks' teeth, and other fossils from the ancient shallow seabed that today makes up much of New Jersey.

"Other kids played baseball," he said as we sat down for dinner at the camp's single table. "I had a museum in my basement."

He first came out to the Bighorn Basin when he was an undergraduate in 1968 and has come back nearly every summer since, earning an MA degree from Harvard University and a PhD from the University of Michigan along the way.

I had contacted him because I wanted to get as close an understanding as I could of the first horses. I wanted to try to see what the first horses looked like and imagine their journey from the dawn of mammals to the present day. But I also wanted to understand how this long history has shaped the recent history of wild horses. We talked a few times by phone, and then he said, "If you really want to get a feel for it, you should just come out to the field."

Before we turned in for the night, he unrolled a large topographical map to decide where his team would focus the next day. The decades-old sheet was peppered with neat pencil notes showing the dates he had collected in each spot. Some showed two or three passes. Every decade or two, he said, he returns to see if erosion has turned up anything new. His map also acts as the unpublished modern history of the Willwood. Here and there, a few words recorded the dates and places of notable occurrences observed over the decades that broke the normally timeless silence of the badlands: the scorpion bite, the nudist, the madman at the sheep camp.

Several of the pencil inscriptions prompted stories he told the students by the light of the camp lantern. I pointed to one note: *The day of 427 jaws*. I asked what it meant.

"That was maybe the greatest collecting day we've ever had," Rose said.

Jaws, it turns out, are what Rose's crew is after. Often, they are all that is left of a mammal after fifty million years. Dying is a pretty brutal process. Even if an animal dies peacefully, it is almost always picked apart by scavengers, the remains scattered and broken and nibbled into oblivion. It is almost astronomically unlikely that a carcass is left intact to be buried. And even then, to be discovered fifty million years later, it has to survive the slow, uncertain process of fossilization, then the uplift of the formation, then erosion. Almost nothing does. But jaws, it turns out, are sturdy, and that is a very lucky thing. More than any other part of the skeleton, jaws carry a wealth of clues about ancient mammals: size, diet, evolutionary lineage, even social structure.

"Full skeletons are pretty to look at but not scientifically valuable," Rose said. "They don't tell us much. Jaws tell us a lot."

Rose now has tens of thousands of jaws in his collection. Over the years, his teams of students have collected so many that they can see how the population changed over millennia and start to describe not just what was in the Bighorn fifty million years ago but also how twenty or so species changed over three million years as the Earth rapidly warmed.

"We can't do that for animals today," Rose said that night, right before he turned off the camp lantern. "In some ways we know more about these ancient horses than we know about the animal today."

At dawn, Rose's students gathered for coffee and a quick breakfast of fruit and granola, seeking shelter in the cook tent from the sun, which felt searing on the skin at 6 a.m. Amid the clatter of spoons and bowls, Rose, who likes to begin each day by reading a passage from a notable paleontologist, opened a marked page in a book by

A 50 MILLION-YEAR-OLD FRAGMENT OF JAW FROM THE FIRST HORSE, *HYRACOTHERIUM*, IN BIG HORN BASIN, WYOMING.

George Gaylord Simpson, one of the greatest evolutionary biologists of the twentieth century. Rose handed the open book, which detailed Simpson's explorations of Patagonia, to a student, who began to read:

> Fossil hunting is far the most fascinating of all sports. I speak for myself, although I do not see how any true sportsman could fail to agree with me if he had tried bone digging. It has some danger, enough to give it zest and probably about as much as in the average modern engineered big-game hunt, and the danger is wholly to the hunter. It has uncertainty and excitement and all the thrills of gambling with none of its vicious features. The hunter never knows what his bag may be, perhaps nothing, perhaps a creature never before seen by human eyes. Over the next hill may lie a great discovery! It requires knowledge, skill, and some degree of hardihood. And its results are so much more important, more worthwhile, and more enduring than those of any other sport! The fossil hunter does not kill; he resurrects. And the result of his sport is to add to the sum of human pleasure and to the treasures of human knowledge."[1]

"Hallelujah, well said!" Rose applauded.

With that, the crew climbed into a mud-splattered 1990 Chevrolet Suburban that had the fossil of an early ancestor of the modern deer, called *Diacodexis*, stenciled on the side. Rose stomped on the gas pedal and took off with a lurch through the badlands, speeding like someone who had just robbed a bank. The old Suburban bounced and bounded at sixty miles an hour down a narrow dirt track through the desert. As he sped up over a rise, Rose pushed a cassette into the old tape deck in the dash and the speakers blared the theme song for Indiana Jones—*Dun da dun-dun, dun da-duuuunnnn!*

I gripped the edge of the vinyl seat as the truck flew over rolls and swayed through turns. Rose barely held the loose steering wheel as he flew along. He seemed much more focused on pointing out places where he had gathered fossils than he did on the road. I realized only later, when we stopped at the site where we were going to collect that day, why the distinguished professor drove like such a madman. After more than forty years collecting here, he knew every dip and roll of this country, and knew how much he could push the needle. Also, hunting for Eocene jaws is an agonizingly slow process, requiring sauntering inspection for hours on end. You might cover a mile in a day. Probably less. Do that all day without a little thrill and it could be a very long summer. As George Gaylord Simpson said, fossil hunting should have enough danger to give it zest.

An avid hunter like Rose would probably add that the faster you drive, the sooner you are searching for fossils.

"Horses!" he shouted. He jammed on the brakes. The Suburban skidded to a stop and was enveloped a second later in the gray cloud of dust that had been trailing off the back. As the dust cleared, he pointed to six wild horses on the horizon. We watched them silhouetted in the morning sun. They stood a few seconds, their heads up and ears pricked. Then the lead mare wheeled and disappeared over the horizon. The others followed, dissolving into the badlands.

"Have you ever seen them here before?" I asked. I had no idea wild horses still wandered the Bighorn Basin.

"Oh, lots of them," Rose said. He had seen horses in varying numbers since he first started coming to the basin in the late 1960s. No one quite knows how far back these horses go. The BLM's first record of horses here dates back to 1938, when the bureau's predecessor, the United States Grazing Service, tried unsuccessfully to remove all of them. In the 1940s, one local cowboy claimed to have removed twenty thousand mustangs from the basin with the help of a small plane. But the presence likely goes back much farther, possibly to the Crow and the Shoshone tribes. It was near this area that a few Shoshone became especially skilled at hunting with horses, split from their old tribe, headed east, and became the Comanche. Lewis and Clark had lost some horses not far north of here. It could be their descendants we saw running wild.

The horses we spotted that morning weren't technically supposed to be there. As I mentioned before, the BLM divides wild horse areas into two types: Herd Management Areas and Herd Areas. Herd Management Areas are places where horses are known to live and have the BLM's blessing. Local district offices are supposed to manage those areas primarily for the horses. Herd Areas, on the other hand, are places where horses are known to live, but the BLM has decided they should not be there. Those horses are slated for eventual removal. The horses we saw were in a third situation. They were not in an HMA or an HA. They were completely off the map, not known to exist. Truly wild. Maybe they had wandered through the unfenced badlands from the nearest HMA, a dozen miles away. Maybe they had been here for centuries, unnoticed or unnoted by BLM managers. The Bighorn Basin is a rough, lonely place. A lot can hide out in the Willwood.

After the horses galloped away, we drove on, finally stopping at a broad amphitheater of shale and sandstone, completely bare of vegetation. "This is my empire," Rose said. "Every outcrop in miles I have collected."

We split up to look for fossils. The graduate students went off in pairs, and I teamed up with Rose. He slipped on his sweat-stained cowboy hat and we started walking. Or, rather, we started ambling. Walking suggests a little too much speed. We shambled, shuffled, dallied, and perused, covering maybe ten feet per minute as our eyes scanned the ground.

We were looking for the telltale glint of teeth. In the fossilization process, white teeth turn nearly black. In a museum, they can look like little bits of onyx, but in the sun of Wyoming they have a glint like the brown glass from a broken beer bottle.

"You find that glint," Rose said. "And chances are you have found something good."

The only problem with looking for something that looks like a broken piece of beer bottle in Wyoming is that cowboys have been coming out to the middle of nowhere to shoot beer bottles here for a very long time. I spent a lot of the day bending down, only to find the remains of a distant Saturday night.

If we had been sashaying through the Bighorn Basin fifty-five million years ago, the scene would have looked fantastically different. It might have looked a lot like the coast of Laos or Brazil. The basin, now at about four thousand feet, then sat at sea level next to a shallow sea that once covered much of the Great Plains. Though the latitude was about the same as it is now, the climate was tropical. Paleontologists refer to this time as "greenhouse Earth." There was no ice, even at the poles. Palm trees and crocodiles extended above the Arctic Circle. Forests dominated the planet. Grass, which in modern times came to cover most of the Earth, was relegated to a few small clearings. The prickly brush of windy Wyoming was then steamy jungle with canopies of ginkgoes, sycamore, hickory, and medicine wood rising over a soggy understory of thick green. Turtles of all sizes paddled the slow streams, squirrel-size primates skittered up rough forest trunks.

In the undergrowth, a giant, flightless bird called *Gastornis* stood more than six feet tall on ostrichlike legs. It had a sicklelike beak fifteen inches thick, which might have been an oversize nutcracker for an omnivore or might have been a lethal neck cracker for a predator, used to grab and crush smaller animals. If it was a neck cracker, its typical meal might have been the first-ever horses.

The first horse was not much bigger than a cat and as slender as a deer, with a back hunched a bit like a rabbit's and dainty legs like those of a deer. It was called *Hyracotherium* (pronounced "heer-a-co-theer-ee-um"). It was likely a bounder, not a runner. It had four small toes on its front feet and three on its back. Each toe ended in a nimble hoof, like the trotter of a piglet. Its delicate muzzle was made to nibble tender leaves and berries near the forest floor. A lot remains unknown about this ancient animal, but one thing Rose knows for sure: There were a heck of a lot of them. He finds more *Hyracotherium* jaws in the Willwood than any other fossil. It dominated the forest.

The first fossil of *Hyracotherium* wasn't found anywhere near Bighorn Basin. If it had been, it likely would not be called *Hyracotherium*, a name that George Gaylord Simpson, who spent decades hunting fossil horses, described as "a jawbreaker that is not likely to win so many friends."

The name doesn't have anything to do with horses. It means hyrax-

AN EARLY TWENTIETH-CENTURY RENDERING OF *HYRACOTHERIUM*
IN THE LUSH FORESTS.

like beast. It got the name in an unlikely fashion, a long way from Wyoming. In 1838, a brickmaker digging in the clay near an estuary of the Thames River in England uncovered a tiny fossilized jaw. It found its way to the leading paleontologist of the time, a man named Sir Richard Owen, who was known, among other things, for being such a rabid student of anatomy that he arranged to have right of first refusal on any animal that died at the London Zoo. (His wife is said to have complained about the arrangement after coming home and finding a dead rhinoceros in her front hall.) Owen, who had classified hundreds of species of extinct creatures, examined the primitive jaw. It had pointed, low-crowned teeth that looked nothing like those of a modern horse. He first decided it must be the jaw of a prehistoric monkey. Later, on closer inspection, he decided its teeth looked more like those of a pig. Finally, he decided the teeth resembled those of an obscure rock-dwelling critter from the Middle East called a hyrax, which looks like a groundhog but is more closely related to elephants. In 1841, he published a paper describing a new order, using the teeth as evidence. He called his new find *Hyracotherium*—the hyraxlike beast.

Owen went on to catalogue uncounted thousands of other fossils, including all of the fossils Charles Darwin brought home from his voyage on the *Beagle*. He named hundreds of new species, coined the term *dinosaur*, and founded London's Natural History Museum, but he never did figure out that *Hyracotherium* was not a hyrax. That happened decades later and thousands of miles away in the United States.

In 1866, a dour-looking young man named Othniel Marsh, with a very straight, prominent brow often accentuated with a straw boater hat, was named the first professor of paleontology at Yale University. He got the job primarily because his fabulously rich uncle, the industrialist George Peabody, built a paleontology museum for Yale. Marsh was a passionate, and fairly talented, cataloguer of bones.

And his timing was excellent. Some of the greatest fossil beds in the world were about to become accessible through railroads opening the American West.

In 1868, Marsh bought a ticket on one of the first trains to the frontier. Passing through what is now western Nebraska, at a whistle stop called Antelope Station, he chatted with some workers who told him they had encountered unusual bones while digging a well. They thought the bones were from ancient humans or maybe even tigers. Hopping off the train, Marsh examined them hungrily and, as he later wrote, "soon found many fragments and a number of entire bones, not of man, but of horses, diminutive indeed, but true equine ancestors." With the train waiting, Marsh threw the bones in a sack and went on, but later, on closer examination, found fossils of four separate horse species, including a small, odd-looking horse with not one toe, but multiple toes. Describing it, he wrote, "During life, he was scarcely a yard in height, and each of his slender legs was terminated in three toes."

Marsh went back to the West repeatedly in the next few years to search for bones, often in dangerous and remote regions where native tribes and the US Cavalry clashed. For safety, his researchers carried both rock hammers and Colt revolvers. On one early expedition near Bighorn Basin, he employed a young man named William "Buffalo Bill" Cody as a scout, until Cody had to ride off to respond to some trouble with Pawnee warriors. Within a few years, Marsh had so many crates of fossilized bones stored in the attic of Yale's Peabody Museum that he had to prop up the ceiling with extra beams.

The collection catalogued more than thirty species of horse ancestors that had lived in North America. At Yale, Marsh began to piece together a horse lineage. He started with horses from the relatively recent past. They had a single hoof that marked them distinctly as relatives of the modern horse. These animals, he found, were clearly related to somewhat older, smaller animals, which had a main hoof with two smaller hooves on either side. Those appeared to be related to even older animals that had three fully developed hoofed toes on each foot. Before this, many scientists had given little thought to how the strange beasts they found in fossil deposits were related to the present. But Marsh had found evidence of a lineage that had changed over time. It became a foundational argument for evolution.

In 1876, the world's leading proponent of evolution, a largely self-taught English biologist with broad, drooping sideburns, named Thomas Huxley, sailed to the United States to deliver a series of lectures on the controversial new theory, formally proposed by Charles Darwin twenty years earlier. Evolution had a lot of prominent backers, but it did not have much hard evidence to support it. Huxley argued that evidence could be found in the fossil record, and he focused on fossil horses from Europe that seemed to show a lineage of change over time. But his evidence was thin: three species so distantly related that drawing a line between them was at best sketchy, and not very good for the lecture circuit.

Before lecturing in New York, Huxley made his way to Marsh's museum for what he described in a letter to his wife as a quick "canter over the fossils." He ended up staying for weeks. The two bone hunters hit it off fabulously, studying at the museum by day and going for carriage rides in the evening. "His collection of fossils is the most wonderful thing I ever saw," Huxley wrote to his wife. A biography written by his son described how Huxley would ask if Marsh had a specimen to exemplify each transition. "Marsh would simply turn to his assistant and bid him fetch box number so and so, until Huxley turned upon him and said, 'I believe you are a magician; whatever I want, you just conjure it up.'"[2]

Marsh had dozens of examples of horse ancestors that showed

Eo hippus + Eohomo

THOMAS HUXLEY'S 1876
DRAWING OF THE FIRST
HORSE AND FIRST MAN.

a gradual evolution from three toes down to one hoof. As the two delved through the specimen boxes, Huxley posited that somewhere in the distant past, there must have been an original member of the horse family with four toes. He called this theoretical beast *Eohippus*—the Dawn Horse.

He drew a cartoon for Marsh of a human ancestor riding on a multitoed horse. Yale still has the doodle in its special collections. Months later, after Huxley had sailed back to England, Marsh wrote to tell him that he had found the four-toed *Eohippus*. In fact, it had been at the museum during Huxley's visit, but Marsh had so many crates of fossils from out West that he had not yet had time to clean the mud off all of them.

Unbeknownst to either, the creature Marsh called *Eohippus* was the same one Sir Richard Owen had called *Hyracotherium* thirty-five years earlier. The name *Eohippus* reigned for decades, until 1932, when an English researcher compared *Eohippus* and *Hyracotherium* and concluded they were the same. Since zoological naming rules give priority to the earliest description, *Eohippus* was scrapped. *Hyracotherium* is considered the proper name today. In the United States, you still hear a lot of ancient-horse lovers refer to the first horse by its American name, which has a nicer ring. George Gaylord Simpson, who had an even finer knowledge of horse fossils than Marsh, got around the problem by referring to the first horse as *eohippus* with a lowercase *E*—a sly way of noting that, while it was not the proper name, it was the right one.

I trailed Rose up through a jumble of boulders and out onto a bare shale flat. He moseyed with his arms loosely tucked behind his back, like a man strolling through an art museum but with his eyes trained down, as if all the paintings were screwed to the floor. In one hand he gripped an ice pick, ready to pry a jaw out of the hard ground. To outside observers, it must have looked maddeningly dull to stand out in the heat and wind, slowly scrutinizing each inch of the middle of nowhere, but each step presented a challenge—thousands of new shapes in the ground for the brain to quickly classify. Tan rock, not a fossil. Broken turtle shell, too common, not worth collecting. Sheep poop, not worth collecting. White-colored rock, oblong, requires further inspection. Nope, not a fossil.

The process continued like a mantra with each step, and took considerable concentration. It insisted that in order to better understand the distant past, we remain fixated on the present. After an hour, I began to wonder whether we would ever find a jaw. Then Rose suddenly bent down and bobbed up holding three pieces of beige stone. He fit them together loosely in his hands to form the spreading spade of a scapula bone.

"What is it?" I asked, hopefully.

"Not what I'm looking for," he said. He tossed them back in the dirt. "I'm after the little things. They are much more important. Easier to carry, too."

As he ambled on, I pressed him about the fossil he had just tossed aside. It was a *Coryphodon*, the largest mammal of the Eocene, he said. About three feet high, maybe a thousand pounds—unrelated to the hippopotamus but with a similar heft and love of aquatic plants.

"Smallest brain-to-body ratio of any mammal you find here," he said—an Eocene lummox, and an evolutionary dead end.

We ambled on. I turned my eyes back to the ground, trying to sort through the galaxy of pebbles for something useful.

"Jaw!" Rose yelled. He bent down, then popped up grinning with a fragment of fossil jaw. It was about an inch long, with a back molar still embedded in the bone, glinting in the sun. The small, narrow tooth had four simple peaks for chewing. It did not look like a scale version of modern horse molars, which have a wide maze of ridges used to grind grass with a sideways motion. *Hyracotherium*'s teeth looked more like plain old teeth—a few crests and valleys for chewing and that's about it.

"These are very primitive teeth, not much specialization in the direction of modern horses," Rose said, looking down at the fossil in his palm. "The story of the horse is really the story of its teeth. They have changed so much you wouldn't be able to recognize the species if you couldn't connect them over time."

The sun rose higher and the shadows disappeared. Rose found about twenty more jaws. I found none. Noon is the best time to find jaws because the light glints off the teeth. But it is also the most brutal time to be in the badlands. The searing sun was amplified as it bounced off the light-colored rock. We shambled and sweated. We sweated and shambled. We stopped to drink water. We sweated more. The moisture evaporated instantly in the dry wind, leaving a crust of salt that felt like fine dust. Or maybe it *was* dust. There was plenty of that around, too. I could feel it infiltrating my shoes and grinding between my toes. My neck and ears were crisping. I was wearing an old baseball cap and envied Rose's big straw brim—the only shade in miles. It gave me an appreciation for the modern horses that live out here. There isn't much to eat. There is less to drink, and there is no cover from the sun or wind. I barely made it through a day, and they had been doing it for as long as anyone could remember.

I started to wonder why anyone would want to gather fossils all day, every day, every summer, for a career. I was so hot I wanted to call it quits, speed down to the cool, green Bighorn River and jump in. But it was strangely addicting. Every time I decided to give up and try to find a small rock outcrop that might offer shade, I would see a small shelf or ravine that looked promising. And I would think, *Maybe there are jaws there.*

Then I saw one. A perfect outline of a jaw, the little black teeth glinting just like a broken beer bottle. I picked it up, cupped it in my palm, and felt my heart beat faster. In my hand was the first horse, which didn't look like a horse or eat like a horse, but even so, it was key to understanding the wild horse today—why it developed in the West, and how it was able to do so well here.

The evolutionary saga of the horse is a kind of cast-out-of-Eden story. The horse started in a lush paradise that it lost as the global climate changed. Since then, it has had to find its way over dry, barren ground, where it has managed not just to survive but also to thrive. That evolution helps explain why the animal made such a tight bond with humans, and why it was able to spread all over the world in the modern era when so many other animals disappeared.

The story starts with little bands of *Hyracotherium*. The first of them appear to have evolved on what is now India, when it was still an island in the Indian Ocean. When India slammed into the southern coast of Asia, *Hyracotherium* spread out and feasted on tender leaves and berries all over greenhouse Earth's forests, eventually reaching to Wyoming and beyond.

A few tantalizing fossil finds suggest that then, as now, horses were social. In 1952, George Gaylord Simpson, who at the time was a curator at the American Museum of Natural History in New York, found an array of twenty-six *Hyracotherium* skeletons in southern Colorado. Later analysis showed the group had far more females than males, and the males were bigger, suggesting bands with one dominant male and a harem of females.

That same band structure is still around today wherever horses roam free. Each band numbers anywhere from four to maybe twelve animals. It consists of one dominant stallion, his mares, and their offspring. The stallion acts as security, watching for both competing stallions and for predators. You will often find the stallion standing on a rise overlooking his band. Despite his size, though, he is not in charge. There is always a dominant mare that leads the band. She decides where they go, when they eat, and when they drink. If chased, the mare leads the way, the band follows, and the stallion herds from the rear, keeping his band together while holding a position where he can fight off predators.

There is not enough fossil evidence to know whether *Hyracotherium* bands worked in the same way, but the record suggests that horses have been living in these stallion-dominated family bands for a very long time.

Back in the Eocene, bands of tiny horses nibbled at lush forest growth. One well-preserved fossil from Germany showed a digestive system filled with the preserved leaves and pits from wild grapes. Just as *Hyracotherium* was getting established, about fifty million years ago, Earth began to steadily dry and cool. One of the leading theories is that the cooling was driven by an explosion in aquatic ferns that sucked so much carbon dioxide out of the atmosphere that it turned down the whole planet's thermostat. Whatever the cause, the forests began to thin. An obscure plant family called *grass*, which was once relegated to marshes and riverbanks, started to spread. It now covers almost a third of our planet.

If the spread of grass doesn't seem like a big deal, that's because you've likely never tried to eat it. And for good reason. It's harsh stuff. As a defense mechanism, grass draws abrasive silica from the ground and stores it in its cells. This sand built into the plant wears down herbivores' teeth to nubs. An herbivore with no more teeth is a dead herbivore.

Fossils suggest that, as grass spread, the horse at first stayed in the retreating forests. But then, in the Oligocene Epoch, about thirty-two million years ago, *Hyracotherium* split into two distinct lines in North America: *Miohippus* and *Mesohippus*.

Mesohippus (middle horse) basically carried on the *Hyracotherium* way of life, though there were some notable changes. The fourth toe on its front feet had withered to a bony nodule along the ankle, leaving just three toes on each foot. It was slightly larger, about two feet tall at the shoulder, with longer legs and a longer face. Its back had lost some of *Hyracotherium*'s rabbitlike hunch. It had developed an extra pair of molars for grinding. But its low-crowned teeth showed it continued to browse on lush forest foliage. Fossil beds formed from swampy areas, like the Big Badlands of South Dakota, are full of *Mesohippus* fossils, suggesting it lived in moist forests along rivers, going on as if global cooling had never happened.

Its cousin, *Miohippus* (small horse), struck out on a different path. Like *Mesohippus*, it had three toes, it was bigger than *Hyracotherium* and more horselike, but its upper molars were bigger and wider. Paleontologists see this as evidence it had started eating grass. The difference may seem minor, but it's not. *Mesohippus* is gone. It was an evolutionary dead end. *Miohippus* passed on its genes to modern horses that now cover the earth.

Miohippus's evolution can be explained in part by what it was trying to eat, and in part by what was trying to eat *it*. By thirty-two million years ago, predators had proliferated across North America. Thousand-pound *Hyaenodons*, doglike predators with muscle-piled shoulders and back legs like springs, prowled the continent. *Nimravidae*, early ancestors of the big cats, waited in the trees to pounce. The forest became dangerous. On the grasslands, at least you could see predators coming.

With the constant pressure of predators, *Miohippus* started to show characteristics now inseparable with horses. Its eyes moved farther back on its head, putting it in a better position to spot predators while lowering its head to graze or drink. Its legs became longer, stronger, and faster. Its brain became rapidly larger, perhaps because it needed to navigate new social behavior and make quick decisions about potential threats on the open plains.

The global trend in cooling and drying continued to spread. Forests continued to retreat. Grasslands and tundra continued to expand. Changes occurred gradually until about twenty-three million years ago, when something really big happened—George Gaylord Simpson called it "The Great Transformation." To watch it happen, the "Great Transformation" wouldn't have seemed all that great. But a crucial change allowed horses to increase around the planet and dominate grasslands and savannas. The transformation was this: *Miohippus* had gradually evolved through a series of limbs and branches into a distinct descendant called *Parahippus* (near horse). The big revolution in *Parahippus* was its molars. They were broad and complex—a series of ridges and valleys that could cut grass like a threshing machine. These back teeth also became much, much longer than typical teeth. Most of their length remained below the gums, housed in the jaw. The new teeth acted a bit like a mechanical pencil. As a steady diet of grass wore down the crown of the tooth, more rose out of the socket to replace it. Biologists call this trait hypsodonty—long-toothedness.

The new teeth could grind grass for decades before wearing out, allowing horses to eat a harsh diet of grass and still thrive and reproduce. Modern horse teeth can be up to five inches long and take thirty years to wear down. This, by the way, is where we get the sayings "He is long in the tooth" and "Don't look a gift horse in the mouth." A person could gauge a horse's useful life expectancy by how much of its back teeth it had left.

A similarly crucial transformation happened around the same time in the horse's digestive tract. Most herbivores are ruminants that ferment plant matter in their stomachs. Horses developed a specialized fermentation chamber near the end of their digestive tract, called the cecum. Elephants and rhinoceroses also have a cecum, or "hindgut," which is located between the intestine and the colon.

Hindgut digestion is less efficient than the digestion of most other herbivores, including cows and deer. A horse can extract only 45 percent of nutrients, while a ruminant can extract 60 percent. But a hindgut also gives horses a big advantage: They can eat low-quality food that ruminants can't. Ruminants must selectively graze tender grasses to maintain the slow process of bacterial breakdown in their stomachs. Hindgut herbivores don't have the same limitation. They can eat harsh grasses and shrubs a cow wouldn't touch. Forage passes through a hindgut system relatively quickly, so even though horses get less energy from every bite, they can take a lot more bites, so they end up getting more nutrients. This allows them to survive on forage that is too rough for most other animals.

I remember being out in a wind-whipped stretch of Nevada desert with a rancher who was explaining to me how he had to take his cattle out of a pasture because wild horses had eaten all the grass. If the grass was largely gone, I asked, how were the horses still surviving? "Shoot," he said, "wild horses can get fat in a place where a cow would starve."

About twelve million years ago, a volcano erupted in Idaho and began spewing thick plumes of ash that the wind carried eastward almost a thousand miles, where the ash rained down over what is now eastern Nebraska. By the time it was all over, the fine, silvery ash was a foot deep across the state and ten feet thick where it drifted. As the ash sifted down, large mammals—choking on the dust—made for the nearby water hole, where hundreds collapsed of lung failure and were covered over with more dust.

The ash became rock, preserving that moment in time. Then, starting in the 1970s, it was excavated by paleontologists. You can now visit the stunning jumble of stricken skeletons at Ashfall Fossil Beds State Park: camels, giant tortoises, pint-size North American rhinoceroses, and five species of horses that ranged from a gazellelike three-toed horse called *Protohippus* (first horse), to a medium-size three-toed group called *Hipparion* (ponylike horse), to the ancestor of the modern horse, called *Pliohippus* (horse from the Pliocene Epoch), which stood on one central hoof, its other toes little more than calluses on its ankles.

The epoch when the volcano blew, known as the Miocene, lasted from about twenty-three to five million years ago. It was the boom time for horses. North America boasted at least nineteen species. Like the ungulates of today's African savanna, they fanned into different niches. Some were forest dwellers, some ate grass. Some were almost as big as modern horses, others were small and light like antelope.

One of the most widespread species was *Dinohippus* (terrible horse). It was larger than previous horses, though still pony-size by today's standards—about fifty inches at the shoulder. More important than size, though, were its innovations. *Dinohippus* lived on the open grasslands where predators like dire wolves and saber-toothed cats prowled. *Dinohippus* evolved under the twin pressures of a grass diet and lurking meat eaters. Its mouth became packed with broad, long molars and it had a strong, thick jaw for grinding grass. Its face grew longer, with eyes set farther up on the head so that it could graze while still keeping watch above the grass for predators. These changes to the head made *Dinohippus* look very much like a modern horse.

The leg bones that allow many other mammals, including humans, to rotate their ankles, changed, too. They became fused to allow only forward and backward motions. This made horses stronger and more efficient. *Dinohippus* could stand with leg bones locked in place while grazing to conserve energy, and could run with increased speed.

In terms of evolutionary success, this new design was a hit. During the Miocene, the horse family, in all its variations, spread from North America to the rest of the world. They covered Florida, Oklahoma, and Texas in great herds. They crossed the Bering land bridge—which then was not a narrow bridge, but a plain hundreds of miles wide—and spread all the way to the ends of Europe and the cape in Africa.

"You just find them everywhere," said Rose. "There are places where there are just piles of them in Asia."

Spend any time looking at the history of life in the last fifty million years and what becomes astounding is not only the innovations but the constant beat of catastrophe: volcanic explosions that blotted out the sun, meteor impacts that hit like a nuclear Armageddon, repeated ice ages. Continental collision. Climatic upheaval. Droughts and storms that likely eclipse what we have ever witnessed. And yet horses thrived.

This is significant because an awful lot of other life didn't. Giant sloths, gone. Car-size armadillos, gone. Mammoths and mastodons and any number of other strange pachyderms, all gone. The *Hyaenodons* and *Gastornis* that preyed on horses, gone. Taking the long view, the story of life on Earth is mostly a story of death. Only one out of every thousand species that ever existed is still alive today. Bad things happen all the time. Five million years ago, North and South America reconnected for the first time since dinosaurs roamed the earth. Eight-foot-tall flightless birds called *Phorusrhacidae*, known informally as "terror birds," invaded North American savannas. For two million years, they stalked small horses, hunting with axelike beaks and top speeds estimated at over fifty miles an hour. No doubt they ate their share of horsemeat. But horses are still here, and terror birds are not.

A threat even more fearsome than terror birds popped up around the same time that the two Americas joined. It was a new kind of grass. As the steamy jungles of the Eocene slowly ceded to open savannas, the grass that took over was almost all of one type called C_3 grass, named for the type of photosynthesis it used. Starting about seven million years ago, a type of grass known as C_4 started to spread. C_4 had a more efficient recipe for photosynthesis, so it could grow faster, especially in hot, dry areas where growing seasons were short. But it had another advantage. C_4 grasses could store five times as much abrasive silica as C_3. It was a built-in defense mechanism because it was too gritty for most animals to chew. But not horses. As the abundance of C_4 grasses increased, so did the length of the horses' teeth. Paleontologists have found that horses were some of the first large herbivores to be able to stomach this new food. Herbivores that couldn't adapt either died out or evolved to find sources of C_3 grasses and shrubs.

It was with this last environmental change that many of the horse ancestors disappeared and the modern horse genus, *Equus*, emerged in North America, somewhere between three and six million years ago. What did *Equus* look like? A number of modern examples are still around us: zebras, wild asses in Africa, and a donkeylike resident of the Mongolian steppes called the onager. As for the true wild horse before it was domesticated, forget the image of the lithe Thoroughbred. The best indication we have of their shape and size is from paintings in the caves of southern France. Here, between thirty and fifteen thousand years ago, Paleolithic hunters recorded the shapes and colors of the animals they saw. They were stocky with big heads, short legs, and big, barrel-shaped bodies. They had short manes like those on zebras. They were mostly dun-colored, though some had stripes at the base of the neck and some had spots. For a long time, most paleontologists thought the paintings on the cave walls were just doodles that didn't show what ancient horses looked like, but a 2011 study examining ancient horse DNA found that the paintings were probably right. Ancient horses, like horses today, varied in color.[3]

Some wild horses today still have remnants of stripes on their legs and necks.

At the end of our day collecting fossils in Bighorn Basin, Professor Rose had found dozens of jaws, and I had managed to spot three. Our finds were all small enough to fit in Rose's pocket. "That's the nice thing about Eocene mammal bones," he said as we walked back to the Suburban. "Not much to carry."

Back at camp, I washed off the dust and sweat in a small, plastic tub. After dinner, we gathered at the table in an old RV that Rose uses as his field laboratory, and the students dumped out what Rose called their "goodies"—the day's haul of fossils.

"A lot of what we find doesn't have much significance on its own," Rose said. "It's only when we get it back in the lab and really compare it with everything else we've collected that we can see how things started to change."

I was so spent from a day in the dry heat that I couldn't bear thinking of the team going out day after day, but the slow shuffle in search of the past had left an impression on me. The transformations and tribulations the horse went through, from the jaw I had held in my hand to the wild mustangs we saw on the horizon, were so revolutionary that the change from wild to domestic and then back again seemed minor.

After what I had learned, I felt that the horse deserved to be counted as a native in North America. It had developed here and lived here for more than about fifty-five million years. It had disappeared ten thousand years ago, but then it had returned to its home range when Europeans arrived. Since then, it has thrived, sometimes despite our best efforts.

If the fifty-five-million-year history of horses in North America were condensed into a day, horses would be a native species right up until they became regionally extinct at 11:59:43 p.m. When they returned in the last second of the day, why did they no longer belong?

There was one more part of the story I wanted to understand: the disappearance. Why, after fifty-five million years, had the horse gone AWOL, and what effect did that have on any claims to being a native species?

To try to answer that, I headed to the University of Colorado in Boulder, where a drawer in the offices of anthropologist Douglas Bamforth held some promising evidence.

The office, in a castlelike, 130-year-old stone science building that is one of the oldest on campus, had grand oak specimen drawers and tall windows to let in natural light. In that setting, I half expected Bamforth to arrive with a herringbone jacket and a pipe clenched in his teeth. But Boulder has become a casual place, and he arrived in jeans and a Patagonia pullover, having just come from the gym.

As the local anthropologist, he told me, he gets a lot of calls from the public. "Pretty regularly anyone who finds a triangular rock will come in and ask if it's an arrowhead," he said with a long-suffering sigh.

One of those calls came in on an afternoon in 2008 from a doctor who was having a koi pond built in his backyard at the edge of town. "I went up there to check it out, a bit reluctantly," Bamforth said. "And what I found was really astonishing."

Workers digging a shallow pit had found more than eighty stone tools—scrapers, cutters, and spear points that dated to about thirteen thousand years ago. Some of them were nearly the size of a dinner plate and exquisitely crafted to almond-shaped points with delicate serrated edges made by carefully flaking both sides with precise hits from a stone. These were not just arrowheads—they were rare Clovis points dating back to the period when the first humans arrived in North America. This was also the time when the horses disappeared.

The name *Clovis* comes from an archaeological site near Clovis, New Mexico, where the first points from the era were found amid mammoth bones in 1929. Since then, Clovis sites have been uncovered in all corners of the Americas, and they are almost always associated with the hunting of huge mammals. Though much about the Clovis people is still unknown, the leading theory is that they came across the land bridge from Asia about fifteen thousand years ago, just as the glaciers from the last ice age were retreating. Everywhere they went, they left large, exquisitely crafted, stone spear points. Within a thousand years, these small bands of hunters had reached the tip of South America, a spread that one anthropologist described as "an unprecedented rate of diffusion not seen again until the invention of the hula-hoop."[4]

All evidence suggests Clovis hunters were an even more disastrous introduction for North American fauna than the South American terror birds had been. Within a few thousand years of their arrival, more than thirty large animal species had disappeared from North America, an event known as the Quaternary Extinction. Mammoths, giant sloths, giant beavers, saber-toothed cats—all disappeared. There has been a great deal of debate among scientists as to whether the extinction was caused by hunters, climate change, or both. There is still no consensus, but most think Clovis played a big role.

Professor Bamforth picked up the biggest, most striking stone tool from the drawer, a broad, almond-shaped point so big it filled both of his hands.

It was made of a honey-colored stone with the soft shine of hard toffee, and expertly flaked edges still looked sharp, more than 10,000 years later.

"This stone isn't from around here," he said. "None of this stone is. It comes from hundreds of miles away. What that shows us is that these hunters were highly mobile, highly skilled, and knew the land well."

In 2009, with the permission of the doctor who uncovered the points, Bamforth sent the stone tools to a lab in California to see if any residue containing DNA could be recovered. It was a long shot—the tools had been buried for hundreds of generations—but it was worth a try.

The results came back positive. Three of the tools had ancient DNA. One was of camel, one was of sheep, and one was of horse. Horse DNA has been found at numerous other Clovis sites since then. Horse bones have been found piled next to Clovis hearths. There is no evidence Clovis people dined on horses alone, but evidence does suggest they dined on horses a lot.

So, does that change whether the horse is a native species? If we classify nonnatives as species introduced through the interference of man, how do we adjust when a species may have been wiped out by man? In modern times, we have reintroduced countless species that have been regionally wiped out by men—elk, bighorn sheep, buffalo, mountain goats, condors, falcons. Does it matter if their absence is measured in millennia instead of decades?

Maybe it does matter. If an animal has been gone so long that the rest of the ecosystem has moved on, and left no room, then perhaps the case can be made that a species is no longer a native. I asked Bamforth about this. Are the grasslands of the West much different today than they were ten thousand years ago? "It was cooler then, and drier," he said. "But no, the species are basically the same."

Evolution can have a long memory. The North American prong-horn evolved to outrun a North American cheetahlike cat that was wiped out when Clovis points showed up. The pronghorn can still run at sixty miles per hour, even though it hasn't needed to for millennia. Maybe the horse and the western grass are the same way: After developing together for so long, they still remember in their DNA what it was like to live together.

The Bureau of Land Management, many ranchers, and even some conservationists argue that because the wild horse was introduced, it does not fit in the ecosystem here. It is therefore a damaging invasive and must be tightly controlled. That is in part why round-ups have continued for decades. That is why we have fifty thousand horses in storage.

Any argument against counting the horse as native is biologically naive. Spend time with paleontologists and you learn to take a longer view. They don't use the word *native*. Nor do they talk about a delicate balance in the ecosystem. All they see is upheaval and change. Nothing lasts. From this point of view, it's hard to give a concept like being "native" much value. Everything that was native to the horse has been lost and remade repeatedly in its evolution, including the horse itself. What matters is what lasts. Through its own roundabout history, the horse is still here.

CHAPTER 2

RETURN OF A NATIVE

Two runners walked onto the sun-bleached plaza of Turquoise Pueblo, in what are now the hills south of Santa Fe, New Mexico, one day in the summer of 1680. Young and lean, their feet strung with simple yucca-fiber sandals and powdered with dust from the miles they had covered on the trail, they asked to see the leading men of the village and especially the war chief. They carried a message that would change the course of the West forever—and also the course of America's wild horses.

At the time, the idea of America was still far, far away from the dry hills of the Southwest. The colonies that would become the United States were barely holding onto a few harbors on the East Coast, focused on growing tobacco and executing accused witches. Along the Rio Grande Valley in New Mexico, the native Pueblo tribes had their own culture far removed from the East. They had been growing corn and squash in the powdery soil for centuries. Turquoise Pueblo had prospered as a center of trade in pottery, corn, and semiprecious stones. Over the generations, families had added adobe rooms, one and two stories tall, with fat walls of mud brick, until clusters stood in crooked bunches around a series of oblong plazas. It was one of dozens of pueblos that clung to the land along the Rio Grande, where springs were reliable and soil was good. The tribes followed a calendar of feasts and dances tied to a religion of indigenous spirits: the snake dance, the deer dance, the bean-planting dance. Except for the coming of droughts, little had changed for a very long time.

Then the Spanish came. Conquistadors were the first to arrive, starting with Francisco Vázquez de Coronado in 1540. And though they often left havoc in their wake, they didn't linger long. Spanish settlers started to arrive in 1598, bringing herds of goats, sheep, cattle, and horses. They built Santa Fe, just a day's run to the north. But it was the Catholic priests who moved to Turquoise Pueblo in 1635 that the runners had come to discuss. The priests had come bent on ridding the natives of their religion. When they arrived, they built a church atop a cluster of adobes and renamed the pueblo, calling it San Marcos, in honor of Saint Mark the Evangelist. They brought livestock and useful skills like weaving, which the locals welcomed, but they also demanded labor and tribute from the Pueblos, who often had little to spare. And they insisted on strict adherence to Catholicism.

Few of the Pueblos were ready to abandon their old gods. When the priests, most of whom had grown up during the Inquisition in Spain, discovered Indians still practicing native religions, their punishments were harsh. Whipping was common. The friar at the Hopi Pueblo three hundred miles to the west trampled a man to death with his horse. An inquiry by the Spanish Crown later found that he also opted for burning in turpentine as punishment for "idolaters and children."[1]

On the day in 1680 when the runners arrived at Turquoise Pueblo, they were led from the bleached sunlight of the plaza into the cool shadows of an adobe room where the headmen of the community were gathered. The locals knew tensions were rising. A decade of drought had brought famine and instability. The priests and their new god had not provided the promised protection. And yet Pueblo men who had gone back to asking the old gods for help had been caught and whipped. The governor of New Mexico had ordered native religious masks, altars, and holy objects to be burned, and many of the local underground ceremonial rooms, called *kivas*, were destroyed. He had ordered four men to be hanged in the square in Santa Fe and another forty-three to be flogged for practicing "sorcery."

Rather than bringing the Pueblos back into line, the assault on traditional ways acted as a wedge, each blow driving them farther from the Spanish. The runners spoke of this abuse, and the men of the village nodded. The runners told the men that all across the region, at villages much like theirs, elders in their kivas had decided it was time to rise up and drive the Spanish out. On the appointed day, they would kill the priests and burn the churches. The men of the village nodded. One of the runners held up a cord of yucca fiber punctuated with several knots. Other runners were delivering cords just like it to other pueblos across the region, he reported. Untie one knot each morning. On the morning the last knot is untied, attack.

If you refuse to join the attack, they said, then, when the Spanish are dead, we will come after you.

There were no wild horses in North America when the Spanish arrived. Three centuries later, when American settlers reached the West, horse numbers may have been in the millions. Mustangs on the Great Plains stretched from horizon to horizon. Whole areas of West Texas were marked on early maps with two words: *wild horses*. Explorers talked of uncountable herds that surged over the prairies in waves. It was one of the quickest, most widespread, and most successful introductions of a species in the history of the world. And it was done mostly through warfare.

There are many points where you could start telling the story of the mustang's spread through the West—all of them centered on humans and conflict. You could start with the first horse to set hoof in North America with the Spanish conquistadors, or go back even farther to the Moorish invaders who brought tough, fleet little Barb horses to Spain. You could go back beyond that, too, to the Scythians and Mongols who spread the horse through raiding campaigns that ranged from China to Rome. The closely linked history of horses and war gives added meaning to the term *invasive species*.

But the day when the runners held up the yucca cords at Turquoise Pueblo and the locals agreed to rise up against the Spanish is perhaps the best place to start telling the story of the horse in North America. At that moment, horses were tightly controlled by the Spanish and were kept clustered around a few European settlements. They were like dandelion fluff still arranged tightly on a stem. The 1680 Pueblo Revolt was the great breath that sent them flying.

From that moment, the Spanish were never really in control of the West again, largely because they had lost control of horses. From the Huns to the Sioux, horses not only have almost always been associated with the spread of war, but they have also enabled the spread of war. The side that made best use of horses usually won. The native tribes used horses to dominate not only the Spanish in the West but also, for a time, the Americans.

No one incident was the source of all wild horses. Instead, uncounted thousands of battles, raids, and black-market trades put Spanish horses in the hands of native tribes. No doubt horses got free before the Pueblo Revolt and after. But after the revolt, the trend was clear. Horses kept getting loose, and loose horses kept breeding. And soon there were vast, uncountable seas of horses that made the whole landscape appear to move. These herds changed the history of the West.

By the time American settlers began arriving in numbers nearly two hundred years after the revolt, the land west of the Mississippi River was covered with horses. One ranger passing through the area that is now Nueces County, Texas, in the 1840s said he "met with a drove of mustangs so large that it took us fully an hour to pass it, although they were traveling at a rapid rate in a direction nearly opposite to the one we were going. As far as the eye could extend on a dead level prairie, nothing was visible except a dense mass of horses, and the trampling of their hoofs sounded like the roar of the surf on a rocky coast."[2]

Christopher Columbus brought no horses on his first voyage to the New World in 1492. They were difficult and expensive to care for on long sea voyages. But it must not have taken long to figure out that horses would be worth the trouble in the land across the Atlantic, because he brought fifteen stallions and five mares on his second voyage in 1493. What they were used for, and how long they lasted, is lost to history, but soon after arriving, he wrote to Queen Isabella that every ship from then on should carry brood mares. In voyages that followed, Columbus and other explorers brought both expertly bred war steeds and scabby, near-worthless nags. They also brought pigs, sheep, and chickens, which they bred on the island of Hispaniola and supplied to the conquistadors who had pushed farther west to the mainland. But it was the horses more than any other animal that the conquistadors credited with helping their small numbers conquer much of two continents.

The stories the Spanish told of subduing whole cultures with a small number of soldiers and horses are so stunning that they survive today. Pánfilo de Nárvaez, who conquered Cuba, fought off

A NAVAJO PETROGLYPH IN CANYON DE CHELLY IN ARIZONA RECORDS NATIVE AMERICAN CONTACT WITH SPANISH EXPLORERS ON HORSEBACK.

a surprise attack by several thousand warriors one night by jumping on his horse, galloping among them, and ringing bells. In Peru, Francisco Pizarro cantered in circles in front of the Inca royal court to show his power, then ran at full speed toward the emperor, stopping only feet away. In the battle that followed, charges of Spanish horses, with the conquistadors blasting their guns and ringing bells, sent the Incas running, allowing Pizarro to defeat an army of eighty thousand Incas with 106 men on foot and sixty-two in the saddle. Hernán Cortés landed in Mexico in 1519 with five hundred men and just sixteen horses. When his men came riding four abreast into the capital, Tenochtitlan, which was built on a great lake, canoes came paddling from every corner so people could gape at the monsters, who seemed to be half-human, half-deer, and able to come apart. The Spanish quickly realized the horse was their secret weapon, or, as Bernal Díaz, a soldier who fought with Cortés, later called them, "our fortress." Within two years, Cortés had conquered the Aztec empire—the most powerful civilization in the New World.

"Next to God we owed our victory to the horses," wrote a chronicler of Francisco Coronado's expedition. When the Pueblo tribes of New Mexico first saw the horses of Coronado's expedition in 1540, they were so awestruck that they smeared sweat from the horses on their chests to transfer the power to themselves. The shock value of horses wore off, of course, but the strategic value of being stronger and faster on horseback than an enemy on foot was permanent. Such an advantage was not to be squandered. As the Spanish settled in what is now New Mexico, they were outnumbered by the natives. To retain control, they passed laws banning natives from owning horses or even learning to ride. Similar laws in the American South later kept slaves from riding horses for similar reasons.

But the value of horses for conquest depended in large part on the landscape. Where the land was wide, open, and dry, horses flew across the terrain, giving conquerors the powers of gods. Dense forests and steep mountains took away those advantages. Where the land was thick and wet, horses literally bogged down and often became liabilities. Central America's jungle civilizations took decades to pacify. There is a reason that ships, not horses, play an outsize role in the story of settling New England—horses could not get around in the thick forests.

In 1540, Hernando de Soto landed in Florida with 250 horses. As he fumbled his way through the South, almost all of his animals sank into marshes, disappeared into the woods, or were shot full of arrows by the locals. After two years of wandering fruitlessly, fewer than ten of the expedition's horses remained and de Soto had died of fever on the banks of the Mississippi River. Eventually, the remaining members of his party built barges, loaded their few horses, and retreated down the Mississippi. These last survivors were grazing along a river one day when a local tribe launched a surprise attack. The Spanish scurried to their barges under a hail of arrows, unable to bring the horses.

Some have supposed that de Soto's horses, abandoned in 1542, were the first wild mustangs in the West. Mark Van Doren, a poet writing in New York City, in a prefatory note to a poem called "The Distant Runners," posited that: "Six great horses of Spain, set free after his death by de Soto's men, ran west and restored to America the wild race there lost some thousands of years ago."[3] But an account from de Soto's expedition suggests those Barb horses never got the chance to run west. As the Spanish floated away from their attackers, a chronicler of the expedition said, they watched the natives "hurl arrows at the horses with great fiesta and rejoicing until all had fallen."[4]

Even if de Soto's horses had lived, it is not clear whether they would have spread. Horses were not as suited for the wet forests of the Southeast as they were for the West. They had evolved for arid grasslands. In order to flourish, in warfare or on their own, they needed dry, wide-open acreage. But once they got loose on the right ground, almost nothing could stop them.

The Spanish plan to keep horses from the natives in New Mexico began to unravel almost as soon as it was in place. The Spanish came to colonize the Rio Grande in 1598, led by Juan de Oñate, the wealthy son of Spanish silver-mine owners. His wagon train of settlers brought with them a few thousand sheep, goats, and cattle and 316 horses. These were not the first horses ever to set foot in the area, but they are the first that could plausibly lay claim to being the origins of wild horses in the West. Fifty years earlier, Francisco Coronado had come through the area with an army and fifteen hundred horses, and journals from the expedition mention a few lost horses, but Oñate's settlers never reported seeing any horses among the natives or loose on the plains. Whatever happened to Coronado's horses, they don't appear to have reproduced.

Oñate's expedition settled among the Pueblo Indians, who, like them, were farmers. Over the first few decades, the horses they brought multiplied, prompting a visitor in 1630 named Fray Alonso de Benavides to report, "Our herds have already propagated much there," noting the land had no horses when the Spanish first arrived, but now had many "famous horses, particularly for military use."[5]

The Spanish set up a feudal system of huge ranches with natives serving as peasants. In the end, the system they designed to give them every advantage led to their downfall. Each Spanish ranch owner was expected to pay tribute back to the Spanish government in Mexico, and in exchange he was allowed to treat the natives on his land as serfs, forcing them to pay tribute to him. Though the natives were not officially allowed to ride horses under this system, as ranch hands they learned how to care for and breed them. In 1621, the Spanish governor in New Mexico relaxed the law to allow Indian ranch workers to ride horses, as long as they had converted to Catholicism. Before long, the region had a growing population of poorly treated underlings who knew everything there was to know about Spain's secret weapon.

These underlings also had plenty of chances to escape. The ranches of New Mexico were surrounded on all sides by nomadic tribes—the Navajo, the Apache, and the Ute, among others. Many of the Pueblos had longstanding trade ties to their nomadic neighbors. Some spoke the same languages, and they often intermarried. A Pueblo man fed up with life as a serf could light out for the mountains, and if he had been taught to care for horses, he had a ready means of escape. The runaways shared what they had learned with the nomadic tribes. By the 1640s, a few chiefs in the Navajo and Apache tribes had learned to ride.

Looking back through the centuries, there may be no way to fully appreciate what horses meant to the tribes, or how potent was the thrill of looking into a horse's eyes, feeling its hot breath, and realizing its strength could be your strength, its speed your speed. A horse and rider could be inestimably more than the sum of their parts. For the tribes, it was everything. The distance and space in the West that had been once oppressive and impoverishing suddenly could become a source of power. Vast grasslands that had been deserts could be turned into muscle, speed, wealth, and weapons of war that, in the right hands, could turn bands of meager scroungers into a fighting force powerful enough to terrorize modern empires and keep both the Spanish and the American armies at bay.

Almost every tribe immediately yearned for horses, dreamed of them, sang of them, painted them on canyon walls, named moons in their annual calendar after them, and welcomed them into their cultures so completely that before long they were sure the horse had always been there. The Apache said the Creator made the horse, using lightning for its breath, rainbows for its hooves, the evening star for its eyes, crescent moons for its ears, and a whirlwind for its power and speed. The Navajo said that every day the sun god rode across the sky on a turquoise mustang with a joyous neigh.

One buffalo hunter recalled in his memoir that by the 1850s the Comanche "were boasting in all seriousness that the horse was created by the Good Spirit for the particular benefit of the Comanches, and that the Comanches had introduced it to the whites."[6]

Maybe the tribes knew at first glimpse that the animals would change everything. Or maybe they just saw such beautiful animals and in their gut knew they had to have them. But this is sure: They did anything to get them. And some Spanish were willing to make secret deals for a price. In the 1650s, Alonso de Posada, a Franciscan missionary at the Pecos Pueblo on the edge of the Great Plains, saw

Pueblos illegally trading Spanish horses to the Apache in exchange for buffalo robes. A number of the region's governors also had been accused over the years of trading horses for Apache buffalo hides. The Apache, probably the first tribe to get horses, transformed from a group of humble nomads into a feared fighting force. Posada, one of the earliest chroniclers of the Southwest, complained that by the 1650s the Apache were "running off day and night the horse herds of the Spaniards and inflicting all the rest of the injuries which the force of their fierce arrogance imposes."[7]

With their newfound skill in horse raiding, the Apaches didn't just raid the Spanish. They raided other tribes. "There is a nation which they call the Apacha which possesses and is owner of all the plains of *Cíbola*," Posada wrote. "The Indians of this nation are so arrogant, haughty and such boastful warriors that they are the common enemy of all nations who live below the northern region. They hold them as cowards. They have destroyed, ruined or driven most of them from their lands."[8]

Native tribes' history with the horse may not seem to have any connection to the species' fossil past in North America, but I think it does. Over millions of years of hardships on the ever-growing grasslands of North America, horses developed both toughness and a willingness to cooperate in bands that made them exceptionally suited to the needs of man. The adaptation of their gut to be able to subsist on poor-quality feed in dry grasslands and their legs to walk long miles between water as well as have bursts of speed to avoid predators became natural assets for long campaigns of war and exploration where long miles were expected and good feed was rarely found. The social structure that horses developed also became a critical asset. Bands operated through complex social interactions. Horses formed relationships, took cues from dominant animals, helped one another watch for danger, and learned to be submissive. Animals with this innate sense of social order easily integrate with humans. Other animals were domesticated—sheep, pigs, goats, even reindeer—but few became working companion animals like the horse because they lacked the social smarts and stamina created by the horse's long and complex coevolution with grass.

Horse stealing became a positive-feedback loop. The more horses that the Apache, Ute, and Navajo stole, the more they were able to steal. The more they relied on raiding, the more they needed to raid. The Spanish started calling the Apache *los farones*—the pharaohs—because they were like the swift Egyptian cavalry of Exodus. The raids grew so constant that, by 1676, the Spanish in New Mexico had few horses left. The governor was forced to send a message to Mexico asking for a thousand horses and fifty saddles to replace those stolen by the natives.

The raiding caused uncertainty and shortages in the Spanish settlements. The Spanish often took it out on the Pueblos. And, by 1680, the Pueblos had had enough.

In the summer of 1680, men in kivas all along the Rio Grande untied the knots on their yucca cords, counting down the days until revolt. At dawn on August 10, they untied the final knot. That morning, men blocked the roads leading to the capital in Santa Fe and seized the Spanish horses that could have spread the alarm. The natives then turned on those Spaniards who were the closest to them and the most hated—the priests. At Santo Domingo Pueblo, three friars were cut down in their mission convent. Their bodies were dragged to the church and heaped before the altar. At Acoma Pueblo, friars were stoned to death. At Sandia Pueblo, Indians tore the doors off the church and hacked the limbs off a statue of St. Francis standing above the altar. They tossed chalices and religious statues in a bucket of manure, whipped the crucifix until it was nearly bare of paint, and, as if to make sure their point wasn't missed, someone took a crap on the main alter. At Jemez Pueblo, attackers rode the priest through the village like a horse, whipping him. Then a young warrior stabbed him through the heart.

Some of the Spanish managed to escape to the safety of Santa Fe, driving ahead of them what horses and livestock they could gather. They barricaded themselves in the low, adobe buildings that made up the governor's headquarters. Thousands of miles from reinforcements, all they could do was wait. On August 15, they spotted five hundred Pueblo warriors approaching, burning cornfields and houses as they came. At the lead was an Indian armed with a Spanish long gun, a sword, and a dagger. He was riding on a Spanish horse.

A battle raged over six days. The Indians cut off the Spanish water supply and tried to burn them out. The Spanish countered with a daring dawn raid that left hundreds of Indians dead. In the end, the Spanish governor, knowing that he had no hope of reinforcements, decided to retreat to El Paso. A thousand survivors limped southward, abandoning the region to the native tribes. The Spanish left three thousand horses around Santa Fe, and more scattered at every ranch. This was the true beginning of the horse in the West, the violent breath that scattered the seeds. It is one of those events so significant in regional history that scholars of the West have given the moment its own name. They call it "the great horse dispersal."

For more than a decade, the Spanish did not return. When they finally formed an army and pushed up the Rio Grande to retake the territory, they were greeted at Santa Fe by Pueblo warriors on horseback. Their leader came riding out to defy the Spanish wearing a mother-of-pearl shell on his head like a crown, and riding what one witness called "a beautiful horse."

The age of the Horse Nations had begun. It would last almost two hundred years and burn itself so deeply into the world's imagination that it is still, more than a century later, almost impossible to imagine Indians without also imagining the horse. The horse made some tribes so powerful that for centuries they held at bay the three most powerful European empires—the Spanish, the French, and the English. The tribes who fell most heavily under the spell of horses—the Horse Nations—became the most successful and hardest to defeat: the Sioux, the Apache, the Crow, the Comanche, the Nez Perce, the Blackfoot. The tribes that didn't adopt horses are largely forgotten by history.

The Spanish managed to hold Santa Fe after returning. They established colonies in Texas and along the coast of California, but they never really took control of the West, in large part because of horses. Instead, they fell into a repetitive cycle where they imported more horses to battle the horse raiders, only increasing their losses. The Apache and Ute, who lived closest to the Spanish, were probably the first tribes to learn to ride, with a few having horses even before the Pueblo Revolt. The Navajo were likely next. From there, scholars have mapped the spread of horses from the journals of explorers and the recollections of tribes. The trade spread like twin vines up both sides of the Rockies. To the east, on the Great Plains, the Apache gave horses to the Pawnee, the Pawnee to the Arapaho, the Arapaho to the Kiowa, the Kiowa to the Mandan. Horses stolen from the Spanish on the western side of the mountains went first to the Ute, then to the Shoshone around 1700, then to the Nez Perce around 1730, then to the Crow and Blackfoot around 1740, and finally to the Cree around 1750. In 1790, trappers spotted horses with Spanish brands in Canada. Though much of the spread came through raiding and warfare, peaceful trade and cultural exchange must also have been part of the deal. After all, stealing a horse is one thing, learning to care for it and ride is another.

Horses stolen from the Spanish could also be traded to the

French, a few hundred miles to the east, for guns that could be used to steal more horses. Which could then be traded for guns. Like furs, mustangs fueled a rabid exchange in manufactured goods. Even tribes like the sedentary Mandan, who farmed river banks and did not rely on horses for nomadic hunting, prospered as middlemen in the market.

"The horse is the most important article of their trade," a French trader named Antoine Tabeau wrote after a visit to tribes on the upper Missouri River in 1803, when a good horse could fetch "a gun, a hundred charges of powder and balls, a knife and other trifles."[9]

A tribe's first encounter with the horse was often so momentous that the story lived for generations. A Piegan elder named Saukamaupee interviewed by a fur trader in the 1780s remembered first seeing a horse from the neighboring Snake tribe killed during a battle. "Numbers of us went to see him, and we all admired him. He put us in mind of a stag that had lost his horns, and we did not know what name to give him. But as he was a slave to Man, like the dog, which carried our things, he was named the Big Dog." Later, they started calling horses "elk dogs." Other tribes called them "holy dogs" or "sky dogs."[10]

Before the horse, the Great Plains had been largely devoid of people. For centuries, a few tribes lived near rivers, where they farmed corn, squash, and beans and lived in earthen mound houses, but surviving in the sea of grass on foot was like surviving in the open ocean in a rowboat. There was no shelter from sun or wind and there were long stretches without water. Families dragged their meager possessions on the backs of dogs and women. Though game was abundant, sneaking within killing range with a handmade bow was tough. Buffalo could be driven off cliffs, but to do that you needed a cliff. You only need to drive across Nebraska to know this is no easy proposition. To live on the Great Plains was to live near starvation.

Those who did live there, survived in part off of roots and roasted grasshoppers.

The horse turned the grass that had been an oppressive void into a near-limitless resource. With it, tribes could suddenly harness the power of the plains—a power mighty enough to sustain eighty million buffalo. Within a generation, whole societies were transformed. Small family bands came together into mobile towns of hundreds and sometimes thousands. Raiding and war, once rare, became frequent. The main prize was horses.

The Ute sometimes used raids on other tribes to capture women and children whom they could trade to the Spanish for more horses. When other children weren't available for trade, they traded their own.[11] The Apache and Kiowa gave up lives of farming to hunt and raid on horseback. The Osage, Sioux, Cheyenne, and Arapaho, living in the forests on the eastern edge of the plains, were drawn westward with horses, leaving behind wood lodges in favor of new buffalo-skin tents called *teepees*. With horses replacing dogs as beasts of burden, the modest teepee soon doubled in diameter to fifteen feet.

The Indian pony was a true mustang—a free-born horse that came from Spanish stock. Before the name *mustang* became dominant, the Spanish also called these horses *cimarrones*—a word that comes from the Spanish word *maroon*—an escaped slave. The horses were small, with short legs and thick bodies. One explorer making his way into the northern plains in 1754 estimated they were "fine tractible [*sic*] animals, about 14 hands high; lively and clean made." They were of every color, about seven hundred pounds, with large, round chests, heavy shoulders and hips.[12]

Americans coming west were often dismayed at the sorry state of Indian horses. They were scrawny, short-legged, sore-backed, crow-pecked, and often mercilessly abused by their owners. It is now often posited that the Spanish brought over finely bred horses that, through neglect, devolved into the mongrel nags of the Horse Nations. I'm not so sure. No doubt Coronado and Cortés, or the governors in Santa Fe, rode well-regarded horses. But most of the Spanish outposts along the Rio Grande were desperately poor, and most settlers there rode simple peasant horses if they rode at all. No doubt the small, crow-pecked nags the tribes had were not so different from the average Spanish stock.

The mustangs of the Horse Nations may not have been much to look at, but Americans writing home were constantly amazed at the ability of these sorry-looking beasts. Surveying the herds on the southern plains, the painter George Ruxton saw "only now and then noble animals of beautiful form." But, he added, "It is unbelievable how much the Indians can accomplish with their horses, what burdens they are able to carry, and what great distances they can cover in short time."[13]

After watching strings of Lakota warriors gallop past his fort in 1867, a cavalry colonel stationed along the Missouri River in what is now North Dakota wrote, "The Indian pony without stopping can cover a distance of from sixty to eighty miles between sunrise and sunset, while most of our horses would be on their knees at the end of thirty or forty miles."[14]

The horse in the hands of the Shoshone tribe was so powerful that it caused the tribe, which had been living in the high basins of Wyoming, to split. One group headed east onto the Great Plains and followed the buffalo southward, where they began ferocious raids against the Spanish and other tribes. The Ute began referring to these new raiders by a word meaning "foreigner" or "enemy," and the Spanish began using the Ute word too. They were called the Comanche.

No tribe was transformed by the horse like the Comanche. What had been a hard-luck band surviving on small game, roots, and ber-

WARLIKE EXERCISES OF COMANCHES.

AN ENGRAVING IN A BOOK PUBLISHED IN 1873 SHOWS HOW THE COMANCHE, ONCE
HUMBLE HUNTER-GATHERERS, WERE TRANSFORMED BY HORSES.

ries in humble brush lean-tos changed within the course of a few
generations into the emperors of the southern plains, running an
area stretching from the Rockies to Louisiana and from the Platte
River in Nebraska down into Mexico.

"They compare their number to that of the stars. They are so
skilled in horsemanship that they have no equal, so daring that
they never ask for or grant truces," according to Athanase de
Mézières, a French explorer who worked as a Spanish Indian liai-
son in the 1770s.[15]

The Comanche were not noted for being tall or good looking,
or having much in the way of culture or arts, but man, could they
ride. Most tribes used horses to cover ground but fought on foot.
The Comanche learned to be a cavalry force. They trained by chasing down buffalo. Boys started riding at four and by adulthood were
expected to be able to sweep a fallen man up off the ground at a gal-

lop, wield a fourteen-foot lance among galloping bison, and shoot twenty arrows in the time a soldier could unholster his rifle.

George Catlin, who himself relied on a tamed mustang named Charlie to carry his painting supplies, camped with the Comanche in 1834, making several sketches of young men riding horses. "On their feet they are one of the most unattractive and slovenly looking races of Indians I have ever seen," he later wrote. "But the moment they mount their horses, they seem at once metamorphosed."[16]

Astride a horse, they seemed to gain superhuman abilities, he observed:

> Amongst their feats of riding, there is one that has astonished me more than anything of the kind I have ever seen, or expect to see, in my life:—a stratagem of war, learned and practiced by every young man in the tribe; by which he is able to drop his body upon the side of his horse at the instant he is passing, effectually screened from his enemies' weapons as he lays in a horizontal position behind the body of his horse, with his heel hanging over the horse's back; by which he has the power of throwing himself up again, and changing to the other side of the horse if necessary. In this wonderful condition, he will hang whilst his horse is at fullest speed, carrying with him his bow and his shield, and also his long lance of fourteen feet in length, all or either of which he will wield upon his enemy as he passes; rising and throwing his arrows over the horse's back, or with equal ease and equal success under the horse's neck.[17]

The Comanche were such expert riders that even the other Horse Nations referred to them as "the horse people." They raided the Spanish mercilessly, in both New Mexico and Texas, sometimes taking as many as fifteen hundred horses at a time. Traveling light, they could strike from a hundred miles away, appear before anyone knew they were there, and disappear just as quickly. Though the plains were their empire, they struck as far as five hundred miles into Mexico and raided the coastal towns of Texas. In a typical raid in San Antonio observed by a French visitor in 1876, the Comanche made off with four hundred horses. Spanish troops pursued for "100 leagues," only to have the Comanche ambush them and steal 150 more horses.

The only reason the Comanche allowed the Spanish to exist in the region, they liked to boast, was to raise more horses for them. The tribe had the power to toy with the Europeans in a way rarely seen among native groups. In 1813, thousands of Comanche warriors appeared in San Antonio demanding gifts. When the governor refused, the tribe destroyed every ranch on the San Antonio River and took all the area's horses along the San Antonio River. Peace only came to the area a few years later, when there were no more horses to steal. Then the Comanche began selling horses back to the Spanish.

When the tribe was finally subdued, decades later, it was in large part because the US Cavalry captured, and immediately slaughtered, thousands of its horses.

Horses became more than just transportation; they were status and wealth, the currency of the plains that could be banked in the endless blonde grass. Young riders customized their horses like hotrods. The Cheyenne decorated them with buffalo or elk horns and red trade cloth. Sioux painted them with red ochre and slit their nostrils to make them breathe more freely. The Kiowa, Arapaho, and Cheyenne all had more than fifteen thousand horses each—about six horses per person. An "industrious" Comanche might own three hundred horses. As with all other kinds of wealth, some men amassed more than seems reasonable. One Crow chief claimed to have ridden off with five thousand Comanche horses in a single raid. A Blackfoot named Middle Sitter amassed more than five hundred and changed his name to Many Horses. A rich Ute chief was said to have more than eight hundred. When he died, his forty best horses were shot so they could accompany him in the afterlife.[18]

The constant raiding and breeding and trading spread horses across the West far more rapidly than they likely would have spread on their own. They were everywhere, and if they weren't, men tried hard to get them there. Once the Horse Nations were established, wild horses were inevitable. In a land with no fences, horses were free to wander off and go wild. Horses were also set loose by constant raiding. When the governor of New Mexico launched a surprise attack on the Comanche at the base of what is now Pikes Peak in 1779, he drove off two thousand horses that escaped onto the plains. The Comanche later counterattacked and drove off two thousand Spanish horses.

Loose horses spread like tumbleweed through any terrain that was dry and open. They ranged from eastern Texas to California and up into Canada. According to early accounts, twenty thousand lived in the San Joaquin Valley, four thousand lived among the tribes on the Columbia River, and twenty thousand lived on the Snake River. On the grasses of south Texas, wild horse herds grew especially thick. In 1777, a missionary, on his way to San Antonio from Mexico City, noted that the wild horses "are so abundant that their trails make the country, utterly uninhabited by people, look as if it were the most populated in the world. All the grass on the vast ranges has been consumed by them, especially around the waterings."[19] The area became known as "The Mustang Desert."

An American named Jacob Fowler traveled up the Arkansas River in 1821, abandoning a number of worn-out horses along the way. Near what is now Pueblo, Colorado, he was charged at full speed by a band of mounted Kiowa who flourished their bows and lances. After a brief parlay, the Kiowa invited him to their camp. The Arkansas River there, with its broad, grassy valleys and thick stands of cotton-woods, was a favorite wintering ground for the Horse Nations. There he discovered bands of Kiowa, Comanche, Arapaho, Cheyenne, and Snake teepees with "about 20,000 horses." The Comanche there boasted they had just stolen twenty-eight horses from a band of Crow they encountered. Later, a few of the men in Fowler's expedition encountered these Crow, who said they had stolen two hundred horses from another tribe. As the Crow were explaining their raid to the hunters, some Arapaho attacked, riding off with a hundred of the horses. In the confusion, the Americans ran, leaving their nine horses loose on the plains. In the week the great camp was assembled, about five hundred horses were stolen, or perhaps went loose. No one seemed to know which.[20]

Tribes that owned thousands of horses often turned out worn-out mounts, planning to collect them later, but they never did. Storms and droughts scattered animals. There was also disease. In 1837, small-pox nearly wiped out whole tribes, leaving herds to wander away.

But really, what made the spread of the horse in the West inevitable was the horse itself. In a very real sense, it was coming home to a place that its genes not only remembered but also had spent millions of years learning to master. Everything the horse needed to thrive immediately was already there when it stepped off the boat.

The first American to record seeing a wild horse was Captain Zebulon Pike. After being captured by the Spanish on an expedition in what is now Colorado, he was taken to Mexico City and, upon being released, started the long overland journey back to the United States in 1807. In Texas, he made several notes about wild horses, including one in which he saw "immense numbers of crossroads made by wild horses." He was the first American to write the word *mustang*. On

June 17, 1807, while riding through Texas, he wrote: "Passed through several herds of mustangs or wild horses."[21]

But Pike was not the first—or the last—to comment on the vast number of mustangs. As a young lieutenant, Ulysses S. Grant rode a recently broken mustang through what is now southern Texas on his way to fight the Mexican army in 1846. Between the Nueces and the Rio Grande Rivers, he later wrote, his Army unit spotted "an immense herd":

> The country was a rolling prairie, and, from the higher ground, the vision was obstructed only by the earth's curvature. As far as the eye could reach to our right, the herd extended. To the left, it extended equally. There was no estimating the number of animals in it; I have no idea that they could all have been corralled in the State of Rhode Island, or Delaware, at one time. If they had been, they would have been so thick that the pasturage would have given out the first day.[22]

Thomas Dwyer, a lawyer from London who started ranching in the same area in 1847, encountered the same uncountable herds. "I well remember when I first came to Texas seeing thousands and tens of thousands of wild horses running in immense herds all over the western country, as far as the eye or telescope could sweep the horizon. The whole country seemed to be running!" Horses would come up and cut off teams, coaxing the tame horses to join their bands. "Time and again I have had to send out my best mounted men to scare away the immense masses of mustangs (charging around and threatening to rush over us), by yelling and firing at them. Then the mustangs would wheel and go thundering away," he said, adding, "The supplies of wild cattle and horses then seemed so abundant as to be inexhaustible."[23]

How many were there? It is impossible to say. Adding up the grossly general observations of various regions by explorers only gives an even more gross general number. Some scholars have suggested there could have been as many as six million. Others have said there were likely never more than a few hundred thousand.

The most commonly repeated estimate is two million. It comes from a man named J. Frank Dobie, who in 1952 published a beautiful summation of wild horses in America called *The Mustangs*. Dobie had been born on a ranch in Texas in 1888 and had grown up among adults who still remembered the days of Indian wars and wild horses. He became a professor of literature and folklore and spent much of his life collecting the yarns and legends of the West. He taught at Cambridge University during World War II, and in Austria and Germany after the defeat of the Nazis. When he returned to teach in Texas, he became a lifelong champion of freedom and a staunch critic against any type of institutional oppression, whether Communism, Fascism, or the McCarthy-era capitalism he found in the United States in the 1950s. He was eventually awarded the Presidential Medal of Freedom. *The Mustangs* was in many ways a summation of his life's work: a monument he penned to the lost wild era of the West and to the ever-enduring spirit of freedom.

When it came to hazarding a guess of how many wild horses had once been out there, Dobie wrote, "All guessed numbers are mournful to history." Then, not being able to resist, he continued, "My own guess is that at no time were there more than a million mustangs in Texas, and no more than a million others scattered over the remainder of the West."[24] It was at best a hunch, but one that has hold on a larger truth—by the end of the era when the Horse Nations ruled the West, there were a lot of mustangs out there. More than anyone could ever count.

On a summer morning about 330 years after the Pueblo Revolt, I visited Turquoise Pueblo. The site is unmarked to keep looters away, but you can find it not too far off the interstate between Santa Fe and Albuquerque by asking around. When I got there, I walked out into a broad arroyo, expecting to find foundations and faint outlines of plazas. There was nothing left. During the horse-driven raids and fighting that followed the revolt, the village was abandoned. Over the centuries, the adobe walls melted back into the earth like sand-castles and were covered over by chamisa brush and cholla cactus.

But not everything from that time is gone. In the rolling valleys around the former village, horses still roam. Locals say they have been roaming free around local Indian reservations for as long as anyone can remember—maybe since 1580. In recent years, commuters from Albuquerque started building houses in the hills where the horses live, and began to complain to the local and state governments about what they called "feral horses."

New Mexico has estray laws that require the roundup of any stray livestock. But when calls came to round up the horses in the hills near Turquoise Pueblo, local horse groups and tribes objected. Is a mustang really a stray, they argued, if its ancestors have been free for hundreds of years? They argued instead that the horses were wildlife.

As part of the case, DNA samples were gathered from the horses and tested in a lab at the University of California at Davis. If analysis showed a mix of ancestors, the court said, the horses would be considered strays. If it showed almost pure Spanish blood, they would be considered mustangs.

Over the centuries, untold thousands of domestic horses from the East have been imported into New Mexico, and many have gotten loose, making it unlikely that any true mustangs still exist. Still, the tests went forward. And something astounding happened. When the results came back, every one showed the horses indisputably were Spanish mustangs.

The case went all the way to the New Mexico Supreme Court in 2016. A judge determined that wild horses were not strays, but not protected wildlife either. They were something in between. They would be allowed to roam, like deer, but they could be shot by land-owners, as is done with coyotes.

Though wild horses were almost entirely wiped out, they are still out there, roaming where the Pueblo Revolt set them free.

CHAPTER 3

THE DOG-FOOD DECADES

In 1923, a round-faced New Yorker in a dark business suit arrived via train in the small but bustling industrial town of Rockford, Illinois. The businessman, whose name was Phillip M. Chappel, made his way through the fray of trucks and horse-drawn wagons on the main street, on his way to a meeting with the stockholders of the local farmers' cooperative's meatpacking plant. The million-dollar plant on the edge of town had been built to slaughter cattle, but it had fallen on hard times because bigger factories in Chicago could undercut its price. The factory, idle for more than a year, was perched on the edge of bankruptcy. Chappel proposed something bold and unheard of. He had a plan that would allow the company to buy meat for almost nothing, sell it at a premium, and make them all rich. It required doing something many of the men found repugnant, but the money was so good that no one left the room. Two words: horse meat.

The town of Rockford, Chappel said, should become horsemeat capital of the United States. Timing was perfect. With the automobile taking over, the market for workhorses had collapsed. Mustangs from the West that once had satisfied a steady need for wagon-pullers in the East were now piling up in places like Montana and Wyoming. Ranchers would almost pay to get rid of them. Horses that once were the most valuable commodity in the West could be had for next to nothing.

The plan was simple: Round up as many mustangs as possible, drive them onto trains, ship them east, prod them up the cattle ramp, pack them into cans, and sell them as dog food. The approach was summarized a few years later by *Time* magazine as "round-up and ground up."[1]

The investors agreed. By 1925, the Chappel Brothers factory in Rockford was up and running. A four-story brick plant rose in the center, bristling with smokestacks and steam pipes. A huge smokestack that towered over anything in town was emblazoned with its

FACTORIES LIKE THE CHAPPEL BROTHERS PLANT IN ILLINOIS TURNED UNCOUNTED MUSTANGS INTO DOG FOOD AND FERTILIZER.

logo. Hammers clanged as workmen expanded the already sprawling complex, building new processing plants and new rail lines.

Every day, more than a dozen train cars wheeled into the complex, their sides often shuddering with the thunder of wild horse hooves trying to break the wooden walls. What those wide-eyed animals, which had grown up knowing only distance and freedom, thought of the stench of the boxcars could be surmised by the high-pitched shrieks and whinnies heard coming from the factory.

When Chappel proposed the idea, there were an estimated two million mustangs in the United States. A few decades later, hardly any were left. Many culprits helped do in the wild horse in the twentieth century: barbed wire, railroads, settlers surging into empty country, competition from cattle and sheep, a warlike campaign by state and federal governments against all wild animals that threatened agriculture, and, of course, plain old greed. But none did a fraction as much damage as Phillip M. Chappel—or P. M., as he was always called. Men had been chasing mustangs for meat and saddle stock for centuries in the West, but only mechanized, marketed, industrial-scale slaughter created both a financial incentive to annihilate wild herds and the practical means to make it happen.

I pieced together the saga of Chappel Brothers through clips from the local newspapers, the *Rockford Daily Republic* and the *Rockford Morning Star*. It is a largely forgotten story, but one that still has deep resonance—not just because it helps explain what happened to the vast wild mustang herds a century ago but also because it is a window into how people still react to the slaughter of horses, an issue that dogs the Bureau of Land Management to this day.

When the Chappel Brothers firm hatched its grand plan to turn mustangs into dog food, the term *animal rights* had yet to be coined. Still, the plan was not without its detractors in its day. People in that era had grown up with domestic horses. Many had used them for transportation or farm work. They respected them. Many found abhorrent the idea of turning a trusted servant into dog food. Some newspapers bemoaned the passing of the mustang and the sad fate of the slaughtered horse. At the same time, the United States was still in the throes of a Manifest Destiny–fueled bender of natural resource plunder, and there was a competing belief that mustangs, like timber and grass and minerals, should be used to fuel the nation's progress.

At the Chappel Brothers slaughterhouse, that societal tension between love of horses and love of money eventually collided in a way that created headlines across the country and nearly destroyed the whole factory. But that wasn't until later, after Chappel Brothers had become one of the largest slaughterhouses in the country.

P. M. Chappel's success came down largely to being in the right place at the right time. Born in England in 1872, he emigrated with his parents as a young boy to Pennsylvania. As an adult, he moved to upstate New York, where he worked as a traveling salesman for Swift and Company—the Chicago meatpacking giant that was so horrifically efficient at slaughtering that it inspired Upton Sinclair's 1906 novel *The Jungle*. In 1911, Chappel became a dealer in horses around the city of Rochester. It was a good time to be in the business. When World War I broke out, it ignited a massive demand for horses to move armies in Europe. In 1916 alone, Europe bought 350,000 horses from the United States. Prices spiked and Americans made good money rounding up excess animals and putting them on boats with a one-way ticket to the front. Chappel got a government contract and claimed to have sold 117,000 horses this way.[2] Many of the horses that went to war were mustangs gathered by ranchers and sold to middlemen like Chappel, who shipped them east and put them on boats.

After the war, the price of horses hit bottom and Europe had exhausted its coffers. In America, the automobile and the tractor had arrived. No one was buying horses. A mustang that brought $30 in 1915 was now worth maybe $1.50. Many dealers got out of the business, but Chappel saw the bust as an opportunity. During the war, he had met a number of French officers, and through them he knew that while the demand for workhorses had dried up, Europe still had a hunger for horse meat. His experience with Swift had familiarized him with the world of large-scale, industrial meatpacking. It didn't take much to put the two together. P. M. would buy old, worn-out horses from midwestern farms and wild horse herds in the West. He'd pay cowboys to bring them to railheads and he'd ship them straight to the killing floor. The good cuts would become pickled meat for Europe. The rest would become a product of his own invention: Ken-L Ration—the first-ever canned dog food.

In 1922, he opened a small New Jersey packing plant, supplied mostly by worn-out city horses, but he soon realized he needed a bigger factory and a bigger supply of horseflesh. He settled on Rockford, in a spot right between the supply lines of the East and the mustangs of the West.

Chappel employed crews of young men on horseback in Montana and Wyoming to gather up horses and drive them to the rails. These drives, sometimes sweeping up a thousand horses, were often punishing, since the cowboys were paid only by the head, not by the condition of the horses. They knew the animals were bound for slaughter, and they only had to get them to the rail line.

"There was little grass and the animals suffered accordingly," one of those "canner" riders, Robert W. Eigell, remembered fifty years later in an article for the Western history magazine *Montana*. "It was one of the most depressing experiences I encountered in the West." His bunch drove the animals twenty-five miles a day, leaving a string of dead horses all the way to the railhead.[3] Mares stopped giving milk and their starving colts started to drop behind. Out of desperation, they nuzzled at the cowboys' horses. One cowboy took out his pistol and dropped behind with the colts. The others heard a shot, then several more. The cowboy came back and said, "Poor little fellers don't have to suffer no more."

Horses arriving in Rockford often had spent days without food or water on the trip east. Packed together, they kicked and sometimes trampled each other. Many arrived dead.

At the factory, huge holding corrals with reinforced fences held hundreds of horses that gathered and broke in waves as cowboys on horseback tried to herd them toward the chutes. The mustangs were pushed up a long covered ramp that led from the final corral to the fourth floor, where a workman known as "the killer" waited with a silencer-equipped rifle. In 1925, the plant was processing two hundred horses a day—one about every two minutes.

On the top floor, carcasses were skinned and drained of blood before being moved to a maze of butchering rooms, where snaking lines of men in white aprons carved down the meat to manageable chunks that were sent down to cooking and baking rooms, then into the clanging machinery that would pack the meat into one-pound cans.

In a sense, the only thing new about what Chappel was doing was the scale. Rounding up mustangs in the West predated Chappel not just by decades but by centuries. As long as wild horses had been roaming free on the land, people had tried to catch them, both because they wanted to have them and because they wanted to get rid of them.

Early in the history of the West, mustangs were a valuable commodity—to be sold, traded, or trained as a new mount. But later, they became so numerous that many locals only wanted to destroy them. In all cases, until the mechanization of the twentieth century, corralling wild horses was extremely hard and often dangerous work, impossible to do on a scale that could ever drain the West of millions of horses.

The earliest way of catching mustangs is the one we still imagine when we think of wild horse roundups: the lone rider clinging to the neck of his pinto in a full gallop, half obscured by the hoof-pounded dust, jutting forward, one wrist cocked with the weight of a swinging lariat, ready to sling it out around a mustang's neck.

The first recorded account of this may be from Washington Irving, the author of *The Legend of Sleepy Hollow* and *Rip Van Winkle*, who visited Comanche territory in what is now Oklahoma in 1832. One evening, after Irving had spotted bands of wild horses cantering over the rolling plains, a young guide in his party, half French, half Osage, came into the camp with a fine, two-year-old colt he had just captured. Around the fire, he told of how he had come across a band of six horses along the river. He chased them through the water, then tried to lasso one with a lariat on a pole, but the rope skipped off the horse's ears. The guide galloped after the band, surging up over a hill and cresting the other side, only to find himself suddenly nearly airborne, plunging down a twenty-foot sand bank. "It was too late to stop. He closed his eyes, held his breath, and went over with them— neck or nothing," Irving wrote.

In the confusion at the bottom, the rider managed to snare the colt, but then the colt jagged back around a tree, pulling the rope loose from the rider's hand. The rider chased the colt out onto open ground and somehow got hold of the rope again, then spent considerable time trying to get the horse back across the river and back to camp. "For the remainder of the evening," wrote Irving, "the camp remained in a high state of excitement: nothing was talked of but the capture of wild horses; every youngster of the troop was for this harum-scarum kind of chase; every one promised himself to return from the campaign in triumph, bestriding one of these wild coursers of the prairies."[4]

That thrill of chasing mustangs never wore off. Westerners continued galloping after mustangs until the practice was outlawed in 1971. Clubs of mustang chasers in places like Salt Lake City and Reno used to rope wild horses on Saturday afternoons in the 1960s the way some people went fishing. Years later, I met a dentist who had grown up in western Colorado. He had become an advocate for wild horses and was working to oppose BLM efforts to remove them from a place called West Douglas Herd Area. As we hiked through the herd area on the lookout for wild horses, he grew wistful describing his days as a teenager in the mesas of the area, crashing through the piñons after mustangs. "I damn near killed myself," he said, "but man, it was exciting."

Chasing mustangs with a lasso, however thrilling, had too many limitations to ever be a good way to catch horses. The first problem was that you could only catch at most one horse per chase. The second was that the biggest, fastest, and most desirable mustangs were the hardest to lasso, especially when the pursuing horse was weighed down by a rider. But the biggest problem was that the mad dash of the chase held too many risks to rider and horse. A valuable saddle horse might step in a badger hole and break a leg chasing a useless old cayuse, or fall on his rider, killing them both. Folks living in Wild Horse Country developed a saying: "Chasing mustangs is throwing good horses after bad."

While roping never went away, it remained a young man's pursuit that was probably more about ego than it was about horses. Instead of lassos, mustang hunters developed more effective techniques. The frontier held many stories of a technique called "creasing," in which a man would aim his rifle at a horse just along the crest of the neck and graze the vertebra—stunning but not harming the animal. The practice had obvious risks. A few inches off the mark and the horse would either run away or drop dead. And early documenters of the frontier often repeated the story but never reported witnessing the practice. It's likely that creasing got far more use as a campfire story than as an actual catching technique.

A more calculated strategy used in Texas was to lie in wait. According to the historian Frank Dobie, some mustangers—as men who pursued the herds were known— would set out salt licks surrounded by hidden snares. A man would hide with a lasso on the ground near the salt, then pull when the right horse stepped in. The problem is that mustangs are smart and have a keen sense of smell. They often wouldn't go near the trap, and men who waited for days eventually learned the strategy wasn't worth the time.

Dobie also tells of a technique in Texas where cowboys would tie a dummy of a man to a mustang and then turn him loose, letting him tire out his entire herd as he tried to run back to them and they fled. When the horses were exhausted, cowboys could come in and rope the ones they wanted. But Dobie didn't say how the cowboys managed to get the dummy on the first mustang—which may be why I found no other references to the practice. Like creasing, the strategy was probably better for storytelling than for catching mustangs.

A more dependable approach was colt catching. At the right time of year, a few months after mares had foaled, when the young were starting to eat grass, riders would charge a herd, chasing until the colts fell behind. The young horses were easy to rope, gentle, train, and sell. The practice was used for generations by the Spanish, the Horse Nations, and the Americans. In 1878, a pair of American surveyors in West Texas came across mustangers from New Mexico who were traveling slowly in a wagon pulled by two cows, leading a chain of thirty colts bound for market. Each was hobbled by a hair rope tied from its tail to its front ankle.[5]

In dry places, where the only water was from isolated springs, men found another approach. They built round corrals around water seeps where horses would come to drink. The corrals would stand open and unattended for most of the year, and horses would get used to going in and out for water, but when a mustanger wanted his catch, he would lie in wait as a herd sauntered in, then quickly close the gate.

In regions where water was too plentiful for these water traps to work, many mustangers used the technique that the BLM still uses in modified form today. They built sturdy, round corrals in places where the land would naturally drive horses together. At the opening, they erected long brush walls, like wings leading into the corral. Then riders working from all directions would drive herds toward the wings and into the mouth of the corral. For centuries, this technique was used in much of Texas, New Mexico, Nevada, and California—nearly any part of the West that had enough natural wood to build corrals. Hundreds of semipermanent corrals dotted the hills, and some can still be seen in remote places today. A few years ago, a rancher in Beaver County, Utah, pointed out a weathering corral built of silver-cedar logs. How long, I asked him, had that been there? "Near as I can tell, forever," he said. "And we used it, too, until the law stopped all that."

In the Wild Horse Desert of Texas, it was typical to gather two to three hundred mustangs per season, but you had to be careful. Too many and the horses would either break down the fences or trample one another in the corral, as the explorer Zebulon Pike noted in 1807, and their rotting carcasses would leave an "insupportable stench" that would make the corrals unusable.[6]

Most outfits lacked the manpower for such massive gathers,

so they simply tried to "walk down" a herd. A small group of men, working in relays, would pursue a group of mustangs over several days. The first rider would set out at a leisurely pace, staying just fast enough behind the herd to keep them from eating and drinking. He would try to work them in a circle, so that twelve hours later he again would be passing by camp, where another rider would take his place. After two or three days, the horses were so exhausted that they could easily be roped or corralled. Often mustangers would mix tame mares with a captured herd to act as leaders when it came time to drive them to captivity.

Slowly, as settlers came into the West, the dynamic of roundups changed. What was once the pursuit of a valuable trade item—the horse—became an effort to clear that item from the land to make room for an even more valuable trade item: cattle. As Texas became more populated, stockmen organized massive roundups. On Mission Prairie in 1875, about 150 riders set out one summer day to drive horses from all sides of the region toward a lake in the middle. They had orders to shoot any horses that broke back. After several hours, a dark line of horses converged like geese. Many broke back and were shot or trampled. It's said the men gathered fifteen thousand horses that day.[7]

These kinds of roundups could produce good riding stock for ranches, and a little extra pocket money, but they rarely netted enough horses to make a dent in the West's vast population. It was like trying to drain a river with a bucket.

When the railroads came after the Civil War, the West finally had quick, easy access to eastern markets. More important, eastern capitalists had quick, easy access to the West. What followed was the wholesale liquidation of anything and everything of value in the West: timber, minerals, wildlife, grass. The federal government, having fought to rid the West of the Horse Nations, threw open the gates and invited settlers in. The historian Vernon Parrington, writing in the 1920s, called this time of rapid resource extraction—when speculators, creditors, railroad companies, and wealthy investors feasted on the virgin West—"the great barbecue."[8]

It was a pattern that originated with the first trappers who stalked up western streams in search of furs and grew exponentially as access and demand snowballed. Bernard DeVoto, a historian who was born in Utah in 1897 during the barbecue era and later taught at Harvard, summed up the pattern of exploitation this way: "You clean up and get out—and you don't give a damn, especially if you are an Eastern stockholder."[9]

The first people to arrive in the West were generally there only to exploit natural resources, and they wrote the laws to protect their pursuits. Even if later settlers wanted to push for a bit of restraint, or even conservation, legally there were few ways to do it. The laws of the region can basically be summarized as "I got here first: it's mine, not yours."

The stock raisers, loggers, and miners in the West went along with it, DeVoto said. "The West does not want to be liberated from the system of exploitation that it has always violently resented," he wrote. "It only wants to buy into it."

Once the railroads reached Wild Horse Country and the Horse Nations were driven onto reservations, the Great Plains slowly became a giant pasture. Teams of hunters killed off the roughly thirty million buffalo within twenty years. They also shot tens of thousands of mustangs and stripped them of their hides, which were sent east. Horsehides had many uses, but the most notable one at the time was in the newly popular game of baseball. It's said that the mustangs' hide, which is softer and more textured than cowhide, made the best leather covers for balls, and made for a better curveball. We'll never know how many baseballs covered with mustang skins were used in the major leagues. Also, at the turn of the twentieth century, horsehair "pony coats" became a fashion rage, boosting the demand for skins.

As the buffalo died off, the legendary drives of longhorn cattle started north from Texas. Less well known is that huge drives of horses also went north to places like Dodge City and Abilene, Kansas. "During the time of the longhorn drives, probably a million range horses were trailed out of Texas," Frank Dobie noted. "Yet so far as print goes, for every paragraph that relates to the driving of these range horses, a hundred pages relate to the trailing of longhorn cattle. . . . The cowboy rode to glory but the horseboy never became a name."[10]

Live horses were packed on boxcars and shipped east, where they were sold as low-end stock and ended up in the most unlikely places. One mustang named Hornet starred in "Professor Bristol's well-known troupe of 22 performing horses," where he did a rocking-horse act and skipped rope.[11] One ended up pulling a smoked fish cart near Coney Island, in New York, where every summer afternoon he went swimming with his owner on the beach. But most of them simply ended up as anonymous, low-cost muscle that fueled country and city life in the nineteenth century.

One of their main destinations was New York City. Its bustling streets had an insatiable need for horses—the cheaper and smaller, the better. "The time for the degrading slavery of the wild Western mustang has come," a reporter noted in the *New York Times* in 1889. "Within a very few months he has been brought to this city in droves and, at present, on the Third-avenue surface railway, at least, he outnumbers the Eastern horse in the ratio of nearly five to one."[12]

The little weather-beaten horses had become the favorite power source for streetcars, the newspaper noted, because they were stronger and healthier. And since they were not much larger than ponies, they also ate less. "After they are once trained they work together with quite as much ease as their more civilized brothers. But before they are trained they are not inclined to peace," the reporter said, noting they came off the train "as wild as a Manitoba blizzard" and often bit their handlers.[13]

On streetcar teams, mustangs were harnessed with tame horses until they learned the job. "Two days are generally sufficient to convince the mustangs that there is a point where obstinacy ceases to become a praiseworthy attribute," the newspaper said. After two weeks, they are used to the noises and smells of the city, and have "an appreciation of the dull realities of Eastern life."[14]

Of course, not all mustangs gave in so easily. Breathless reports of the latest mustang gone wild in Gotham were so common in the late nineteenth century that they became almost their own genre in the city papers. In one, a policeman made a daring rescue straight out of a dime novel, jumping onto mustangs bareback and riding through Central Park until he could calm the frightened animal. In another, a mustang got spooked by the clatter of a passing elevated train and took off down Forty-Second Street, dragging a wagon behind. It knocked down a little girl, plowed into another parked horse, smashed its wagon, and thundered down the street dragging the splintered wreckage through a crowd of strikers picketing a carpet works. Another, fresh off the train from the West, got away from a peddler and dashed through the carriage traffic of the Upper West Side, clattering onto a crowded sidewalk. "The broncho [sic] again played havoc with the throngs on the sidewalk, for it galloped at a terrific pace for five blocks, while thousands rushed into nearby doorways," a report in that evening's paper read. The mustang outran a police horse in pursuit, tripped over its own lead rope and tumbled twice, sprang back to its feet, turned a sharp corner and knocked over a beloved theater manager, and was headed for a park. On the corner, it was suddenly shocked to a standstill by a crowd of men who opened their umbrellas.[15]

The railroads continued to deliver fresh carloads of wild horses to the East from the 1880s through at least 1910. The West continued to replenish the population with little reported impact on the wild herds. But as the West grew more crowded and ranchers turned out more sheep and cattle, the naturally replenishing spring of horses started to be viewed not as a resource but as a problem. The vast herds on the prairie, which had so impressed explorers, exasperated the settlers who wanted to farm and raise livestock. Wild horses came at night, knocking down fences to abscond with domestic horses. "Large numbers of wild horses abound on the prairies between the Arkansas and Smoky Hill Rivers," the *Topeka Commonwealth* reported in 1882. "They are of all sizes and colors, and are the wildest of all wild horses. . . . Settlers on the frontier would hail speedy extinction as a blessing, for when domestic animals get with them their recovery is simply out of the question."[16]

Settlers began comparing the predations of wild horses with the raids of the Horse Nations they had recently driven onto reservations. "Not satisfied with its own freedom the wild horse has adopted the tactics of the Apache and the Sioux and stampedes its brethren," a Colorado journalist noted in 1897. "Novelists have taught us to believe that the wild mustang is emblematic of freedom pure and noble. The Texas ranchman regards him as an emissary of the evil one, for he brings to his ranch despair and loss."[17]

The simple solution, one many in the West yearned for, was to get rid of the mustangs, permanently. And, if possible, make money in the process. Where it was economical to ship them east, they did, but the Far West's leagues of canyons and mountains gave herds too many places to hide. Even if horses could be caught, they were often far from rail lines, so there was no economical way to get them to market.

In places where wild horses had no realizable value, settlers treated them like they treated coyotes, prairie dogs, or any other critter they labeled "varmints." They shot them. Starting in the 1870s, ranchers in Texas began cooperative hunts to try to eradicate mustangs on the Gulf Coast. Local and state governments got into the act, passing laws allowing open season on free-roaming horses. On the plains around Cheyenne, Wyoming, in 1884, one reporter wrote: "Wild horses have become so numerous on the Plains that some of the stockmen in this vicinity have organized a hunting party whose object will be to thin them out. The hunters are provided with long-range rifles, fleet ponies, and supplies and forage enough to last all Winter."[18]

In the red mesas around Kanab, Utah, ranchers organized yearly hunts. Sometimes horses were shot on the run, but: "If possible the horses will be driven into some 'blind' canyon, where the work of slaughter will be made easy," one observer noted.[19]

Though the myth of the West puts the cowboy and the wild horse on the same team, they were more often adversaries. "There!" one Wyoming rancher cursed in 1888, as he stooped over an immense black stallion bleeding from a bullet hole in its neck: "I guess you won't steal anymore of my mares, you old rascal, you."

"It seems a pity to kill such a fine animal," said a journalist who had witnessed the kill, as the two looked down at the dying mustang.

"A fine old thief," the rancher corrected him. "Why, man, do you know that cuss has stolen more than a dozen of my mares, and I reckon $1,000 wouldn't cover the damage he's done to this valley in the past summer."[20]

Area ranchers took up collections to pay bounties for wild horses. Much of the killing was done by professional hunters, called "wolfers," who made their living killing wolves, mountain lions, and any other offending critters. A lone wolfer traveling on horseback with a packhorse in tow could get up into the remote benchlands where mustangs hid. The aim was not to lasso the mustangs, but to shoot them. After dropping several from a distance with a rifle, a wolfer would lie in wait for wolves and lions that showed up to feed on the carcasses. A pair of wolf ears could be worth $4. A wild stallion's scalp could bring up to $25.

In 1893, Nevada passed a law allowing anyone to shoot mustangs on sight. "There are now in Nevada more than 200,000 head of these horses," a railroad agent in Reno told the *San Francisco Examiner* in 1894. "And they are increasing so fast that they are getting to be a great nuisance." The herds were beautiful and included many fine horses as tough as pine knots, he said. "The trouble is, they are eating off the grass, so that sheep and cattle owners are having a tough time of it in some sections."[21]

It is up for debate whether there were really more mustangs or whether there were just more settlers after the grass. Regardless, Nevada ranchers started shooting any mustangs that came in range. "They use long-range rifles, however, and ride fleet domestic horses, and in this way pick off a great many," said the railroad agent. "Every rancher or wild cattle owner in Nevada, when he sees a wild stallion and has a weapon with him, turns loose at it."[22]

Hunting pushed horses into rough, remote country. The hunters followed. It was hot, dangerous, difficult work. Most of the hunters were young men who lived outdoors for weeks at a time. But at least one was a woman. "She is a Californian, and a young woman, only 23 years old. Moreover she is respected for her many good qualities," noted an 1899 newspaper profile of the lady mustang hunter. Her name was Maud Whiteman, and she was "an affectionate mother" and a "hospitable soul." She would lie in wait at desert watering

SHOOTS WILD HORSES.

WHEN WESTERNERS COULD NOT CAPTURE MUSTANGS, THEY OFTEN SHOT THEM, AS THIS 1899 ENGRAVING SHOWS.

holes. When a band of horses came to drink, she would shoot the lead horse, aiming not to kill but to maim. The band would scatter at the crack of the rifle but then return to check on the disabled horse. Maud would then "rush from hiding, shoot as many as possible, and follow fleeing victims until all or nearly all are killed." She skinned the horses and sold their hides for $2 each in California.[23]

Nevada eventually repealed the law allowing open season on mustangs because domestic horses started disappearing, and branded hides showed up in shipments of mustang hides.

The West's desperation to rid the region of horses was a theme in some areas long before the coming of the railroads. In California, where the Spanish missions had bred horses for centuries, wild runaways flourished in the dry hills until they eventually outnumbered tame stock. One explorer in the San Joaquin Valley in the early 1800s said that "frequently, the plain would be covered, with thousands and thousands flying in a living flood towards the hills. Huge masses of dust hung upon their rear, and marked their track across the plain; and even after they had passed entirely beyond the reach [of] vision, we could still see the dust, which they were throwing in vast clouds into the air, moving over the highlands."[24]

These herds, which had evolved to thrive in the dry West, outcompeted imported cattle and sheep. California's small and isolated human population had no use for so many horses, and no easy way to trade them in the East. So Spanish ranchers simply drove the animals into the ocean. Reports from the missions show that in 1805 the Spanish drove 7,500 horses over the sea cliffs in San Jose. In 1806, another 7,200 were sent into the waves in Santa Barbara. In some roundups, horses were driven into corrals, lanced with long spears, and left to die.[25]

"An intimate story of the wild horses of the Southwest and the war waged against them would read like a dime novel romance. In everyday parlance, however, they are a nuisance and a pest," a reporter wrote in the *New York Times* in 1912, echoing the growing frustrations that settlers likely had for generations. "As horses they are valueless and useless. They can no more be tamed and domesticated than the hyena. The stallions infest the tame herds of the ranges and taint them with strains of wild blood that make the offspring worthless."[26]

Of course, generations of trappers and cowboys knew that wild horses were among the best horses in the world. But their ability to outcompete livestock and their skill in stealing domestic horses is hard to dispute. Often locals felt powerless against these fleet raiders.

"Their hiding places are all but impenetrable," the *Times* reporter continued. "Like mountain sheep, no trail is too rough for them.

The most intrepid riders have failed to round them up. A mounted man appearing is a signal for them to break for the wilds. No horse with a rider can keep their pace. Their endurance seems to be without limit."[27]

As time went on, ranchers tried to improve on the old roundup strategy. They replaced wood-and-brush wings on traps with long swaths of canvas wings that were easier to set up than wood. They introduced tame mares into wild herds to make them easier to corral. A hunter in Utah announced he planned to shoot horses with a drug that would put them to sleep long enough to be roped and hobbled. Another in Nevada filled a water trough with a narcotic that left the horses dazed and easily captured. But he stopped the practice because a number of horses overdosed, and so did a number of cattle.

Then came barbed wire. In the 1870s, farmers and ranchers started stringing it across the West. By 1900, contemporary government statistics said Americans had put up more than 100,000 miles of wire fence. The spread of fences swept wild horses out of the Great Plains and most of Texas. They were pushed back to the broken, jagged country of the intermountain West that could not be easily fenced. This was particularly true in Nevada, where most of the range remained open, and long, rough ranges of mountains provided endless hiding spots for herds.

With increased fences and resources, ranchers redoubled their efforts to finally get rid of the mustang. In 1902, ranchers in Lander County, in the middle of Nevada, organized a massive horse hunt. They hoped that with the help of a hundred riders, "between 4000 and 6000 wild animals will be slaughtered and left as food for the carrion crows."

"These animals dash wildly about the hills and valleys, destroying crops as well as scattering herded cattle," a reporter for the *San Francisco Call* wrote of the planned hunt. "The horses are of no value.

They cannot be tamed, and, in fact, cannot even be caught." Here was the horse not as a natural resource but as a threat—a party crasher at the Great Barbecue. And like mountain lions or wolves or Comanche raiders, the westerners had a way of dealing with their unwanted guests. "Many of the animals will be shot on the run," the reporter noted. "At the point where a meeting is expected pits have been dug, into which the horses will be run to their death."[28]

Rarely were reports of the results of these roundups published, though when they were, the buckaroos—as cowboys are still called in Nevada—often spent way more time trapping far fewer horses than they had hoped. Even so, they kept at it. The largest wild horse hunt ever staged in Nevada was organized in Washoe County in 1909. Five hundred buckaroos swept a swath of territory fifty miles long, bringing horses to a central point near the northern end of the Nightingale Mountains. Desirable young horses were roped and sold. The rest were shot.

Ranchers in Nevada were so desperate to rid themselves of the herds that they lobbied for a federally funded war against mustangs. The manager of the state's forest reserves asked Washington to call in the Army to kill horses, requesting that "sixty days of each year be set apart for the purpose, and that the horses might be exterminated under the skirmish conditions of general warfare."[29]

"No fence is strong enough to stop these horses, and when they appear in force they have even been known to knock down and kill cows and calves," said a story on the problem in the *Los Angeles Herald*. "Any one who finally finds an effective method to settle this problem will have done a great service for the stockmen of every state west of the Missouri River. As an old and experienced stockman, now in the employ of Uncle Sam, said of this wild horse problem: 'Theoretically it seems a very simple matter to handle, but practically it is quite the reverse.'"[30]

The coming of the automobile complicated things further. The ready market for fresh horses to draw wagons and pull plows began to dry up. In New York in 1912, traffic counts showed more cars than horses for the first time. Streetcars went electric. Suddenly no one wanted mustangs anymore. The last horse-drawn streetcar in Manhattan trotted down Bleecker Street in 1917. The horse market collapsed and mustangs on the range were no longer worth the cost of catching. Ranchers decided to just kill them. In 1927, that forest ranger in Eureka, Nevada, reported that he shot 1,046 wild horses to get them off the range.[31]

But shooting was often time consuming and only marginally effective, so ranchers kept searching for creative ways to rid the West of mustangs. In Oregon, they asked the US Army to fly in with bombers to destroy the state's wild horse herds. In Utah's Skull Valley, they tried to recruit tourists to do the work. "Americans who like adventure and excitement in a hunt are advised to try their hand at hunting wild horses," a 1920 announcement in *Popular Mechanics* declared. "They will find this sport quite as thrilling as cornering a tiger." An expedition had shot 102 horses, the notice stated, and "ranchers in Skull Valley invite shooting parties to go after the wild horses and [will] furnish guides and other necessary supplies."[32]

Despite these sustained efforts, mustangs did not face annihilation until the rise of meat factories like Chappel Brothers. The mechanized plants started springing up on the edges of the West at the turn of the twentieth century—always next to rail lines that reached into Wild Horse Country like long straws. Their thirst knew no end. And they would eventually nearly drink the West dry. The first reference I can find of wild horse meat processing is from 1895, when a Portland, Oregon, canning factory specializing in wild horses announced its grand opening, noting: "This is a legitimate industry, and there is a large supply of raw material in Oregon, consisting of half-wild horses—the majority of them young, and substantially all of them, presumably, in wholesome condition—for which there is no other market"[33]

In 1911, there is another reference to a group of cowboys in Colorado who got a contract with California soap factories to round up thousands of wild horses for $5 a head.

In 1919, Congress changed laws to allow for federal health inspection of horse meat, and, along with Chappel Brothers, a number of canneries opened around the West. In Los Angeles, Ross Dog and Cat Food became a destination for horses and burros in the Southwest. In San Francisco, the chicken-feed plant in Petaluma was a pipeline that drained much of Nevada. In Portland, Oregon, the Schlesser Brothers plant feasted on the huge herds in the state's eastern deserts, packing the remains of hundreds of horses a day into big barrels to be shipped east to New York, then across the ocean to the Netherlands.

With the steady price from canneries, ranchers could plan bigger and more ambitious roundups, knowing that the maw of the meatpacking industry would pay for everything they caught. In New Mexico, ranchers banded together on a drive in 1928 to push thousands of horses to a fertilizer plant in El Paso. One reporter called it "the journey of death." This was the reality of the mustang that the dime novels of the time often ignored. There were no gallant young men in chaps. With little forage or water on the way, scores of mustangs collapsed and were left in the dust. "Some of the doomed horses were wild and spirited at their start across the desert, but none were at the end. Those that survived death gave little indication of ever being free."[34]

Some bemoaned the passing of the West, but their eulogies were hardly enough to hault the liquidation of the open range. It was seen, in a way, as inevitable. "The wild horse—a symbol of pioneer America—is making its last stand," one easterner said in 1935 on observing the relentless roundups. "The wild buffalo is gone; the traders and prospectors have vanished; the Indian is on his reservation; the blue-coated cavalry-men of the old United States Army are history. Sole survivor of the era which carved out Western America from the wilderness is the wild horse. With the swift flight of the years the bands of wild horses become smaller. Ranges which once thundered to their battering hoofs are silent."[35]

The biggest buyer of mustangs by far was the gleaming new Chappel Brothers plant in Illinois, which contracted mainly with cowboys in Montana, Wyoming, and Colorado.

"The first chapter has been written in the greatest wild horse roundup ever held in the west," a correspondent for the *New York Times* breathlessly reported in 1929. "Hundreds of horses large and small, vicious and indifferent, mustangs, 'fuzz tails' and 'broncos'— are in pastures ready for the first sale and elimination." In the wide-open plains of central Montana, a young rodeo cowboy and movie actor named Carl Skelton, wearing chaps and a six-shooter, was running the show and invited newspapermen to go along as his cowpunchers gathered wild horses on the range along the Missouri River. "There's six or seven thousand wild horses on the Cascade range," he told reporters. "I'll bring in five thousand or more."[36]

Reporters covered the roundup like a real-live Western—a snapshot of the last wild moments of the frontier. What they didn't report, and perhaps Skelton had failed to mention, was that the main character in this Western was the midwestern meat canner, Chappel, who paid Skelton and his men to do the work.

Chappel Brothers's big product was its canned dog food, Ken-L Ration, which Phillip M. Chappel had invented. Before Ken-L Ration, most dogs had just eaten whatever scraps owners dropped.

Chappel family lore has it that Phillip Chappel got the idea for canned horse-meat dog food from watching dogs fight over horse offal at his slaughterhouse. Another inspiration might have been the canned "trench rations" developed for troops during World War I. Ken-L Ration cans rolling out of the factory featured a colorful label with a picture of dogs playing poker, and emblazoned with the slogans *quality made it famous* and *a horse-meat product.*

To get Americans used to the idea of canned horse meat, Chappel enlisted the country's biggest dog celebrity, the silent film star Rin Tin Tin. When Chappel made the proposal to the owner of Rin Tin Tin, he balked at feeding horse meat to his dog. But Chappel opened a can and ate a piece himself to show how good it was. It worked. In ads on his weekly radio show, the German shepherd plugged Ken-L Ration as a delicious, nutritious treat, and cans flew off the shelves. By the time the factory was at full capacity, it was churning out nearly six million cans a year.

Not everyone celebrated the Chappel Brothers innovation. The local humane society in Rockford complained about the gaunt, stumbling horses coming off the packed railroad cars. Many in the public thought shooting horses for dog food was just plain wrong. The United States has never been much for eating horses. While it was not always necessarily taboo, horse meat was always a sign that something had gone wrong. The public equated it with disreputable butchers selling it as beef. Though many mountain men learned to love the flavor and tenderness of colts from tribes like the Comanche and the Apache, who prized the meat, frontier lore turned eating horses into an example of ultimate desperation—a deed only slightly less ghoulish than cannibalism, done only when all options were exhausted. To turn a trusted companion into chunks of meat was bad enough. To do it for dogs was more than many people could stomach.

Charles Russell, a Montana painter whose vivid scenes of cowboys and Indians on horseback helped create the myth of the West, decried the practice of shipping unwanted mustangs east for slaughter. "If we killed men off as soon as they were useless," Russell wrote, "Montana would be a lot less crowded."[37]

In 1928, a journalist named Russell Lord traveled the West to report on the rapidly disappearing mustang. Writing in the magazine *The Cattleman*, he started out determined not to be sentimental. "The romantic story of the American wild horse is being brought, of necessity, to an end," he wrote. "In strict accord with the practical necessities of range agricultures, the work of ridding the Plains of wild horses goes on. They eat too much grass, these horses drink too much from streams which else would sustain peaceful and profitable herds and flocks of cattle and sheep. . . . In a word, the wild horse has become a pest. He must go. Whether you like it or not, there it is," he wrote.[38]

But then Lord visited one of the western slaughterhouses—a forlorn, ramshackle place where he found 450 "miserable, slabsided, bedraggled horses." He sat down with the owner, who complained of the work. Cranks wrote letters accusing him of cruelty. "Sentimental old ladies" came sniffing around, he said. No matter how kind he tried to be, he was a hated man. Worse, by 1928 the easy-to-reach herds had all been ground up. Supplies were down, costs were up. "It's a rotten business," the owner said. "It's on the skids. There isn't anything in it. It is being overdone. It would soon be over and I'll be damn glad of it."

A small band of five mustangers moseyed toward the plant as Lord watched, driving sixty horses gathered from the surrounding country. They were a sorry group, both men and horses silent, shambling, beaten, with their heads down. They'd get $5 a head for their trouble. A railroad brakeman in the yard with Lord looked at them, shook his head, and said, "Three hundred dollars will keep those five birds in liquor for a week or so. Then they'll ride out again."

Lord talked to the lead mustanger about his business. He didn't like it, he said. It was just a dirty job. He would only take the horses as far as the rail yard. "You couldn't pay me, not for money, to drive a bunch of horses up to the slaughter house," he said, adding, "All along the line, as one seeks facts, one encounters as to the horse meat business a confusion between hot, instinctive repugnance and cold, calculating common sense."[39]

In the end, the journalist was unable to reconcile the myth of the noble mustang and the maw of the meatpacking plant. He still thought horses were a pest on the range, but he decided canneries were a desecration for such a proud animal. "Forget the five dollars a head," he said. "Shoot the mustangs where you find them. Let them go back to the earth out there in the open, where they lived."[40]

The Chappel Brothers factory churned on, despite people's grousing. More trainloads of mustangs went up the ramp each day. And the Chappel brothers themselves were getting rich. But in October 1925, strange things started to happen. First a fire erupted one night in a corner of the plant, where it appeared someone had splashed gasoline on the back doors. Then a 2,300-volt power line snapped, sending arcs of electricity through the night and making the factory floor go dark. Closer inspection showed the cable had been cut. A few days later, another fire broke out in a different corner of the plant. Workers rushing to put out the flames found cans of gasoline stacked in a corner to feed the inferno.

It was clearly the work of a saboteur, but managers didn't know what to make of it—perhaps some union agitator from a radical group like the Industrial Workers of the World was bent on bringing them down. But they knew of no labor problems at the plant. If anything, P. M. Chappel, who called nearly everyone in the plant "honey boy," paid well and was liked by the workers. But there could be little doubt that someone was trying to destroy the factory.

For a few weeks after the second fire, all was quiet. The cannery kept humming. Droves of mustangs went up the chute. Then, on November 21, 1925, an off-duty fireman driving home late at night saw flames leaping from a window in the plant's west wing. He sounded the alarm, but by the time engine crews responded, fire was bursting from all the windows on three floors. Embers rained into the corrals, causing hundreds of horses to stampede in panic. The glow could be seen from all over town.

The thick brick walls of the factory withstood the fire, but the insides didn't. Flames raged hot, spreading up walls and licking across rafters. The top killing floor collapsed. Then the carving floor. Then the canning floor. Dark cyclones of smoke must have poured out as thousands of pounds of canned meat exploded and burned. Two boxcars loaded with Ken-L Ration caught fire, burning so hot that only their iron trucks remained. Firefighters fought to keep the flames from the refrigeration wing, where enough ammonia gas was stored to level half the town. They succeeded, but it was one of their few victories. When the flames were finally doused the next day, most of the slaughterhouse was gutted. The Chappel Brothers firm had lost more than $75,000 in horse meat.

But if the saboteur thought he had stopped the factory, he was wrong. P. M. Chappel told the local newspaper that he would reopen again in a matter of weeks.

Though investigators could not find sure signs of arson, Chappel was convinced someone was trying to destroy his factory. He ordered workers to build a ten-foot fence around the grounds, and he hired private detectives to patrol with shotguns. For weeks, armed guards walked the complex at night, searching the shadows with flashlights for a saboteur. Managers interrogated the workers, looking for anarchists or union radicals, but found nothing.

Then one night in early December of 1925, well past midnight, a guard on his rounds came around the power plant and saw an inky figure slink into the shadows beneath the huge KEN-L RATION smokestack. When the guard crept over for a closer look, he saw the figure crouched in front of a bulging shape at the base of the smoke-stack. "Stop! What are you doing?" the guard yelled. When there was no answer, the guard raised his shotgun and ordered the prowler to come out.

A shot rang out as the prowler fired a pistol from the shadows and then turned and ran. The guard fired his shotgun, then fired again. When the intruder stumbled at the edge of the darkness, the guard took a few steps forward. But then the prowler sprang to his feet, fired back, and disappeared into the night. The guard sounded the alarm and men poured out along the perimeters, checking the fence and sweeping the shadows with flashlights, but the trespasser was gone.

Walking back to where the man had first been spotted, the guards found a black suitcase. It was so overstuffed that it had been held closed with baling wire. They untwisted the wire and opened it. Inside were 150 sticks of dynamite—enough to destroy the whole plant. A nine-foot-long white fuse snaked out along the ground. Someone noticed it was lit and slowly sizzling toward the charge. The guards quickly snuffed it out.

That night, a cold December storm swept in, and gusting winds beat rain against the town. Police fanned out over the city, looking for the bomber. They searched all night and through the next day. They checked the hospitals and hotels. It looked like the saboteur had gotten away. Then, late that afternoon, two boys walking home from high school found a man passed out in a field. His clothes were soaked with rain, his back was caked in blood. His hand gripped a large revolver. The authorities had their man.

A shotgun blast had hit the man in the back, and pellets had lodged in his lung. He was barely conscious from pneumonia and loss of blood. He was taken first to the jail, then moved to the hospital. Fortunately for him, the Chappel Brothers guards were only packing birdshot, which had left him bloodied but had not pierced too deeply.

The man was small and thin, pale in complexion, with neat dark hair he parted sharply to the right, and light blue eyes that bulged slightly out of his face. Police searched his hotel room and found Industrial Workers of the World literature that encouraged violent action against unfair employers. The police told the local paper they were "convinced he was one of the most dangerous anarchists ever apprehended in the area."

Late that night, the man recovered enough to speak. With the state's attorney and a stenographer in the room, he made a bedside confession—one he likely thought would be his last. His name was Francis Litts, but everyone called him Frank. He was polite and well spoken. He was calm and sincere as he spoke. He said he was forty-one years old. He had been born in upstate New York but raised in Montana and Idaho, where his father kept sheep and drove them up into the mountains each summer. He had grown up around horses, and he loved them very much. As an adult, he had wandered the West, working in mines in Alaska and California. He was a kind man who sent money home to New York to buy Christmas

FLED ASYLUM IN THE WEST

Frank Litts, cowboy-dynamiter, who escaped the Portland, Ore., asylum to come here for a try at blowing up the Chappel Bros. packing plant. Dr. Sidney Wilgus declares he is suffering from religious paranoia.

A MUGSHOT OF FRANK LITTS.

presents for his relatives, and sometimes he sent chocolates. But he could also be unpredictable. His brother's granddaughter told me that family lore held that he once attacked a man for whistling.

In the hospital, the prosecutor pressed Litts about his labor activism. A reporter from the *Rockford Daily Republic* was there to record the conversation. The prosecutor pressed Litts about the pamphlets the police had found. Litts said something that surprised them. He admitted, calmly, that he had tried to blow up the plant. But he was not trying to destroy Chappel Brothers in solidarity with the workers. He was trying to destroy it in solidarity with the mustangs.

"I was in Miles City, Montana, when I first heard about range horses being shipped east to be killed for food purposes. I believe that the killing and corralling of wild horses is wrong," he said.[41]

In Montana, he had seen the mustangs being loaded for the Chappel Brothers plant, he said, and decided the only way to stop such an evil factory was to destroy it. He headed east on the same train line. He applied for a job at Chappel Brothers so he could case the factory, he said, but soon left because he couldn't bear seeing the horror inside.

He told of the first night he tried to burn the place down, pouring gas on the back doors. "After I touched it off, I ran through the fields, reached the business section, and went to sleep in my room at a hotel," he said, his voice growing raspy with exhaustion. "I didn't wait to see if the fire was going to damage the building or not, but I guess it did, but not enough."

A nurse stopped him and made him drink water. She urged him to rest, but he pushed on. He said he kept watching the plant, and the sight of more trainloads of mustangs arriving enraged him. He tried again to set fires with more gasoline. And again. He thought the big fire in November had done the trick, but, after repairs, the plant kept churning out cans of meat.

So, he said, "I went last week and bought 150 sticks of dynamite."

His plan was not to kill anyone. He had about ten minutes' worth of fuse, he said, which would give him just enough time to warn the workers to get out.

Throughout his interview, he was courteous and clear-headed, but he showed no remorse. "I would rather see my body or my mother's ground up and used for fertilizer than to have horses killed like they are here," he said, adding that he was looking forward to standing trial, because he was sure the public would feel the same way.

Though the decision of Litts to dynamite a dog-food factory is extreme, his deep respect for horses is hardly rare. It's often said that one of the reasons horses became such successful domestic companions is that they are innately social animals. Horses have lived in family bands for millions of years, and they are all wired to be attuned to the moods and signals of other members. People successfully domesticated horses because we were able to tap into that capacity for trust and dependence. What gets less attention is that this domestication is a two-way street. We, too, are also wired to be social animals. The urge to reach out and connect with animals is something so basic in our fabric that it is universal across cultures and arises shortly after birth. Horses have also tapped into our capacity for trust and dependence. We forge relationships with them that are in ways very human. We talk to them. We give them names. We connect. And when we do, we implicitly extend to them the social contract of humanity: fairness, kindness, honesty, trust. The word *humane*, which is how we are supposed to treat horses, comes from the word *human*. It is perhaps because of this social contract Americans have extended to the horse that we do not eat them, and since the time of Chappel Brothers, we have done away with horse slaughterhouses in this country entirely.

Litts, like most people of his era, grew up with horses. He respected them. To him, they were not meat or marauders but companions. To him, slaughter was akin to murder. What choice did he have but to try to stop it?

The principle of animal rights was beyond a fringe idea in 1925. Vegetarianism was essentially nonexistent. In terms of radical activists, Litts was at least fifty years ahead of his time. People living on farms slaughtered animals themselves, and the practical economics of farm life didn't allow much room for the rights of other creatures. But horses did have a special place in many people's minds. Families often kept workhorses long after they could work—they were "put out to pasture." A century ago, these horses even had a name: Old Dobbin. Most people of the time grew up knowing at least one Old Dobbin they would visit in the back pasture. Perhaps because of this widespread support of horses, the story of the mad cowboy trying to save mustangs from the cannery went out on the wires and ran in newspapers all over the country. Many in the public were sympathetic. Telegrams of support addressed to "the cowboy" began to flood the jail from all over the country.

The authorities in Rockford tried to head off the idea of Litts as a dime-novel folk hero by portraying him as a hopeless nutcase. Ernest Chappel, P. M.'s brother, questioned whether Litts really was a Montana cowboy and suggested he was, in fact, really a miner—a job that at the time was synonymous with violent anarchists. If Litts were a real cowboy, he said, he would support what Chappel Brothers was doing. "The people of Montana are eager to get rid of these wild horses as they take the feed the cattle need," he told reporters.

The Horse Association of America also got in on the public relations campaign, saying the animals being slaughtered at the plant were not really horses, but "worthless Cayuses, descended from the mustang, but inferior, having deteriorated from inbreeding and lack of food." A spokesman told the Associated Press that "it was more humane to slaughter them than to let them starve to death on the range in old age."

The press took up the drumbeat, calling Litts "the eccentric Montana cowboy" and "the little man with a cow pony complex." They wondered whether he was truly crazy or just "a tool of an organization trying to destroy the horsemeat industry." But many in the public sided with Litts, and some even joined in his cause. A week after he had been arrested, police again surrounded the Chappel Brothers plant after Chappel saw what he thought were suspicious figures casing his plant, and he got a call from a man who said, "We'll get you, look out."

In jail, Litts spent his days reading books on his cot and writing letters to senators, city councilmen, and anyone else he thought would listen. He wrote a letter to Grace Coolidge, wife of President Calvin Coolidge. A noted animal lover, she had once spared a raccoon sent to the president for Thanksgiving dinner, then let it live in the White House. In his letter, Litts described the sadness of the horses as they learned their fate, and the tears that rolled out of their eyes.

We don't know what books Litts read in his cell, but we do know many of the best sellers in the years leading up to the bombing attempt were romantic portrayals of the West, including Zane Grey's *The Vanishing American*—a tale about a greedy capitalist who tries to round up wild horses for profit.

Frank Litts seemed to be looking forward to his trial as a public platform. "I'm going to tell the world about the conditions down there at the packing plant," he told a local reporter. "I'm not sore at anyone around here, but I just want a chance to tell what I know." Prosecutors seemed intent on not letting that happen. They decided to test Litts's sanity, so they hired a local "alienist" named Dr. Sidney Winglus to evaluate him. In an interview with Litts, the alienist discovered that Litts had previously been in two insane asylums.

Eleven years before his arrest, Litts was locked in the Morningside Hospital for the insane in Portland, Oregon. There, too, he advocated against what he thought was injustice, sending a letter to his state senator complaining about poor conditions where inmates ate bowls of watery gruel with no spoons and were packed by the dozen into rooms with no chairs. Shortly before traveling to Illinois, Litts had been put in Morningside again after what he said was an argument with his father over a girl Litts wanted to marry. Litts escaped from that asylum in Oregon and went to Montana, where he heard about Chappel Brothers and headed east.

The alienist asked Litts why he tried to blow up the Chappel Brothers plant. Because horse slaughter was morally wrong, Litts said. He listed a number of reasons, including the Bible's ban on eating meat from animals that don't have a cloven hoof. The alienist asked Litts whether he felt specially called upon to destroy the plant. Litts said yes. "Religious paranoia" was the alienist's diagnosis. Cautioning that it would gradually grow worse, he suggested locking Litts in an institution for the criminally insane as soon as possible.

Other people who came in contact with the well-spoken little cowboy thought he seemed fine, and fully aware of what he was doing. "I don't claim to be an alienist," the physician treating him for the gunshot wounds told the local paper. "But in my opinion, Litts appears sane."

If Litts'a state of mind was debatable, his aim was clear. He wanted to destroy the factory, and he wasn't going to stop just because he had been jailed. During his arraignment, a week after his arrest, he found himself sitting on a bench near the front of a busy courtroom as a crowd of attorneys sorted out the day's docket. Seeing a chance, he suddenly sprang up, sprinted down the aisle, and disappeared out the door. The deputy in charge chased after him. All eyes remained fixed on the doorway. Eventually the breathless deputy appeared with his quarry after tackling Litts near the elevators.

The deputy put Litts back on the bench and stood behind him, ready for any move. Litts sat quietly as he waited to enter his plea. Suddenly, he dove forward again, crashing through a crowd of lawyers toward a door to the jury room. The deputy caught him by the knees. For the rest of the morning, he sat handcuffed. "Why'd you do that?" asked the deputy later. "You knew you only had a one in a million chance." "I had a chance didn't I?" Litts said. "And why not take the chance?"

The bombing attempt barely caused a hiccup in production at Chappel Brothers. A few weeks after Litts was arrested, the local newspaper reported that "one thousand Montana mustangs have been slaughtered the last week by Chappel Brothers." The meat would go to Europe for Christmas feasts, the article said: "Whole carcasses are barreled for exportation, but corn beef, soup, mince meat and other products are also made." The reporter noted, "No horse meat is sold for human consumption in this country, but occasional visitors to the plant are given the opportunity to sample the steaks, and greatly to the surprise of most of them, find the meats real delicacies—tender and of excellent flavor."[42]

Charged with arson, Litts pleaded not guilty. When his trial started, in February of 1926, he entered court with dozens of pages of handwritten notes held in a tight roll. This, he had told his jailers, was his defense.

The first day of trial, Litts's court-appointed defense attorney called Dr. Winglus, the alienist, to testify that Litts was insane. Litts sprang to his feet. He was willing to be found guilty, but there was no way he wanted to be dismissed as crazy. He shouted that he did not want the doctor to speak. "I'm being tried for arson, not for sanity," he told the judge. His lawyer stood and began to make the case to the jury that they could not convict Litts because of his mental state. "Now you cut that out!" Litts shouted. He made his attorney sit down, then gave what the newspapers called "an eloquent speech" to the jury about how the horse was man's best friend.

Litts's lawyer interrupted and asked about previous stints in asylums. Litts shot back that he was being tried for arson, not his past. He asked for the county humane inspector to testify, but the judge refused to call him. His attorney again tried to make the case that his client was incompetent. "I am sane, I can control my acts," Litts insisted. Litts turned to the judge and said, "He's throwing me down, trying to make me out that I'm crazy when I'm not!"

The jury deliberated for eleven hours, with two men holding out because they didn't believe Litts was crazy. Eventually, though, they came back and told the judge that the fires and attempted dynamiting were "the acts of a lunatic."

Litts immediately stood up and asked for a new trial. "How can a jury deciding if I'm guilty of arson find me insane?" he asked. The judge banged his gavel, calling for order, and sentenced Litts indefinitely to the Illinois Asylum for the Criminally Insane.

It must have been a hard moment for Litts. He had hoped that he could reason with the jury and show them that what he had done was justified by the horror inside the factory. If they found him guilty, he could go to prison with a clean conscience, knowing that even if society was wrong, he had done right. But by finding him insane, the jury denied him any morality. It wasn't just that they denied he had made the right judgment, they denied he was even capable of making a judgment, and they stripped him of the very thing that was most central to him—his sense of right and wrong.

It was a long drive down to the insane asylum in the southern part of the state, in the town of Chester. Litts sat calmly in the back seat as the sheriff of Rockford drove. According to the local papers, Litts told the sheriff unapologetically that he would one day return to Rockford, and the next time he tried to destroy the Chappel Brothers plant, he would "do it right."

The asylum had castlelike stone walls. Litts walked down the long corridor of cells that echoed with the shrieking and mumbling madmen. He wouldn't stay long. Seven days after he arrived, he went out in the circular exercise yard with the rest of the inmates, and, under the watch of armed guards, he disappeared. The guards only noticed him missing after an hour, when they counted the inmates before dinner. Some later theorized the tiny man had slipped out through a small opening in a gate while exercising. Others thought he had hidden under some mats in the yard, then escaped in the chaos as guards rushed out to search for him. Either way, he was loose.

The next day, a bold headline in the *Rockford Daily Republic* blared what Chappel likely immediately thought when hearing the news: DYNAMITER FLEES CHESTER, FEAR LITTS MAY RETURN TO ROCKFORD.

When he slipped out of the asylum gates in March 1926, teams of guards with dogs swept the farms around the grounds and combed the banks of the nearby Mississippi River, but they couldn't find him. People around the Chappel Brothers plant in Rockford worried he would come back for another try at the plant. Locals flooded the police station with calls saying they had spotted him. He was driving by the plant, one said. He had been spied walking down an alley, another said. The Chappel Brothers firm beefed up its squad of armed guards and erected floodlights around the plant. The cops doubted the runaway cowboy would return right away—first he would need to earn money and devise a new plan—but they had no doubt he would be back.

Over the next several months, Litts became the town's version of Boo Radley—a half-real, half-myth dynamite cowboy bogeyman who lurked in every shadow. Any report of a suspicious figure or odd occurrence was immediately ascribed to Litts. A local train was robbed and authorities suspected Litts. A drunk wandered over to the fence of the Chappel corrals where colts were kept. He was rushed by armed guards and was hauled to jail until he could prove he wasn't Litts. A religious fanatic shot a man at a rural dance, miles outside of town. It was immediately assumed to be Litts. A small, thin drifter stabbed a rodeo cowboy in Oregon; Rockford newspapers blamed Litts. Rumors gradually cooled after all these reports turned out to be false. Maybe he wasn't coming back. Maybe he had drowned trying to swim the Mississippi, or gone back to the wilds of Alaska. Maybe he was riding the range in Montana. This was certain: He wasn't in Rockford.

Trainloads of mustangs kept pulling into Chappel Brothers. The operation expanded. It opened new factories. It added new products. It even began leasing ranch land in Wyoming and Montana, where it could gather even more mustangs. It soon controlled 1.6 million acres in the West—an area the size of Delaware. Then, one afternoon in November 1927, a tidy little man with hair parted sharply to the right checked into a hotel in Rockford under the name of Joseph Stewart. He asked for one of the cheap rooms and went upstairs to put away his suitcase. A few minutes later, he came down to listen to the lobby radio, which was tuned to a Notre Dame football game. He leaned back in one of the hotel's armchairs and eventually fell asleep.

Some time later, a woman doing the evening shift at the front desk walked into the lobby to start work. Before taking a job at the hotel, she had worked for years as a matron at the county jail, where she took food to inmates and tended to their needs. She passed by the sleeping man and immediately recognized his dark, flat hair; his thin face; and his protruding eyes. It was Frank Litts.

A few minutes later, Litts was shaken awake by the sheriff's deputy who had arrested him two years earlier. "Come on, Frank," he said, "you're coming with me." The man looked up at him, politely smiled, looking genuinely perplexed, and said, "Who's Frank?" Then he made a break for it.

The deputy tackled him by the door. He put him in handcuffs and searched his pockets, finding a packet of red pepper Litts was carrying in case he needed to throw it in someone's eyes to escape. The officer also found a bill for 150 pounds of dynamite that had recently been shipped by train. At the jail, the suspect continued to insist he was not Frank Litts, but Joseph Stewart. To end the debate, the sheriff pulled up the man's shirt and found scars from two years earlier, when a guard at the Chappel plant had hit him with a shotgun. The next day, police found three boxes of dynamite hidden in a pile of lumber near the train station.

In jail, when a group of newspapermen interviewed Litts, he continued to insist he was a victim of mistaken identity. "Who is this Frank Litts and what has he done?" he asked, appearing befuddled. But when the reporters got him onto the subject of horses, he lost his composure. "The people of this country owe their existences to horses," he said. "It's a terrible shame to take these animals that have done so much for us out and kill them. Suppose we take all the old men in our country out and kill them after they have worked hard all their lives? It is just as horrible to kill horses."

A little over a week later, the sheriff who had taken him to the asylum less than two years earlier locked Litts in leg irons with a chain on his waist tied to a deputy. Afraid that sympathizers might try a rescue, the sheriff sneaked Litts out of the jail at 4 a.m. On the long drive back to the asylum, Litts said to the sheriff, "Take care of that dynamite, because I intend to be back some day."

Litts was a man of his word. Four years later, in 1931, while 175 men were exercising in the walled yard of the asylum, he and eleven other inmates tried to scale a fire escape of a building that made up one of the walls. A guard peppered the group with shotgun blasts and Litts fell back into the yard with a punctured lung. The report of his shooting was the last time his name ever appears in the newspapers.

Though the warden at the time was unsure whether Litts would survive the night, he lived seven more years, eventually dying of a lung ailment in 1938, at age fifty.

The moral outrage Litts so explosively expressed in the 1920s has become much more widespread in the United States. You will not find horse meat these days on supermarket shelves. People refuse even to feed it to their dogs. During the 2000s, there were three slaughterhouses left in the United States—two in Texas and one in Illinois—that survived by sending frozen meat to Europe. But they closed down in 2007 after Congress, under pressure from horse welfare groups, defunded the federal horse-meat inspection program, effectively blocking all sales. Today, more than 100,000 American horses are still slaughtered every year for meat, but they are exported to big plants in Mexico and Canada, where most of the meat is packed into frozen containers and shipped to Asia and Europe.

The story of Frank Litts has been all but forgotten. But as the nation struggles to find a sustainable solution for wild horses in the West, we might do well to remember it, because its themes continue to reappear. When Litts was sentenced, the *Rockford Morning Star* called him "A remarkable example of the insanity that carries a humane and noble impulse a step beyond common sense into psychosis." But that noble impulse—to treat animals fairly and to love and respect wildness—is one that has defined how people have viewed wild horses ever since. The instinct that drove Litts is the same one that drove people to later pass laws to protect mustangs. It is the instinct that shut down all horse slaughterhouses in the country. It is the instinct now that drives advocates to file lawsuits and block roundups. Any management policy that dismisses this viewpoint as sentimental or unrealistic is a policy that is bound to fail. And as Litts's story shows, it may fail violently.

There are still people like Frank Litts out there—likely many more than there were when he was arrested in 1925. One night in 1997, after media reports revealed that the Bureau of Land Management was letting horses secretly go to slaughter, an anonymous group calling itself the Animal Liberation Front sneaked into a BLM corral complex near Burns, Oregon, and set fire to a barn and a tractor. The activists blocked entrances, so fire trucks couldn't approach, and freed almost five hundred horses. They likely had never heard of Frank Litts, but they were his unwitting comrades. According to a communiqué they later released, they did it to "help halt the BLM's illegal and immoral business of rounding up wild horses from public lands and funneling them to slaughter." That same year, the group burned down a horse slaughterhouse in Redmond, Oregon. The plant never reopened.

One night in the summer of 2001, Animal Liberation Front members sneaked into the BLM's big corrals in Litchfield, California, and planted firebombs in the barn, the office, and two trucks. Once again, they cut the fences to free hundreds of captured mustangs. The group released a statement saying, "In the name of all that is wild we will continue to target industries and organizations that seek to profit by destroying the Earth."

Several members of the group were eventually caught and prosecuted under federal terrorism laws, but the BLM continues its roundups, knowing that the threat of a new Frank Litts or Animal Liberation Front is an ever-present danger. In 2008, in minutes of confidential meetings about what to do with "excess" horses, the

BLM explored euthanizing them or selling them for slaughter. While the move would be legal, staff said, it could lead to "threats to BLM property and BLM staff." After considering the risks, they quietly backed off.

Frank Litts was never able to destroy Chappel Brothers, but Chappel Brothers eventually destroyed itself—or, rather, burned itself out. The whole mustang slaughter industry declined steadily during the 1930s as the factories depleted the once-innumerable herds. In 1930, the United States processed ten million pounds of horse meat. By 1938, it processed less than two million. Mustangs were increasingly hard to find and expensive to gather. Chappel tried to boost his supply by introducing hefty draft-horse stallions to the mustangs of Montana to make them heavier, but the domestic studs were driven off by the tougher, more aggressive mustang stallions and had little impact on the genetic makeup of the herds. Drought and decades of unsustainable grazing brought numbers even lower. The vast sea of mustangs was going dry.

Chappel Brothers slipped into debt. During the depression, the factory started slaughtering dust-bowl cattle to can for government relief rations, but it still lost money. Like so many businesses that flourished during the Great Barbecue, it was only designed to function with unbounded plenty. It never invested in sustaining its resources—it just made money while it was there for the making. And when it was over, it closed shop.

In 1937, the company's board of directors dismissed P. M. Chappel as president. He moved to Argentina to start another horse canning factory, drawing from horses on the wide-open pampas, but he died two years later. The Quaker Oats Company bought the Rockford factory and continued to churn out canned horse meat at a much smaller scale, but, after World War II, it turned to beef.

The horse-meat plant in Portland, Oregon, also eventually shifted over to beef. So did the plant in El Paso. A few small slaughterhouses remained, but in terms of grinding up huge herds of mustangs, by 1950, the Great Barbecue was over.

A few still haunted the mesas here or there, but the galloping thousands that once made the land appear as if it were moving were gone forever. It was, many thought, the end of the wild horse. A few more years would bring extinction. When J. Frank Dobie published his epic appraisal, *The Mustangs*, in 1952, the remaining herds were so scant that his book amounted to an elegy. He finished the book this way:

> Well, the wild ones—the coyote duns, the smokies, the blues, the blue roans, the snip-nosed pintos, the flea-bitten grays and the black-skinned whites, the shining blacks and the rusty browns, the red roans, the toasted sorrels and the stockinged bays, the splotched appaloosas and the cream-maned palominos and all the others in shadings of color as various as the hues that show and fade on the clouds at sunset—they are all gone now, gone as completely as the free grass they vivified.[43]

CHAPTER 4

PRINT THE LEGEND

I n 1832, a dusty group of scouts and trappers gathered in the humble glow of a campfire out in the boundless night of the western prairie. They had trekked for weeks upriver into what would one day be Oklahoma but was still at that point simply marked on maps as "Indian country." Gathered in the light of the fire, they sat talking idly, propped against their saddles as they chewed on buffalo ribs.

In the circle sat one of the most famous writers of the time, a forty-nine-year-old Manhattanite named Washington Irving. By 1832, Irving had established his literary reputation with popular tales like *The Legend of Sleepy Hollow* and *Rip Van Winkle*, and had spent years living in Paris and London. A well-connected aristocrat, he had talked his way onto an expedition into Indian Country led by the Secretary of Indian Affairs. The group had been traveling west among the warring Horse Nations of the plains, who at the time were at the peak of their mustang-fueled expansion. Wild horses had brought wealth but also near-constant warfare as tribes tried to gain hunting grounds. Stopping to meet with each tribe they encountered, the secretary would give a speech, according to Irving's later account, saying it was the intention of "their father at Washington to put an end to all war among his red children; and assure them that he was sent to the frontier to establish a universal peace." (One group of Osage warriors responded that if the great father was really going to impose peace, they had better get moving, because they had many horses to steal.[1])

Around the fire that night, Irving raised the subject of mustangs. He had spied one for the first time that day while riding across the plains. At first his party thought it was a buffalo, and gave chase, but the animal wheeled and galloped, throwing its mane like a horse. The cavalrymen charged off after it, but the horse turned and ran, too fleet to catch.

Irving watched it go, "ample mane and tail streaming in the wind," he wrote later in his book *A Tour on the Prairies*. "He paused in the open field beyond, glanced back at us again, with a beautiful bend of the neck, snuffed the air, then tossing his head again, broke into a gallop." He added: "It was the first time I had ever seen a horse scouring his native wilderness in all the pride and freedom of his nature. How different from the poor, mutilated, harnessed, checked, reined-up victim of luxury, caprice, and avarice, in our cities!"[2]

Irving's fascination for the animal hinted at the power the mustang would come to have in the American mind—a power that only grew stronger as the great herds were slaughtered and the country grew more urbanized. Even in Irving's time, when most of the continent was still wild, the mustang evoked freedom and defiance—an antidote to the woes of city life.

By the campfire that night, after Irving told the other men about spotting the mustang, the men started offering their own stories. There was an especially good one about a legendary mustang that no one could catch: the White Stallion. All the men who had spent any time in the West had heard of him, and some claimed to have seen him. Each man around the fire began offering what he knew about the glorious animal, interrupting one another to pile on their own details. The stallion was faster than any horse in existence. Instead of galloping, he paced. But with his long, muscled legs, his walking gait could still outdistance any pursuer. For years, men had tried to catch him. The best ropers could not get close enough to throw a lariat. Seasoned mustangers had set traps, but the stallion was too smart to enter. They tried to snare him at water holes, corner him in canyons, chase him off cliffs, lure him with the most beautiful mares, but every time, just as it seemed he was finally caught, he slipped away.

Irving jotted notes on these stories in his journal. Though he did not know it at the time, he was recording the first-ever written account of the myth of the mustang that would be repeated for more than a century.

The legend of the White Stallion was told in uncounted variations as long as the free and open West existed. And it often grew in the telling. He was tall and noble. Some said he was stark white, others who swore they had seen him said that he had a touch of gray, or black ears. His head and neck were unmistakably Arabian, some said. Others said he was pure Spanish Barb. His mane was like spun silk. It glowed like moonlight. Some called him the White Steed of the Prairies. Some called him the Ghost Horse. Some said he was the devil disguised as a mustang. Some compared him to a god.

He inevitably roamed the most open, wild, far-flung places. Some said he frequented the staked plains in the panhandle of Oklahoma. Some said he ran near the mesas on the Wyoming/Colorado border. Some said he haunted the deserts of the Texas border country, or the upper reaches of the Columbia River west of the Rockies.

He was always spotted on the horizon, tossing his head in defiance. But try to pursue him and you were sure to come back empty-handed, if you came back at all. Men in three relays with packs of hounds chased him across Texas. The best mustanger in the Brazos country set snares near his favorite shade trees. Some hunters tried to catch him in springtime when he was weak, or by the water hole when he was heavy after a long drink. But no rope ever touched him.

A doctor in San Antonio offered $500 for the stallion's capture, one story goes. Some say it was actually P. T. Barnum who made the offer, and the price was $5,000. No matter. It couldn't be done. One group of Blackfoot warriors trapped the stallion in a corral, only to have him leap the seven-foot fence. Some say a group of soldiers, after chasing him eighty miles, were sure they shot him dead along the Llano River, but the next day he returned to his favorite water hole. Another cowboy chased him through a storm near midnight out in the cliffs of the Cimarron country. After hours of pursuit, he cornered the stallion on a cliff a hundred feet above a rocky gully. The stallion, unwilling to surrender, leapt into the void. The next morning, the cowboy came back to look for the body, but the horse was gone.

In a few cases, the White Stallion led to the pursuers' downfall. Two gamblers named Wild Jake and Kentuck are said to have set out from Santa Fe in the 1850s, determined to either return to the town riding the legendary stallion or "pursue him until the great prairies were swept by the fires of the Day of Judgment."[3] Dodging Indians and living off buffalo, they searched for weeks without a sign of the mustang. The longer they searched, the more they were consumed by obsession. Talk of the wild steed was always on Jake's lips, and Kentuck could even hear him muttering about it in his sleep.

The weeks stretched into months. Winter was drawing near. Kentuck started to wonder whether they should turn back to Santa Fe, but Jake would only snap back that he aimed to find that horse or keep looking until the Day of Judgment. Finally, on a stormy night on the plains, they spotted him—standing only 100 yards ahead in the moonlight, a glowing white beauty of perfect proportions.

They charged as though the whole Comanche nation was pursuing them. But the horse paced away, gliding noiselessly into the darkness. No matter how hard they rode, they never got closer. After hours of chase, Kentuck yelled to Jake to stop. They should go back, he urged, it was no use.

In the moonlight, Jake turned and looked at Kentuck with a maniacal grin. His hat had fallen off and his long hair dangled around his darting eyes. His lips had a thin foam and a hint of blood where he had bitten them. "I'll follow him—yes—to the Day of Judgment." Jake sped off after the horse, not seeing a cliff ahead of him. Kentuck watched Jake sail into the canyon below, calling as he fell, "'Till the Day of Judgment!"[4]

In a way, the White Stallion is just another larger-than-life folk hero like Paul Bunyan or Pecos Bill—a way to spin a mythical yarn that was a variation on a theme: How is the horse going to get away this time? But it represents much more. We never made a national symbol out of Paul Bunyan. He is the story of power. The wild horse is the story of independence.

The White Stallion made it into a number of best-selling accounts of adventures out West, including Irving's, and soaked into the literary Zeitgeist of the country. It became the basis of Herman Melville's whaling classic, *Moby-Dick*—a story of the maniacal pursuit of a legendary white beast that could not be caught.

Melville—who, like Irving, grew up in New York City—likely heard the tale of the white horse as a young author, either through accounts of frontier yarns that appeared in popular magazines at the time or through the book-length sagas of Irving and another literary explorer, George Wilkins Kendall, who published an account of exploring the area in 1844. He probably also took inspiration from the tall tales of a white whale said to have escaped more than a hundred encounters with whalers off the coast of Chile. And the stories of the white whale and the White Stallion, which both emerged from groups of explorers in the early nineteenth century, may have the same root in the era's yearning to explore and subdue. In any case, Melville makes it quite clear in *Moby-Dick* that he had given a great deal of thought to the horse before writing.

"Most famous in our Western annals and Indian traditions is that of the White Steed of the Prairies," he wrote in a chapter about the whale's "whiteness":

A magnificent milk-white charger, large-eyed, small-headed, bluff-chested, and with the dignity of a thousand monarchs in his lofty, overscorning carriage. He was the elected Xerxes of vast herds of wild horses, whose pastures in those days were only fenced by the Rocky Mountains and the Alleghenies. At their flaming head he westward trooped it like that chosen star which every evening leads on the hosts of light. The flashing cascade of his mane, the curving comet of his tail, invested him with housings more resplendent than gold and silver-beaters could have furnished him. A most imperial and archangelical apparition of that unfallen, western world, which to the eyes of the old trappers and hunters revived the glories of those primeval times when Adam walked majestic as a god, bluff-browed and fearless as this mighty steed.[5]

The folklorist Frank Dobie spent decades tracking every reference to the legend of the White Stallion and eventually gave up, finding that there were simply too many, and the "Zane Grey assembly line and pulp magazines have published stories on the horse without end."[6] The myth changed and grew over time as other writers and other generations added their own takes, but in the nearly two hundred years since, it has remained essentially the same: The mustang is always pursued by man, and always gets away. He is proud and regal and prizes freedom above all else, including his own life. He stands as a proof that some things can never be had. Despite the many industrious plans of man, there is a certain wild nobility that can't be captured. This is an idea so linked to wild horses that most Americans know it, even if they know nothing about the myth of the White Stallion, and it has resonated through the generations because it expresses an idea that runs deep in the country's identity.

There is no other animal in America that we have heaped with so much meaning. Though the bald eagle is the country's official symbol, it isn't as American as the mustang. The eagle is too regal and aloof—a symbol of federal power but not of American grit. Besides, the bald eagle is known for stealing fish from other birds, which prompted Benjamin Franklin to call it a bird of "bad moral character." The mustang, on the other hand, embodies the core ideals of America. It is not pedigreed. It has no stature. Instead, it derives its nobility from the simple toughness of its upbringing in a free and open land. It is beholden to no one. It will not be subjugated. It is superior to its domestic brethren because it has the one thing Americans say they yearn for most: freedom. It is the hoofed version of Jeffersonian democracy.

Why the mustang? When the experience of settling North America produced such a menagerie of animal characters—the mule, the oxen, the longhorn, the sheep, the herding dog—why was it only the wild horse that crossed into legend? Why was the story of the White Stallion told and retold, and heaped with so much meaning?

To try to answer these questions, I made my way, one muggy July morning, down a winding road on the Lackawaxen River in the mountains of northeastern Pennsylvania, where everything was a wall of green—lush and still and close. The Appalachian forest leaned so far over the narrow road along the river that only a few palm-size patches of sun hit the pavement. The thick smell of breathing trees and aging leaves hung on the breeze.

I pulled my car up to a spot where the lacy riffles of the Lackawaxen emptied into the broad, smooth Delaware River at a place called Cottage Point. It could not have been farther from the vast, dry vistas of Wild Horse Country. There were no long views or mesas, no cactus or sage. That morning, a steady stream of candy-colored kayaks drifted by, slowly turning in the glassy emerald water under galaxies of flies and midges that glowed in the early light. But on a small rise on the riverbank stood a two-story white-clapboard farmhouse with dark green shutters and a broad front porch opening on the river that is so tightly bound to the legend of wild horses in America that you can't understand what has happened in the West unless you look at what happened in this quiet house in the East.

I pushed open the oak front door, stepped through the parlor, and walked down the creaky wood hall of the farmhouse. The last door on the left revealed a spacious study. Its walls were covered with Navajo weavings and paintings of Hopi Kachinas. The bookshelves were filled with the adventure tales of James Fenimore Cooper and Rudyard Kipling. And in one corner, near the woodstove, stood a broad armchair with a maple lapboard still leaning against it. Here one of the best-selling Western authors of all time, Zane Grey, spent eight hours a day penning pulp novels.

If the pueblos of New Mexico are the place that set wild horses free on the West, then this quiet spot in the Appalachian Mountains is the place that set free the icon. Grey helped build the myth of the West from campfire stories into an industry. Along the way, he, more than anyone else, molded the wild horse into an enduring American legend. The riders of the purple sage, the damsel in distress, the lowborn cowboy with a strong moral code. The noble mustang that will only submit to the hero, and, despite a lack of pedigree and a fiery temper, is the best horse under the sun—these are all stereotypes popularized by Grey. One film critic called Westerns the Genesis and Exodus of the American story. Grey's stories and thousands others like them glorified the Western hero and the idealized Western code of honor as a way of explaining our origins to ourselves.

Grey didn't invent the Western genre or the legend of the wild horse. Instead, he was the myth's Henry Ford. His genius was in designing an attractive, streamlined, accessible product for the masses. Like an assembly line, he was constantly churning out books: *The Last of the Plainsmen*, *The Heritage of the Desert*, *Riders of the Purple Sage*, *Spirit of the Border*, *The Last Trail*, *Wanderer of the Wasteland*, *The Thundering Herd*. Through simple language, vivid scenery and characters, and sheer output, he modernized, mechanized, marketed, and democratized a myth so powerful that, in a big way, it became a key chapter in the story we tell about ourselves as a nation. In a writing career spanning thirty-six years, he published more than forty books. When he died in 1939, his publisher noted he had sold seventeen million copies, outselling every book but the Bible, and calling him "the greatest selling author of all time." He has since sold more than twenty million more. You can find copies in nearly every library and bookstore. They were made into magazines, comics, radio plays, and more than 110 movies and television episodes. They inspired countless other Westerns and anti-Westerns. The Lone Ranger and his horse Silver, Randolph Scott in a white hat, Gary Cooper with his six-shooter, John Wayne riding shotgun— all the most famous tall, silent archetypes got their start in stories thought up by Grey. And the myth he popularized led to the law that now protects wild horses.

Myths live in the mind, not on the land. And where the myth of the West really took root was not in the West but in the East, where a handful of men like Irving and Grey—almost all of them wealthy men in New York City—turned the herds of galloping mustangs into something more than just horses. Through dime novels, pulp fiction, stage shows, and eventually Hollywood movies, they made the mustang an indelible part of the myth of America, forever linked to a set of ideals: quiet toughness, steadfast loyalty, plainspoken common sense, an insistence on independence, the pursuit of certain inalienable rights endowed by the Creator.

Sure, most Westerns were idealized parodies of the West written for eastern audiences, and they offered a message often designed to resonate with the quiet desperation of urban lives. But Grey appeared to be aware of this, and comfortable with it. When I walked into the old farmhouse in Lackawaxen, Pennsylvania, which is now a museum run by the National Park Service, I was greeted by this quote from his 1921 novel *To the Last Man*: "In this materialistic age, this hard, practical, swift, greedy age of realism, it seems there is no place for writers of romance, no place for romance itself. I have loved the West for its vastness, its contrast its beauty and color and life, for its wildness and violence, and for the fact that I have seen how it developed great men and women who died unknown and unsung. Romance is only another name for idealism; and I contend that life without ideals is not worth living."

Another quote on the wall read: "Realism is death to me. I cannot stand life as it is."

As I read it, I thought about all the forgotten, yellowing newspaper clips from a century ago that I had tracked down to try to understand the long war between ranchers and horses. How obscure, and even beside the point, those snippets of fact seemed when compared to the story we tell now about the horse as a noble companion. The myth had more weight than the real history. I couldn't help but remember the last scene of the classic 1962 movie *The Man Who Shot Liberty Valance*. Slumped back in an armchair, a three-term governor of a Western state finally reveals the truth: He had built his career on a reputation for having killed a no-good outlaw, but, in fact, he had never shot the man at all. On hearing this, a newspaperman interviewing the governor rips up his notepad.

"You're not going to use the story?" the governor asks.

"No, sir," the newspaperman says. "This is the West, sir. When the legend becomes fact, print the legend."

Myth always tries to find meaning in the past, and, in the process, it often discards many of the facts. A lot of the legend of the West that we now carry in our popular imagination was never true, including aspects of the story of wild horses, but at this point there is so much cultural heft behind it that it hardly matters.

———

To find resonance, every myth has to have some foundation in reality. As generations shaped the myth of the wild horse, it slowly changed from one of majestic wildness to one of noble and willing servitude—reflecting changes in the country itself. The men sitting around the campfire with Washington Irving in the 1830s, and the cowpunchers and trappers who came after them, had all left civilization to try to make it in the West. The leagues of endless grass, uncut forests, and tumbling mountain rivers appeared to offer resources without end, but a man had to figure out how to seize them and make them his own. They knew well the raw power of the land and its nobility. In a way, their telling and retelling the story of the White Stallion pacing away was a sign of respect for their place in the West. They admired the land and the bounty it could produce. They pursued its riches, but ultimately they knew they could not possess the one thing they loved most about it: the wildness.

Of course, the West changed, and, as it did, so did the myth of the wild horse. Railroads cut the plains into pieces; the buffalo and the Horse Nations both were nearly eradicated. Barbed wire was patented in 1874 and rolled out across the West. The stories told about the White Stallion changed too.

Frank Dobie made a habit of talking to old-timers who had ridden the range back in the 1870s and 1880s. He observed that as the West was settled, the story of the White Stallion slowly changed from a stallion that couldn't be caught to a stallion that couldn't be tamed. It would choose death over subjugation. Live free or die. Some men told Dobie the stallion was eventually shot by a group of frustrated cowboys. Some said he was chased ten days and finally caught in the desert hills near Phoenix by a bunch of ranch hands. They penned him in a high and sturdy corral, but he refused to eat or drink. No one was ever able to ride him. He died of starvation after ten days.

About the same time the White Stallion reportedly died, the Wild West pretty much rode into the sunset too. The last big cattle drives ended in 1886. Geronimo and his small band of Apaches surrendered the same year. The Horse Nations were defeated, their horses confiscated. For decades, the census had been marking the western march of the frontier, but in 1890, the Census Bureau said the frontier was gone. The country was now civilized.

In 1893, historian Frederick Jackson Turner, in a small lecture to other historians at the World's Columbian Exposition in Chicago, announced that the period of westward expansion that had marked and molded the American psyche since the time of the *Mayflower* was over. In his "frontier thesis," the thirty-two-year-old history professor said the frontier had been the defining feature of Americanness. The "Great West," with its endless wild lands, had created the

American identity: practical, inventive, egalitarian, fiercely independent, and distrustful of government. The values he was tying to the frontier were the same ones writers would give to the mustang.

"The frontier," he told the audience, "is the line of most rapid and effective Americanization." He continued: "Since the days when the fleet of Columbus sailed into the waters of the New World, America has been another name for opportunity, and the people of the United States have taken their tone from the incessant expansion which has not only been open but has even been forced upon them. . . . Each frontier did indeed furnish a new field of opportunity, a gate of escape from the bondage of the past; and freshness, and confidence, and scorn of older society, impatience of its restraints and its ideas, and indifference to its lessons."[7]

In a way, though he did not know it, he was arguing that Americans were a lot like mustangs: European imports of various stations, who were defined not by their birth but by the freewheeling life they encountered in the West.

If the wild period of the frontier, when mustangs and Americans had been created, was ending, the myth was just getting its start. Across the street from where Professor Turner delivered his speech—a speech that largely went unnoticed at the time, and was only later recognized as one of the most significant lectures ever on American history—William "Buffalo Bill" Cody was putting on his Wild West Show to a daily audience of eighteen thousand. It was pure spectacle, the weaving of history into myth, right before the audience's eyes. Riders on real mustangs reenacted the Pony Express days. Lakota warriors carrying bows and rifles played out the Battle of the Little Bighorn. Cody, who had been an explorer on the plains long enough to have heard the legends of the plains dozens of times, started every show by galloping into the arena astride a regal white stallion.

It was around this time that a myth of the mustang took a turn. In this new version, the mustang would submit to a man and become a willing servant—but only if the man's heart was true. It is this version that has largely endured. In radio plays of *The Lone Ranger* generations later, the ranger's white stallion, Silver, is wild and untamable until the ranger saves him from a buffalo attack. In gratitude, Silver becomes his companion.

The new myth got its start with dime novels about Buffalo Bill and other explorers. Buffalo Bill alone was the subject of more than 1,700 pulp novels. Often myth and reality worked side by side in ways that might strike even a reality TV producer as odd. Early on, Buffalo Bill, for example, was a scout in the West in the summers and played himself in musicals in Chicago in the winters. These early accounts were full of stories of tough mustangs and their incredible feats. Buffalo Bill told of riding one little Indian pony named Buckskin Joe nearly two hundred miles while being pursued by plains tribes. The horse never gave out, but he was so exhausted by the end that he went blind.

In a way, the new version of the wild horse myth, which made the horse into a noble companion, was a melding of the two myths. America had long championed noble adventurers like Daniel Boone and Natty "Leatherstocking" Bumppo. The horse had long symbolized the evasive nature of the wild. In the new myth, they were side by side. The mustang remained noble and independent but was willing to work with the right guy. It was Manifest Destiny, the wild yielding to American exceptionalism.

Zane Grey grew up reading those early dime novels. But he was in many ways an unlikely godfather of the Western myth. He was born Pearl Zane Grey in 1872 in Zanesville, Ohio, the son of a strict and often disapproving dentist. As a boy, Pearl, who maybe not surprisingly eventually started going by his middle name, devoured boys' adventure books: James Fenimore Cooper's tales of Leatherstocking, Robert Louis Stevenson's *Treasure Island*, and the constant churn of dime novels featuring Western yarns about Buffalo Bill and Deadwood Dick. Grey's study still contains volume after volume of these classic adventure books. Growing up, he loved the outdoors, baseball, and writing, but his father insisted he go into dentistry. By age sixteen, Grey was making rural house calls to pull teeth. A smart, athletic kid, he eventually won a baseball scholarship to the University of Pennsylvania, graduating with a dentistry degree in 1896. Soon afterward, he opened his own practice in New York City.

In his old farmhouse, the rooms are now filled with glass cases stocked with relics of Grey's writing career: pristine first editions, journals, binoculars, fishing rods, and black-and-white photographs. A photo near the door shows him as a dentist—lean, taut, and broad-shouldered like an athlete, but yoked in a black suit and stiff

THE PROLIFIC
NOVELIST ZANE GREY.

paper collar. His costume is staid, his look is stern, but his eyes blaze under a deep, intense brow, making him look like a caged animal—a maniac desperate to escape.

Throughout his life, Grey was stalked by what he called "black moods," and he had an intensity and wildness that life as a dentist could not satiate. Only outdoor adventure seemed to lift his spirits. When his city life of pulling teeth became too much, Grey would often catch a train out of Penn Station to take fishing trips around Lackawaxen. He dreamed of one day leaving the city entirely to live out in the mountains, writing about his adventures. In 1900, while canoeing on the Delaware, he met a sharp and beautiful seventeen-year-old girl named Lina "Dolly" Roth and fell in love. They had a long courtship, writing letters back and forth as she finished college, and eventually married in 1905.

Dolly seemed to understand that her husband needed something beyond pulling teeth. She had a small inheritance and encouraged him to quit dentistry and follow his dream to move to a farmhouse on the bank of the Lackawaxen and become a writer.

"I need this wild life, this freedom," he told her in a letter. "To be alive, to look into nature, and so into my soul."[8]

By 1907, Grey was living on the Lackawaxen. He had quit dentistry and written an adventure novel about the Revolutionary War, but it was quickly rejected by New York publishers. He kept writing, scraping together something close to a living by penning articles here and there about fishing. That year, he attended a lecture in New York by a Buffalo Bill–type adventurer named Buffalo Jones—a longtime frontiersman who had rounded up some of the last buffalo and was trying to breed them at a ranch north of the Grand Canyon. Jones regaled the crowd with tales about hunting mountain lions and once lassoing an unruly bear. Intrigued, Grey pulled Jones aside after the lecture and asked to go with him to the Grand Canyon to write about his life. Jones agreed. They spent months traversing the wilds of northern Arizona—fording rivers, encountering gun-toting cowpokes, and hunting mountain lions. After the trip, Grey returned home and in the space of a few months wrote what would be his first Western, *The Last of the Plainsmen.*

His last chapter included his own retelling of the legend of the White Stallion.

"He can't be ketched," the Buffalo Jones character says. "We seen him an' his band of blacks a few days ago, headin' fer a water-hole down where Nail Canyon runs into Kanab Canyon. He's so cunnin' he'll never water at any of our trap corrals. An' we believe he can go without water fer two weeks, unless mebbe he has a secret hole we've never trailed him to. . . . He never makes a mistake. Mebbe you'll get to see him cum by like a white streak. Why, I've heerd thet mustang's hoofs ring like bells on the rocks a mile away. His hoofs are harder'n any iron shoe as was ever made."[9]

The book ends with the cowboys coursing down a dead-end box canyon at a full gallop, sure that there is no way the stallion can escape. He does.

After *The Last of the Plainsmen*, Grey almost immediately headed back west in search of more stories. Though he was gone for long periods of time, his wife encouraged him, knowing that adventure was one of the few cures for his depression. Writing in longhand in his study back in Lackawaxen, Grey began turning out one hit novel after another: *The Heritage of the Desert, Riders of the Purple Sage, The Lone Star Ranger.* He was on the best-seller list every year for the next decade.

The books coined the idea of the Western hero who was honest, steadfast, and loyal. Ironically, Grey was anything but. Most notably, he had an unquenchable appetite for sex. At sixteen, he'd been arrested in a brothel. A few years later, he was the subject of a paternity suit. He kept sleeping with other women throughout his courtship with Dolly, and he slept with even more women after they married. Fame only fueled his exploits. For his whole writing life, he traveled with a series of "secretaries" and "nieces"—sometimes as many as four at a time—keeping journals (written in code) of his sexual encounters.

"A pair of dark blue eyes makes me a tiger," he once wrote. "I love, I love my wife, yet such iron I am that there is no change."[10] In a way, by creating characters driven by honesty, loyalty, and trust, he was expressing a life he wished he could live.

If the myth of the White Stallion had originated with men in the West, who were intimately familiar with the power of the western landscape, the myth of the horse as noble companion, which endures today, was one devised in the East, generally by men like Grey, who yearned to be free in the West but were instead entangled in eastern society.

At first, the heroes of the myth were all explorers, but they were eventually replaced by a more blue-collar hero, the cowboy. For that, we can thank a not very blue-collar eastern blueblood named Owen Wister, who in 1902 published what is often called the first Western novel, *The Virginian: A Horseman of the Plains*.

Wister was an even odder choice as father of the Western than Zane Grey. He grew up the privileged son of a doctor and a southern lady whose family had owned hundreds of slaves before the Civil War. He attended the best boarding schools in Switzerland and New England, then graduated from Harvard. In school he excelled at music and theater, and he wanted to become a composer, but his father pushed him into a desk job at a Philadelphia bank. It didn't take long for Wister to suffer a nervous breakdown. In 1885, a doctor recommended that the best way to recuperate was to go west. Stepping off the train in Wyoming a few weeks later, he encountered the plain-talking ranch hands who inspired the cowboy archetype. Like the wild horse, the man was defined by the freedom of the place, not his lineage.

"The grim long-haired type," he called them. Ones that "wore their pistols, and rode gallantly, and out of them nature and simplicity did undoubtedly forge manlier, cleaner men than what our streets breed of no worse material. . . . They developed heartiness and honesty in virtue and in vice alike. Their evil deeds were not of the sneaking kind, but had always the saving grace of courage. Their code had no place for the man who steals a pocket-book or stabs in the back."[11]

That is an interesting idea, because Wister was, among other things, a first-class, Gilded Age bigot. He laid out his feelings clearly in an 1895 essay for *Harper's* magazine called "The Evolution of the Cow-Puncher," which became the blueprint for his version of the cowboy myth. He believed, first off, that the West only worked its magic on Anglo-Saxons. He saw Philadelphia, and America as a

THE NOVELIST OWEN WISTER,
AUTHOR OF *THE VIRGINIAN*.

whole, as being a flagging "compound of new hotels, electric lights, and invincible ignorance," infested with Catholics, Jews, and immigrants. Or, as he called them, "hordes of encroaching alien vermin, that turn our cities to Babels and our citizenship to a hybrid farce, who degrade our commonwealth from a nation into something half pawn-shop, half broker's office."[12]

Democracy was falling apart, he contended. But his visits to the West had inspired him, because out there he had encountered, he said, the most noble breed of man in his natural setting: the rural Anglo-Saxon. He believed the Anglo-Saxon, dropped into the raw, wild West, free of the mongrel horde, reawakened a natural superiority that had been present in Viking warriors, the knights of Camelot, the other brave explorers of yore, but had gone dormant in his deskbound generation. He wrote:

Watching for Indians, guarding huge herds at night, chasing cattle, wild as deer, over rocks and counties, sleeping in the dust and waking in the snow, cooking in the open, swimming the swollen rivers. Such gymnasium for mind and body develops a like pattern in the unlike. Thus, late in the nineteenth century, was the race once again subjected to battles and darkness, rain and shine, to the fierceness and generosity of the desert. Destiny tried her latest experiment upon the Saxon, and plucking him from the library, the haystack, and the gutter, set him upon his horse; then it was that, face to face with the eternal simplicity of death, his modern guise fell away and showed once again the mediaeval man. It was no new type, no product of the frontier, but just the original kernel of the nut with the shell broken.[13]

This was only true of Anglo-Saxons, he observed. "To survive in the clean cattle country requires spirit of adventure, courage, and self-sufficiency; you will not find many Poles or Huns or Russian Jews."[14]

A crucial ingredient, he said, was the horse—specifically, the cow pony, or mustang, or Cayuse—the wild horse of the West:

A few words about this horse—the horse of the plains. Whether or not his forefathers looked on when Montezuma fell, they certainly hailed from Spain. And whether it was missionaries or thieves who carried them northward from Mexico, until the Sioux heard of the new animal, certain it also is that this pony ran wild for a century or two, either alone or with various red-skinned owners; and as he gathered the sundry experiences of war and peace, of being stolen, and of being abandoned in the snow at inconvenient distances from home, of being ridden by two women and a baby at once, and of being eaten by a bear, his wide range of contretemps brought him a wit sharper than the street Arab's, and an attitude towards life more blasé than in the united capitals of Europe. I have frequently caught him watching me with an eye of such sardonic depreciation that I felt it quite vain to attempt any hiding from him of my incompetence; and as for surprising him, a locomotive cannot do it, for I have tried this.[15]

In the West, both man and horse had undergone renewal, he argued. And like steel and flint, or bow and arrow, the man needed the horse and the horse needed the man: "Deprive the Saxon of his horse, and put him to forest-clearing or in a counting-house for a couple of generations, and you may pass him by without ever seeing that his legs are designed for the gripping of saddles."[16]

Wister wrote several short stories on this theme, culminating in *The Virginian*, his only full-length Western novel, about a nameless ranch hand in Wyoming, which announced to the world the archetype of the lowborn natural aristocrat cowboy hero that is still in broad circulation today:

> His broad, soft hat was pushed back; a loose-knotted, dull-scarlet handkerchief sagged from his throat; and one casual thumb was hooked in the cartridge-belt that slanted across his hips. He had plainly come many miles from somewhere across the vast horizon, as the dust upon him showed. His boots were white with it. His over-alls were gray with it. The weather-beaten bloom of his face shone through it duskily, as the ripe peaches look upon their trees in a dry season. But no dinginess of travel or shabbiness of attire could tarnish the splendor that radiated from his youth and strength.[17]

Of course the Virginian rode a mustang. His name was Buck.

The gunslinging and galloping adventures made *The Virginian*—a yearning Easterner's portrait of time past—a best seller. The strong, silent drifter, an unlikely Sir Galahad of the plains, would live on with Grey and a crowd of other imitators. Grey studied *The Virginian* before writing his first book. Other writers, in turn, saw Grey's success and copied him. Fred Faust, a Berkeley dropout, aspiring poet, and practiced alcoholic in Manhattan, writing under the name Max Brand, churned out scores of Western pulp novels in the 1920s and 1930s with names like *Riders of the Silences*, *The Untamed*, and *The Night Horseman*. Ernest Haycox, a beat reporter at the newspaper in Portland, Oregon, in the 1920s, was also inspired by Grey's work, and a steady stream of titles followed: *Starlight Rider*, *Riders West*, *Man in the Saddle*, *The Wild Bunch*.

There were many, many more imitators. Westerns dominated nearly every medium for the next fifty years. The action-packed stories naturally translated into movies and radio. In 1925, Douglas Fairbanks starred in a silent film based on Grey's 1928 book *Wild Horse Mesa*, about a rancher, desperate for money, who tries to trap and sell wild horses but is stopped by the hero and a wily White Stallion. After that box office success, more than a hundred films were made from Grey's work. Hundreds more were inspired by the writers who followed him. By 1950, the golden age of the genre, Westerns outnumbered all other movie categories combined.

You can see the reach of the myth as it percolated into the rest of America. During World War II, when the Americans developed a tough little one-seater fighter plane that could cover long distances at high speeds, they called it the P-51 Mustang. In 1964, when Ford came out with a little two-seater with surprising power and affordability, a marketing manager who had just read a J. Frank Dobie book

ONE OF THE FIRST ADS TO INTRODUCE THE FORD MUSTANG PLAYED ON THE MYTH OF THE WHITE STALLION.

suggested *The Mustang*. At the time, more than stories of the Revolution or the building of cities or the digging of canals, mustangs and the cowboy myth were a way we explained our origins and connected ourselves to the past. Even if it was a past that never was.

After several best sellers, Zane Grey moved from his farmhouse in Pennsylvania to California in 1918. He continued to write feverishly, but he also pressed farther and farther from civilization, looking for adventure. He descended rivers in Mexico, hunting for new fishing grounds. He bought a $250,000 yacht and traveled first to the Galapagos, then out into the South Pacific, where he spent months fishing and became a real-life Captain Ahab as he nearly pushed his crew to mutiny in the hunt to land a world-record marlin. He continued to pursue new women, even while keeping up a relationship with his wife, who reliably, if rarely happily, put up with his affairs and managed the business side of his writing, often signing her letters, "Your wife, in name only."

As I walked through the rooms of Zane Grey's house, looking at carefully labeled fishing rods, camp stoves, and canteens, I couldn't help but feel a little sorry for him. Grey had been born wild and spent the rest of his life trying to break free of a world that was increasingly haltered. He was constantly pushing himself to run farther, to experience more, to bite into life deeply and drink the juices. That is a hard thing to live with for a lifetime. But at the same time I admired him. That constant itch had made him disregard the comfortable life given to him and really live. He wandered the globe drinking life to the lees, hunted mountain lions on canyon rims, and rode mustangs through desert valleys. He spread a cowboy mythology that is still with us. He lived a life of wildness. How long would he have lasted if he had stayed a dentist?

I doubt Grey thought much about the impact of his stories beyond his own life, but the people who grew up with the myth he helped spread are the people who, as adults, passed the 1971 law protecting wild horses. Would it have happened at any other time, with a population that wasn't raised with the stories of the Noble Mustang and the White Stallion? I have my doubts.

In the house at Cottage Point, the National Park Service had a volunteer docent working the front desk. He looked to be about sixteen, and the sleeves on his short-sleeved shirt hung down past his elbows. He was probably too young to have had much exposure to the cowboy myth. Baby boomers grew up saturated in cowboys: TV, radio, the movies, toys. I was born in the 1970s. By that time, all the heroes on the screen were mostly in space. Westerns were complex, full of anti-heroes, and no more trusty mustangs. The faithful mustang had morphed into R2-D2 in an X-wing fighter. With younger generations, cowboys are even more obscure. Few people anymore know the story of the White Stallion.

There was no one else in the museum, so I went up and asked the volunteer to name his favorite Zane Grey book. He paused, mouth half open, then said, "I've never really read his books."

He explained that he was volunteering not because he had a huge affinity with the author but because he lived nearby. The few people who drifted in and out during my visit all appeared to be in their seventies—people who were young parents when the 1971 law passed. I wondered what the younger generations, who had not grown up surrounded by Zane Grey–style Westerns, thought of wild horses.

I told the volunteer I was writing about wild horses, and I thought Grey was a pivotal part of why they still existed. He nodded in the way kids do when they are old enough to realize that all adults are really weird.

"Wild horses," he muttered. "Are they still around?"

CHAPTER 5

WILD HORSE ANNIE

In the spring of 1950, a thirty-eight-year-old secretary named Velma Bronn Johnston was driving to work at an insurance company in Reno. Cigarette in hand, smoke curling out of the window in the early morning light, she sped down a gravel road through a rocky desert valley in Nevada where a green patchwork of small ranches clung to the Truckee River. The road snaked along the water, following almost every bend, but Velma knew the turns well from weekly trips between the sixteen-acre hobby ranch where she lived with her husband, three horses, and two cocker spaniels on the weekends, and Reno, where she lived and worked the rest of the week.

If there is a rugged, rural type of person most people would expect to live in a desert valley in Nevada, Velma Johnston was not it. She was well read and well spoken, with none of the Texas twang that in recent years became an affect of many rural westerners. She wore heels, not boots, and painted her nails to a flawless pearl sheen. She was also jarringly disfigured—the result of a childhood bout with polio that left her back twisted and the left side of her face askew like a Picasso portrait. But her looks had never deterred her. She was confident, smart, and determined to be the best secretary any boss had ever had.

After a few miles of bumpy dirt road, she turned onto the paved road to Reno. The city was thirty miles away, through a pass in the Virginia Mountains, and she put the pedal down to make time. It was normally open road that early in the day. Reno only had forty thousand people, and the Great Basin in her rearview mirror was almost entirely unpopulated. Traffic was never a problem. But not long after turning onto the highway, she came up behind an old stock truck rolling slowly alongside the river. Its bed had high wooden-slat sides and a canvas roof. She could tell by the way it swayed and sagged that it was fully loaded. Johnston, in a hurry to get to work, came up close behind it. The highway between her ranch and Reno was winding, and there was no easy place to pass, so she was forced to stare in frustration at the back of the tottering truck.

She noticed something glistening on the back bumper. It was dark, like oil. As she got closer, she realized it was blood. There was a steady dribble leaking out of the truck bed and dripping off the bumper.

Johnston stayed behind the truck, studying the blood. What was in the back of the truck that was bleeding—was it an injured cow or sheep? Certainly the rancher driving would want to know, she thought, and she decided to alert him as soon as she could.

The flow of blood increased as the truck rolled down the highway. By the outskirts of Reno, it was a constant stream. The truck pulled off at the stockyards in Sparks, Nevada, and Johnston followed. When the truck parked, she went up to peer through the slats. What she saw stole her breath. The bed was packed full of mustangs, many of them bleeding from wounds as though they had been blasted with shotguns, others bleeding from torn hooves. One stallion had both his eyes gouged out. As the horses jostled and shifted, she saw a colt on the floor, trampled to a pulp by the crowd.

She asked the driver where the horses had come from, and why they were in such ghastly shape.

He pointed to the Virginia Mountains and said the horses had just been rounded up by plane out there and were headed for the slaughterhouse in California.

Johnston began to weep.

"No use crying your eyes out over a bunch of useless mustangs," the driver said. "They will all be dead soon anyway."

That moment forever changed Johnston's life. She decided that day to work on saving Nevada's remaining mustangs. Within a few years, she had built a national movement. Tens of thousands of people were demanding protection for wild horses. They began calling Johnston by a nickname, "Wild Horse Annie." And she eventually, after an effort that lasted more than twenty years, led them all to victory.

———

When the Chappel Brothers plant stopped slaughtering horses in the 1940s, the slaughter business never really recovered, but it didn't entirely go away. The remaining herds were too small and too hard to reach to be viable for big factories. There was no money in it. But then a new efficiency came along that kept mustanging viable: airplanes.

A plane could skim low over the roughest terrain, flushing herds out of rough country. One pilot could see for miles and the plane never grew winded. It did the work of a hundred men and erased the problem of sending "good horses after bad" through perilous country.

A California pilot named Floyd Hanson, described as "a tall, gangling, cheerful fellow," became one of the first sky wranglers in 1938, when he took an old open-cockpit biplane to the Owyhee Desert of southeastern Oregon. He was getting $5 a head, as men had done decades before, but he could gather many times more horses in a day. He claimed to have collected ten thousand wild horses in Oregon.

He swept over the sage, coaxing the animals out of the canyons, looping, diving, sideslipping like a "skidding billiard ball," according to a writer who flew with him for a profile in *Popular Mechanics*. After ten miles, the writer reported, "the herd has been run to the verge of exhaustion. Their most heroic effort just can't match the 'bird that never tires.'"[1]

Once on the ground, Hanson related to the writer a modern version of the legend of the White Stallion. There was a horse called Silver King, he said—pure white and uncatchable by even the fastest riders. Every rancher in the area had tried, but no one had come close. One day Hanson scared up Silver King with his plane. He chased him for miles, but the stallion seemed never to tire. Then, just as the plane was about to push Silver King into the corral, the horse reared and broke back, escaping into the badlands.

Eventually, during another flight, Hanson said he managed to catch Silver King, but he held him only long enough for the other wranglers to see him, before turning him loose again. It was, in a way, a fitting update for the legend of the White Stallion. Man, bolstered by technical innovations, could finally tame nature. And yet, he let it go. It was the first inkling of a budding ethic of conservation that later spurred Velma Johnston to pursue her work.

But the airborne mustangers of the 1930s and 1940s gave little actual thought to conservation. A cowboy named Frank Robbins in the Red Desert of Wyoming also started using planes. By his telling, he at first tried to round up horses the old-fashioned way when a band he was pursing on horseback got scared by a mail plane in 1938. He hired one plane, then two. At times, he was pulling in three hundred horses a month, which he mostly shipped east to slaughter. He worked the open range of the Red Desert for twenty-seven years, claiming to have gathered more than thirty thousand horses. "Eleven years we worked on the Red Desert, which is about 150 miles by 150 miles," he later said in an oral history. "We pretty well cleaned out the area except for a few. Then they outlawed the plane for roundups and since then the horses have had it easier. I'm kind of glad, because if they hadn't there wouldn't be a one left."[2]

After World War II, small-time mustang operations using army veterans as pilots traveled Wild Horse Country, subsisting on a combination of what they could get from the meatpackers who desired the horses and what they could get from the ranchers who didn't. By the 1950s, the Department of the Interior estimated there were only twenty thousand horses left, almost all pushed into the driest, most forbidding, and most inaccessible corners of the West.

It was, many thought, the end of the wild horse. A few more years would see its extinction. When Frank Dobie published *The Mustangs* in Texas in 1952, he reckoned that the only true mustangs that remained were those that still roamed the American imagination. On the very last page, he broke into poetry:

I see them vanishing, vanishing, vanished,
The seas of grass shriveled to pens of barbwired property,
The wind-racers and wind-drinkers bred into property also.

But winds still blow free and grass still greens,
And the core of that something which men live on believing
Is always freedom.

So sometimes yet, in the realities of silence and solitude,
For a few people unhampered a while by things,
The mustangs walk out with dawn, stand high, then

Sweep away, wild with sheer life, and free, free, free—
Free of all confines of time and flesh.[3]

What Dobie could not foresee was that at the same time he was finishing his manuscript, a thousand miles away a young secretary in Nevada was about to throw a saddle and bridle on the legend of the mustang and make everything change.

Rarely does anyone encounter a single, crystalline moment that abruptly alters the course of life—not just one life, but the whole country's. But the morning Velma Johnston peered into that truck full of mutilated mustangs, she suddenly forgot about getting to work on time.

"I went home that night and I knew I couldn't live with myself unless I did something about it," she later told the author and activist Hope Ryden. "I decided right then that I would not rest until I had done everything humanly possible to stop such atrocities."[4]

After recovering from the sight of the bloodied horses in the back of the truck, Johnston dried her eyes, got back in her car, and drove to work. Within a few years, she was leading a movement to save wild horses that eventually reached the halls of Congress.

No movement probably ever had a more unlikely leader. Johnston was not a trained activist, and she had likely never met one. She had no funding, few connections, and only a high school education. She was often introduced as a "ranch wife," and she told people she was "more accustomed to a hitching post than Emily Post." As she was rising to national prominence, a best-selling children's novel based on her life, called *Mustang: Wild Spirit of the West* and featuring a girl named Wild Horse Annie, made her out to be a simple cowgirl with a heart of gold straight out of a 1950s Western. The public cast Johnston as the flesh-and-blood protagonist who brought the myth to life. She was the cowgirl, the woman with the white hat, the hero.

VELMA BRONN JOHNSTON, BETTER KNOWN AS WILD HORSE ANNIE, WITH FELLOW WILD HORSE ADVOCATE DAWN LAPPIN (LEFT) AT STONE CABIN ROUNDUP, NEVADA, IN 1975.

The White Stallion would escape once again, but this time with the help of a little "ranch wife" and the United States Congress.

Johnston, however, was hardly the naive country wife she often pretended to be. She was much more at home behind a typewriter than in the saddle. She was head of her local executive secretaries association and could type a hundred words per minute, but she was allergic to horses. Though she owned a few, she rarely rode. She was clever and funny, sentimental on occasion but practical as a rule. She was aware that in the 1950s and 1960s, she was navigating a world run by men, but she was hardly intimidated by it. "All I need is a tight girdle and a case of hair spray to keep me going," she once wrote to a friend.[5]

She enjoyed stiff cocktails and banging out show tunes on her mother's piano. She smoked constantly and traveled with a flask of whiskey in her purse. One would think her health alone should have kept her from taking on the momentous wild horse issue. Her twisted spine kept her in constant pain and she had trouble sleeping at night. She once told a friend that she was able to keep going with what she called "slow pills and go pills." None of this even once deterred her.

"I'm 5'6", 104 pounds, a 62-year-old widow and I'm tired and overworked," she said in an interview years later. "But I'm unbelievably tough."[6]

Johnston's story has been told in wild horse circles often enough that it has become a blend of fact and legend that is sometimes hard to untangle. When the fictional story of Wild Horse Annie helped her cause, she went with it. By the end of her life, even people close to her couldn't for sure say which parts of her past were Velma and which were Annie. And maybe it doesn't matter. *When the legend becomes fact, print the legend.*

Johnston had the luck to begin her life of activism just when the legend of the mustang was at its cultural peak and the herds in the West were still at a level where swift action could save them. In 1950, when she encountered the truck full of mustangs, Westerns were the main genre in Hollywood. Just that year, she could have gone to the theater in Reno and seen *Branded*, *The Baron of Arizona*, *Broken Arrow*, *Comanche Territory*, *High Lonesome*, *The Nevadan*, *Rio Grande*, *Sierra*, John Ford's *Wagon Master*, and dozens of other films. *The Cisco Kid* and *The Lone Ranger* were on TV. *My Friend Flicka*, the 1941 novel about a boy and his mustang, had become a classic of children's literature. The nation was saturated with stories that told and retold the legend of the West, and the mustang played a starring role. Annie was successful not only because she revered wild horses but also because at the time nearly everybody did.

Johnston's family arrived in Nevada in 1882, and her grandfather got work in a silver-mining town called Ione, which was tucked in the Shoshone Mountains in the middle of the state. The family had been there six years when one of the major mines closed and they were forced to leave to look for work. The story goes that shortly before they set out for California, two hundred miles to the west, her grandmother gave birth to her father, Joseph Bronn. The family headed out in a covered wagon pulled by two domestic horses and leading a half-tamed mustang mare from a rope on the back. A few days into the journey across the desert, Johnston's grandmother's milk gave out, and she could no longer feed Joseph. Unsure what to do, her grandfather milked the mustang mare and gave the milk to the child, saving his life. It's a story Johnston later told often to show how much she owed to mustangs.

The town of Ione today is a ghost town, with just a few residents who cater to tourists looking through the abandoned buildings. Wild horses still roam the hills all around it. Johnston's father, Joseph Bronn, grew up to be a freight driver in Reno, and he used the tough little wild horses captured from the hills to pull his wagons. He had three children in a small, tidy house with a white picket fence on the edge of town. Velma was the oldest, born in 1912. To earn extra money when the kids were small, Joseph would catch mustangs in the hills near town. The start of World War I doubled the price, and he spent his weekends hunting them. Johnston later talked about seeing him gentle them in a small corral in the backyard.

In 1923, when Johnston was eleven, something happened that might have been her defining characteristic if not for wild horses. She contracted polio. What started as a fever soon changed to throbbing in her joints. Paralysis set in and she was hospitalized. With polio nearly eradicated today, it is easy to forget what a vicious affliction it is. In severe cases, the virus infects the brain and spinal cord, causing muscles to go limp as nerves fail. But this failure is uneven.

Some muscles go limp while the complementary muscles continue to pull, so limbs slowly twist into wracked and painful poses. Johnston's paralysis attacked her back, pulling her spine and neck in different directions.

Unsure what else to do, her parents sent her to Children's Hospital in San Francisco, where she was put in a body cast to try to hold her spine in place. The skinny girl was covered in white plaster from her hips to her head. With her spindly legs and arms sticking out, she later joked that she looked like Humpty Dumpty. According to one account, during her long days in the cast, she liked to gaze at a painting in the ward that featured a band of mustangs tossing their manes as they galloped across the sage. With their unbound freedom and strength, they were everything her little plaster-encased life was not. Though we don't know for sure whether that picture is just part of the legend, it's easy to imagine the little girl looking at those horses and yearning to be home, where she could be healthy, safe, and free.

When the cast was finally removed, Johnston's family was shocked. Months of straining against the plaster had disfigured her face. Her jaw was pushed back, making her top teeth jut out. The left half of her face, starting above her brow, slumped down and away from the rest of her face, giving the appearance that she was starting to melt. Her back and neck were twisted in a cruel S shape that made her look forever off balance. Before she went home, her parents hid all the mirrors in the house.

Polio may have been a pivotal experience for Velma Johnston. It left her disfigured and unable to have children, which at the time was all that was expected of girls like her in Reno. Instead, the fallout of the disease steered her to focus on her studies, her career, and ultimately, wild horses.

After graduating from high school in 1930, she got a job as the personal secretary to the president of an insurance company in Reno. It was a job she kept the rest of her life. Like polio, secretarial work became an unexpected resource in the struggle for wild horses. Johnston learned to fire off clear, error-free letters at a machine-gun pace. Her smooth voice, given a slight velvety edge by cigarettes, carried none of the shock that her face did, and she became an expert at working the phones. At a time when making copies—or mimeograph copies, as they were known then—was still a specialized skill, she could roll out hundreds in short order. It all sounds so basic, but these skills turned out to be as crucial as a love of horses, because the main obstacle to saving the last remaining mustangs was getting the word out. At the time, before television had really taken over and the Internet was not even a glimmer, an efficient secretary was maybe the best weapon anyone could have in the information war.

A few days after Johnston encountered the truck of bloody mustangs, she went to alert the BLM about the theft of animals from public land and their mistreatment. According to her account, the regional range manager at the Reno office assumed she had come to complain about wild horses grazing on the land, and he assured her that the bureau was doing as much as it could to rid the land of the pests. Even better, he boasted, because the bureau relied on freelance mustangers who sold the horses to slaughter, the eradication wasn't costing the taxpayer a penny. This was Johnston's first indication that the federal agency that policed the range was not going to be an ally in the fight to save the mustang. There was no law to protect wild horses, and no agency to stick up for them. As Johnston later told her biographer, Marguerite Henry, "We had to be our own law."[7]

Faced with the realization that there was no legal way to protect horses, Johnston chose the same path as Frank Litts had done a generation earlier: When the law protects something morally abhorrent, break the law. Though she did not resort to dynamite, she was unwilling to let mustangs go to slaughter, so she and her husband, an incrementally employed construction worker who rolled his own cigarettes and liked to quote Persian poetry, began driving the deserted mountain valleys of western Nevada on the weekends, searching for the corrals the mustangers used to collect their catch. When they found unattended corrals, they slipped open the gates and watched the horses run free into the hills. At the time, mustang roundups were regulated by Nevada county commissioners in the state, and entirely legal. Setting free the legally collected horses was not. This part of Johnston's story doesn't make it into most accounts of her life. In *Mustang: Wild Spirit of the West*, a fictional account of her life written for children, Wild Horse Annie takes pictures of the horses trapped in corrals to alert the world, but she never sets them free.

From those first acts of defiance, Johnston became an activist and quickly learned her talents could be better used on the legal side of things. The road between her ranch and Reno cut through the Virginia Mountains in Storey County, Nevada. In 1952, she learned the Storey County commissioners were considering a permit for another roundup, and they were going to take a vote at the next commissioners' meeting. She showed up the night of the meeting, intending only to take notes. The room was packed with locals who liked having the horses roam the hills and didn't want a roundup. A mailman from the county seat, Virginia City, stood up and said he had a petition signed by more than a hundred people opposing the mustang roundups. "These roundups are completely against the spirit and tradition of the West!" he said.[8]

In fact, they were right in line with the tradition of the West but completely against the legend crafted by so many pulp novels and Saturday matinees. Ranchers in Nevada had been warring with mustangs for generations, but increasingly people in the West didn't make their living off the land, and many of them wanted protection for the mustang.

After the mailman finished, he sat down, and it appeared no one else planned to speak. With the commissioners about to vote, Johnston stood up. Using shorthand she had taken during a conversation with local BLM officials—a worthy secretary always took detailed dictation—she laid out the facts as she saw them.

"Mr. Chairman, I'm just a simple secretary," she began. The mustangers, she said, were making thousands of dollars by sending public property to the fertilizer factory. The federal managers at the BLM were encouraging it. The mustang was nearly extinct and there was no one to stick up for it. The commissioners had to act, she said, to keep greedy men from wiping out a piece of the West.

The crowd cheered. The roundup was unanimously voted down.

Johnston gained a friend in Lucius Beebe, editor of the *Territorial Enterprise*. "Every so often there is put in motion agitation for the destruction of one means or another of the bands of wild horses which still roam the hills," he wrote in an editorial. "The current pressure is being applied solely for the benefit of two sheep ranchers who claim their grazing lands are being impaired by the horses. In view of the practically unlimited grazing lands in western Nevada and the absurdly small number of the horses, such claims are purely fictional. The wild horses, harmless and picturesque as they are, are a pleasant reminder of a time when all the west was wilder and more free and any suggestion of their elimination or the abatement of the protection they now enjoy deserves a flat and instant rejection from the authorities from within whose province the matter now lies."[9]

At the next meeting, Johnston and a few other locals persuaded the county commissioners to ban the use of aircraft altogether in roundups in the county. It was her first taste of success.

Johnston soon started working with a handful of other local wild horse lovers in Reno to draw up a bill for the state legislature that would extend the ban on aerial roundups to all of Nevada. It was a long shot. The only people in the Nevada establishment who were not ranchers were miners, and neither groups were likely to stick up for wild horses. So Johnston started building grassroots support to pressure lawmakers. She assembled a mailing list of anyone she could think of who might be sympathetic: riding clubs, 4-H clubs, humane societies, school groups, editors of papers and magazines of all sizes. To each she sent a hand-signed letter and a small bulletin laying out the basic argument that something had to be done before the greedy dog-food factories and the cruel mustang wranglers drove the last remaining wild horses to extinction. Letters of support started to pour into the Capitol. Before long, the governor of Nevada was getting more mail on the mustang than any other issue.

The BLM, however, continued to round up horses at a frenzied pace. One of their go-to pilots was Chester "Chug" Utter from Reno, who was proud to say he had rounded up forty thousand horses for the agency. "You need every spear of grass for deer, antelope and cattle," he once said in an interview. "I'd much rather have wild game than a bunch of horses you can't do anything with."[10]

In 1955, at Johnston's urging, a state senator named James Slattery introduced Johnston's bill banning the mechanized hunt of wild horses. Many of Nevada's newspapers began to take up her cause. If the United States passed laws protecting the bald eagle, an editorial in the *Nevada State Journal* asked, "Why cannot we in Nevada afford some protection to an animal which, more than any other, symbolizes the history, the strength, the progress of Nevada and the west—the wild horse."[11]

The BLM fought the proposed ban. The agency had grown out of the United States Grazing Service—a New Deal agency established in 1934 to bring needed order to the free-for-all grazing on the open range of the West. Before the Grazing Service, grass on the public lands belonged to anyone who wanted it, which resulted in disastrous overgrazing and often-violent disputes over territory. In 1934, Congress passed the Taylor Grazing Act to establish a system of leases to regulate grazing and the Grazing Service to enforce them. The Grazing Service, and then the BLM, was staffed by livestock men who thought only in terms of livestock.

When Johnston showed up lobbying for bans, the BLM and the ranchers were likely at first dumbfounded. They had been playing the same game for decades. BLM was the referee, the ranchers were the players, and everyone agreed on the game: maximizing the livestock that could be raised on the public land in an orderly and somewhat sustainable fashion. There might have been grumbling by both bureau and ranchers over stocking numbers or grazing fees, but no one argued that the game should change. Then here was someone—a woman, no less—who, with the help of other women, children, and various outsiders, wanted to change the grazing game completely. She wanted to let in wildness, wilderness, heritage, freedom. No doubt the old players were at first mystified. Then they were likely dismissive. And then, when Johnston started gaining traction, and was seen as a credible threat, they were pissed. She got threatening phone calls from some ranchers. Others had her followed. "I'm about as popular with these people as leprosy," she once said about the stockmen. She began carrying her husband's .38.

The regional BLM director, Dante Solari, when encountering Johnston at a hearing for the proposed state ban, reportedly sneered, "Well, here comes Wild Horse Annie herself." It was probably meant as an insult, but Johnston wore it like a title, telling and retelling the story through interviews and letters until many people thought Annie was her real name.

The Nevada bill to ban mechanized wild horse hunts passed in

1955, but not before the BLM and ranching interests slipped in a provision that made the state regulation not applicable on federal land. That was a big deal, because almost 90 percent of Nevada is federal land—and virtually all wild horses are found there. So Johnston's first statewide victory was a hollow one. Despite all her work, she knew the law would not save many horses.

She was not ready to quit, though. Fueled by cigarettes, "go pills," her love of mustangs, and support from the public, Johnston typed letters late into the night, creating a broad grassroots alliance. She soon had a nationwide alliance of horse lovers, their names all neatly catalogued on index cards. She was also building a stable of sympathetic journalists. The passage of the state bill attracted the attention of the national press. They visited Nevada to meet Wild Horse Annie and see the mustangs firsthand. First came a columnist from the *Sacramento Bee*, then a correspondent from the *Denver Post*, then a reporter from the *New York Times*. *Reader's Digest* and *Life*—two of the most popular magazines in the country, with a combined circulation of millions—both picked up the story. They described Johnston in almost mythic terms as a tiny, tough-as-nails cowgirl fixin' to stampede a law through Congress, and "the most tireless, outspoken friend the mustang ever had."[12]

She was happy to play the part. "I was born on a horse," she told the *Denver Post*. "I love horses tame or wild. I just had to do something about the way they were being treated."

In 1957, Johnston had a visit from an old elementary schoolmate named Walter Baring, who was Nevada's lone representative in Congress. Baring was, in the words of a later *Las Vegas Review-Journal* profile, "a 250-pound bear who liked both his rhetoric and his cigarettes unfiltered."[13] He was a former tax collector and small-town politician who had slipped into office by a razor-thin margin. A Democrat in a Republican state, he reliably voted with Southern

Dixiecrats against civil rights legislation and believed the United Nations, the civil rights movement, and fluoridated drinking water were all Communist plots. But Baring also had a keen sense of politics. He was elected to ten terms and liked to say, "Nobody likes Walter Baring except the voters."

And perhaps he saw in wild horses a chance to grab onto a bill voters would love. He offered to introduce a bill that would ban aerial hunting on federal land and close the gaps in the state bill. If having a disfigured secretary from Reno as the wild horse movement's champion was a bit odd, it was nothing compared to having a congressional ally like Walter Baring.

They made a deal. Johnston and her allies would write the bill, Baring would introduce a bill called HR 2725, and Johnston's vast grassroots network would pressure every congressman to support it. In July 1959, Johnston walked into a hearing room in the US Capitol wearing white heels and white gloves and carrying a white handbag. Her hair was sprayed up into a bouffant, her small frame was wrapped in a crisp sheath of cotton prints. The newspapers that day described her as a "hardy ranch wife," but she looked and spoke like anything but.

"By removing this comparatively easy method of capture, we feel it will no longer be worth the while of the professional hunters to operate, either for themselves or for individual ranchers, or for the government, for it has been the practice of the land management agencies which may not be equipped to carry on the operations within their own personnel to turn over the actual roundup to private professional operators," she told the committee. "My colleagues do not believe that humane herding of the horses and burros can be done by aircraft or mechanized vehicles. We also feel that if they are in such rugged terrain as to preclude the possibility of horseback roundups, then surely that terrain is not usable as range for cattle."[14]

So much for folksy.

"Mr. Chairman and members of the Committee on the judiciary," she continued. "The fight for the mustang has come a long way in the past few years. . . . From a mere handful of fifty or so firm believers in the right of survival, it has come to an awareness throughout the country of his desperate plight, resulting in a mighty plea on his behalf."

The Bureau of Land Management, fearing that horses would once again spread by the tens of thousands, as they had in the nineteenth century, tried to weaken the bill with an amendment that read, "Nothing in the Act shall be construed to conflict with the provisions of any Federal law or regulation which permits the Land Management agencies responsible for administration of the public lands to hunt, drive, round up and dispose of horses, mares, colts or burros by means of airborne or motor driven vehicles."[15]

In other words, it would be business as usual on federal land.

Johnston fired off letters to everyone involved: congressmen sponsoring the bill, groups of animal lovers like the Humane Society, and her grassroots Rolodex of citizens. She let them know the bill must remain as it was written, without interference from the BLM. She pressed her case in newspapers and radio interviews. While a few rural papers opposed her, most of the national papers trumpeted the need to save the mustang. Hundreds of thousands of letters poured into Congress in support of the bill.

At the hearing, a BLM range officer named Gerald Kerr told Congress that the agency needed to keep horse numbers down, and that the horses on the range were not truly wild, but merely unclaimed ranch strays. "Wild horses, as such, do not exist on the public lands today," he said. "The unclaimed and abandoned horses now using the federal ranges are remnants of extensive horse ranch operations which were conducted on the public ranges of the West until the 1930s."[16]

But Johnston eventually prevailed. The bill was passed a few months later without the BLM's amendment. On September 8, 1959, the final version, known as the "Wild Horse Annie Law" became law. It banned all aerial roundups on federal land. Johnston hoped the law would end the era of mustangs being chased down for dog food. It didn't.

Ranchers continued to try to purge the public land of wild horses and the BLM did little to stop them. Often mustangers would get around the new law by releasing some branded animals out into the herds, then using them as an excuse to round up branded and unbranded alike. The BLM openly encouraged the practice, saying in a press release at the time, "The rancher may use any method he wishes . . . including driving the animals with trucks or airplanes . . . if someone intends to round up his own animals, he may accidentally take wild horses at the same time."[17]

Velma Johnston railed against this practice and continually pressed the BLM and local authorities to crack down. In 1967, she got her first shot. A tip came into the office of the White Pine County sheriff that a Nevada rancher named Julian Goicoechea had hired a famed Nevada mustanging pilot named Ted Barber to round up horses on public land near his ranch. The sheriff and the brand inspector drove out in a Jeep and, from a high ridge, spotted the plane diving after a group of mustangs in a remote spot called Long Valley. The pilot and copilot dangled a rope of tin cans and operated a howling siren to scare the band forward. For good measure, they were also firing a shotgun at any that turned back. When confronted, the men said they had been rounding up horses for weeks, but that the unbranded horses belonged to the rancher and were not wild. An investigation found the men had sent more than 150 horses to slaughter, and only four had brands. The men were quickly charged under the Wild Horse Annie Law.

What seemed like an open-and-shut case quickly fell apart. In court, the mustangers argued that the animals were, in fact, branded, but thick winter hair hid the markings. The horses had been in the possession of the mustangers since their arrest. The defense had the horses shaved, and, lo and behold, they had brands. A local jury quickly acquitted the men.

Johnston was furious but did not give up. She next tried to catch another longtime aerial mustanger, Chester "Chug" Utter. In 1969, tipsters had told her that he had built a trap in the Virginia Mountains, introduced domestic horses into the wild herd, and was ready to bring in a plane to round them all up. Johnston organized volunteers to watch for the plane and had the local sheriff on call, ready to arrest Utter. Word may have gotten out, because Utter never showed. Eventually, as a publicity stunt, Johnston got local school kids to dismantle the trap and called the Associated Press to cover it.[18]

In the decade after the law passed, it was as if nothing had happened. Aerial roundups were still sending mustangs to the chicken-feed factory. No one had been successfully prosecuted. Horse numbers had continued to decline. BLM leaders still saw themselves as the good guys, fighting for quality range management against an uninformed public. "I think this whole thing is an emotional issue whetted by Walt Disney movies," Harold Tysk, BLM director, told a reporter in 1967.[19] The BLM estimated that by 1970 there were only about ten thousand wild horses left.

But across the country, attitudes were changing. During the 1960s, Velma Johnston's once-lonely push to save horses turned into a movement. Humane groups brought their thousands of members to the cause. A number of well-connected East Coast women became Johnston's allies. There were Pearl Twine and Joan Blue of Washington DC, who both had been working already for years to improve treatment for domestic horses in the East. There was Hope Ryden, a fashion-model-turned-documentary-filmmaker for ABC News, who in 1970 published a best seller called *America's Last Wild Horses*, which sounded an urgent call for preservation. Popular national magazines such as *Cosmopolitan*, *Life*, *Time*, and *National Geographic* all published big spreads on the disappearing mustang. School groups across the country baked cookies and sold bumper stickers to raise money for Johnston's cause.

"How sweet the ride on the bandwagon is," she wrote to a friend in 1970. "And the politicians are quick to smell out a possible campaign boost."[20]

It's worth taking a step back to realize that Johnston and other horse supporters were not working in a vacuum. Her awakening to the idea of conservation is closely tied to a broader realization among the American public that the wild remnants of the country were nearly gone and desperately needed protection. It was, in a big way, the natural reaction to the abuses of the Great Barbecue.

It had been simmering for decades. In 1949, a year before Johnston encountered the truck of bleeding mustangs, a former US Forest Service game manager-turned-conservationist named Aldo Leopold published the seminal ecology book *A Sand County Almanac*. "Like winds and sunsets, wild things were taken for granted until progress began to do away with them," he argued in the book. "Now we face the question whether a still higher 'standard of living' is worth its cost in things natural, wild, and free."[21]

The answer from an increasing number of Americans was "no."

In the 1950s, the Nature Conservancy was founded and the Sierra Club grew from an outing group into a political force. In the 1960s, laws were passed regulating pollution in air and water and protecting endangered species and wild and scenic rivers. There was a national clamor for more regulation to protect the wild world.

Culture shifted toward environmental ethics, too. In 1942, Disney had released *Bambi*, one of the first mainstream broadsides against cruelty to animals. The 1961 film *The Misfits*, the last film made by stars Clark Gable and Marilyn Monroe before both died, was an anti-Western that revealed the horror of mustangs being sent off and turned into dog food.

By 1970, the public drumbeat for conservation was deafening. That year, the United States celebrated the first Earth Day. In 1971, Dr. Seuss published his classic children's book on conservation, *The Lorax*. During the first years of the 1970s, Congress, with broad bipartisan support, passed the most sweeping environmental laws in the nation's history: the National Environmental Policy Act, the Clean Water Act, the Clean Air Act, the Marine Mammal Protection Act, and the Coastal Zone Management Act.

President Richard Nixon recognized environmental causes as a feel-good issue that would distract voters from the Vietnam War and coopt a campaign issue raised by Democratic opponents. He had never pushed for environmental regulation. He saw environmentalists as "hopeless softheads" and privately dismissed environmentalism as a fad. He notably got in a shouting match with the president of the Sierra Club and stormed out of their private meeting.[22] But he was happy to step in and take credit for saving charismatic symbols of freedom. "Like those in the last century who tilled a plot of land to exhaustion and then moved on to another, we in this country have too casually and too long abused our natural environment," he told Congress in February 1970. "The time has come when we can wait no longer to repair the damage already done."[23]

It was in this context that Velma Johnston went to Washington in April 1971 to push for the passage of the Wild Free-Roaming Horses and Burros Act at a hearing of the House Committee on Public Lands. The act had been introduced by her old friend Nevada Congressman Walter Baring. At the hearing, where forty people were scheduled to speak, Baring introduced only Johnston by name, calling her his "lifelong friend."

The rest of the wild horse bandwagon was there too: the Humane Society, the National Mustang Association, the Sierra Club, the Animal Rescue League, the Citizens Committee on Natural Resources, and the American Horse Protection Association, among others. There were also witnesses who cautioned against the bill, saying that if wild horses were left unchecked, they would soon eat the range to dust.

With Johnston's encouragement, tens of thousands of children had sent letters to their congressmen. Since the beginning, she had always seen kids as her main ally, and she had courted them strategically by speaking to schools and 4-H groups. "You can almost see the Stars and Stripes waving in their eyeballs when you give them a stirring talk," she said in a video interview near the end of her life.[24]

The press jokingly referred to it as a "children's crusade." Fittingly, one of the first representatives to appear before the committee, Gilbert Gude from Maryland, asked if he could let his eleven-year-old son Gregory speak, since he was "really involved in me getting involved in the legislation."

Gregory took the stand. Neither he nor his father had ever been to Wild Horse Country. "Lots of people have read about the wild mustangs," he said. "My dad and I have gotten about 1,000 letters and petitions supporting the bill. We even got a letter from Brazil." He held up a letter from a nine-year-old girl in Mississippi and began reading: "Every time the men come to kill the horses for pet food, I think you kill many children's hearts."

More than a dozen conservation and animal groups pressed for passage of a horse protection bill. There were also enough livestock and BLM representatives that Johnston quipped while testifying, "I am taking a chance turning my back right now on this whole room full of people."

Given the years of animosity toward wild horses and Wild Horse Annie, the BLM and livestock interests staged a fairly tepid defense. No one from the bureau spoke at all. An official from the Department of the Interior, which oversees the BLM, appeared to say only that the agency supported protection and could run the program for about $3 million a year. And though livestock and sportsmen's groups were cautious, none outright opposed protection.

A spokesman for the National Cattleman's Association spoke in favor. In the past, he said, mustangs were "part of the bounty of our great land to be harvested, as needed, for the benefit of mankind. They have been taken for granted." He only tepidly pressed for one consideration: that wild horses not affect the number of cattle on the range, and that ranchers be paid if they do.

A spokesman for the Wyoming Wool Growers Association, the only other livestock group, was more dire in his predictions. The law would be so onerous, he said, that it would "turn every private landowner into a crusader to remove all wild horses." If the "government got into the livestock business," he said, it would soon find its wild herds increasing, and would have to remove animals to control population, as cowboys in Wyoming had done for generations. Only a few mustangs would be suitable to be saddle horses. "The surplus animals each year would have to be disposed of by burying, burning, or some other sanitary disposal method," he warned.

The harshest words came from Lonnie Williamson of the Wildlife Management Institute, a fish and game group. He said mustangs were actually "trespass stock of a not-too-impressive ancestry" that did not belong on the land. "It must be remembered that although mustangs are respected and cherished by a great many people, they are aliens which compete with native species," he said. "To manage wild horses on a priority basis to the detriment of native wildlife would not be in the broad public interest." Failing to limit their numbers, he warned, would change the mustang from "a symbol of unbridled freedom" into "a symbol of environmental degradation."[25]

A few of the committee members from western states were also clearly skeptical, particularly Wayne Aspinall, a longtime congressman from western Colorado who had grown up in Wild Horse Country. "Most of the wild horses are not horses that any of us would look twice at," he said. He worried about crafting a sweeping federal solution that would take away control from counties and states. "What has bothered me throughout the last many years is the fact that every time we can't do something at home we want to look far away in order to get the task taken care of. Uncle Sam is the one who pays all of it."[26]

Ultimately, the critics were too few and their warnings too weak against the urgent message delivered by Velma Johnston.

She appeared poised and ladylike in her stiff bouffant, with impeccably researched testimony that she had been building for more than a decade.

"Since I was one of those who started the fight long ago," she said, "I feel adequate to pass along the feeling of our people in America. The wild horse and burro symbolize the freedom, the independence upon which our country was founded. . . . Perhaps it is because the forbearers [sic] of these wild horses and burros were alien to these shores as were our own forbearers. Perhaps it is because they settled in the wilderness, fought off Indian attacks, enforced law and order, brought civilization to this country," she added. "My mail alone averages 50 letters a day. This fight has captured the interest of young people as no other."[27]

With the passage of the 1959 Wild Horse Annie Law, she said, "We thought we had a happy ending," but the ranchers were determined to continue their campaign against wild horses. "They are fenced off from their grass and water holes. . . . They are indiscriminately shot, trapped or driven off." Mustangers who had been caught red-handed were acquitted or not charged at all. Just a few months earlier, the commissioners of Elko County had approved the roundup of several hundred horses that were sent to the slaughterhouse.

The law, she said, "has not been effective in areas where it is not in the best interests of the elected officials to see that it is enforced."

The Department of the Interior had proposed setting up half a dozen preserves for wild horses. It estimated that ten thousand of the remaining seventeen thousand horses were not Spanish mustangs but domestic strays, and should be killed. The rest would be relocated to preserves and protected. Johnston pushed instead for all wild horses to be managed in the places they lived, as integral parts of the land. She rejected the idea that horses had to be of a certain breed to count as a mustang. All that mattered to her was that they were born free.

She knew that numbers would have to be managed, but she thought the right oversight would ensure it was done humanely. "I asked for a management and control program," she said. "I realized it must be multiple use. The cattle people have contributed greatly."

Congress continued to be deluged by letters from citizens. After receiving bags of mail from grade-schoolers, one representative from Texas wrote to his constituents: "Am I going to be susceptible to pressure? Am I going to be influenced by a bunch of children? Am I going to support a bill because kids . . . are sentimental about wild horses? You bet your cowboy boots I am!"[28]

The law passed easily and was signed on December 17, 1971, by President Nixon, who then sent Velma Johnston a personal letter, thanking her for her "splendid efforts over the years."

In the end, the new Wild Horse Annie Law—officially called the Wild Free-Roaming Horses and Burros Act of 1971—gave Johnston almost everything she had asked for. It protected horses where they were found on federal land, and it imposed stiff fines and jail time for anyone who captured or harassed wild horses. It made releasing domestic horses on public land illegal to end the mustangers favorite pretense for roundups. And, maybe most important, it recognized wild horses' and burros' right to exist.

The law began:

Congress finds and declares that wild free-roaming horses and burros are living symbols of the historic and pioneer spirit of the West; that they contribute to the diversity of life forms within the Nation and enrich the lives of the American people; and that these horses and burros are fast disappearing from the American scene. It is the policy of Congress that wild free-roaming horses and burros shall be protected from capture, branding, harassment, or death; and to accomplish this they are to be considered in the area where presently found, as an integral part of the natural system of the public lands.

With the law, Johnston stopped a century-long killing spree and likely saved the wild horse from annihilation. But she also put the mustang on a future course that was far different from anything she imagined: the one we live with now.

CHAPTER 6

LIFE UNDER THE LAW

I n the years after passage of the Wild Free-Roaming Horses and Burros Act, horse populations rebounded. Valleys in Nevada where once it was rare to see a mustang soon had bands dotting the sage. In a place called the Stone Cabin Valley in Nevada, where once there had been only a scattering of horses, there were nine hundred. The bands grazed placidly around the valley's springs and up in its hills, untroubled by mustangers or ranchers. Wild horses had been saved.

But the success of the law was also increasingly a problem. The Bureau of Land Management determined after the law was passed that there were likely far more than the seventeen thousand horses it had originally estimated. Maybe as many as twenty-five thousand. Freed from the pressures of mustangers, the herds were increasing by about 15 percent a year. They were coming out of the hills and canyons where they once hid and grazing on prime cattle land. Ranchers were calling the BLM to complain about horses eating grass that once fed their herds. BLM range specialists on the ground found that some ranchers were not able to graze at previous levels because horses had taken the forage, and that the problem would grow worse if left unchecked.

During the 1971 testimony in Washington, reproduction had gotten scant attention. Ranchers had warned of growing herds, but mustang advocates had generally either ignored the issue or dismissed it. Hope Ryden, the best-selling author of *America's Last Wild Horses* and the most prominent voice for mustangs after Johnston, insisted that population growth was a myth ranchers fed to the "gullible public," adding, "Left to their own devices, the wild horses do not seem to multiply until they eat themselves out of their habitat."

She and many other horse advocates were sure the talk of multiplying horse herds was yet another ploy by the wild herds' enemies to get them off the land. "Dire prophecies are made regarding an imminent wild horse population explosion by those who would have them removed," she wrote in a revised edition of her book. "Because the horses are not 'culled' by hunters, the public is told it is only a matter of time before the herds will overpopulate and starve. In the case of the wild horse, an animal that is not being 'managed' for game, no such catastrophe has yet been recorded."[1]

But on the land, that was proving to be false. In Nevada's Stone Cabin Valley, BLM range scientists had estimated the land could sustain only about five hundred horses. With nine hundred now in the valley, they said the pasturage would soon collapse. To avoid that, the bureau said, the extras would have to be rounded up.

Velma Johnston visited the Stone Cabin Valley on a blistering day in July 1975. After touring the valley by Jeep and airplane with bureau staff, Johnston agreed to the roundup. The range was in rough shape. Some of the horses would have to go, she said, as long as some of the cattle came off, too.

On the first day of the roundup, Johnston liked what she saw. Wearing a snap-button denim shirt and a mustang belt buckle, and sucking ice cubes to keep cool, she looked out at a tall corral fence set up in a circle around a distant spring with a single gate that could swing shut once mustangs wandered in to drink. It was the same kind of water trap mustangers had used for centuries, but she saw it as a sign of progress.

Where once wild horses were run to death by trucks and planes, mutilated in the pursuit, hunted to the brink of extinction, and sent off to the cannery, now the Bureau of Land Management was protecting and removing the extras humanely. The man they contracted to run the trap—a fireman out of Las Vegas who had been a weekend mustanger before passage of the law—did not chase or abuse the animals. The captives were not sent to the slaughterhouse. Instead, the BLM had found plenty of volunteers it called "foster parents," who planned to train the mustangs as riding horses and pets. To Johnston, it seemed like sensible, cost-effective management that honored both the horses and the land.

"I feel good about myself," she told a reporter as she stood in the sun.

But that feeling wouldn't last more than a few days.

Though Wild Horse Annie herself had given the thumbs-up for a roundup, other wild horse groups were opposed. The Washington-based American Horse Protection Association, once an ally of Johnston, filed suit in federal court to stop the roundup, claiming the BLM was misrepresenting the quality of the range and the number of horses in order to do the bidding of a few ranchers in the valley. Its director had once welcomed Johnston to Washington as a friend. Now they were no longer speaking.

The ranchers whose cattle shared Stone Cabin Valley were not thrilled with the new BLM roundup either. They disagreed not with the roundup plan but with the whole premise that the federal government had authority over stray horses on public lands. It went against every bit of local law since the days of the trappers. Wild animals belonged to the states, not the federal government, they said. They saw the roundup as a potential precedent-setting move that could cede local authority to the feds, and they were not fixing to let that happen. The afternoon when Johnston had stood with a mug of ice cubes, looking out at her achievement, the head of the Nevada Department of Agriculture showed up and told the BLM to stop the roundup. The Wild Free-Roaming Horses and Burros Act was unconstitutional, he said. The feds were stealing horses that rightfully belonged to the state and local ranchers. He impounded the seventy-five horses that had been trapped and shut down the operation.

Being blasted simultaneously by ranchers and conservationists, facing court challenges on both sides while trying to keep order on the land, was a fitting start for the BLM's Wild Horse and Burro Program. Since that day at Stone Cabin Valley, the BLM's main management tool—nearly the entire focus of the program—has been rounding up and removing horses. In the process, it has been buffeted constantly by lawsuits from both ranchers and horse advocates. Its budget has ballooned even as it has slipped farther from its goals. It quickly became clear that the roundup policy had serious flaws and was so dysfunctional that no matter who ran it, and how much money they received, it was continually ending up in the ditch. And yet it is still the approach used today.

In 1975, despite lawsuits from both sides, the BLM eventually completed the roundup in Stone Cabin Valley. A federal appeals judge dismissed the lawsuit by the American Horse Protection Association, saying the BLM had discretion to remove horses under the law. The Nevada Department of Agriculture backed off its assertion that states owned the horses, after the regional BLM manager threatened that if the agency wasn't allowed to take horses, "we're going to have to take a close look at the numbers of livestock on that range." Eventually, about 460 wild horses were removed. But that was not the end of the story.

I went to visit Stone Cabin Valley on a sunny but frigid February morning almost forty years after Johnston looked out at the water trap. I wanted to see how the management of wild horses had evolved since the birth of the law.

When I visited the valley, there were about 750 horses. The BLM planned to remove about five hundred through daily helicopter roundups that would span most of the month. Some would be adopted on-site by locals, but the vast majority would go into the maze of feedlots and storage pastures that the BLM calls "the holding system."

I called the local BLM office in the southern Nevada town of Tonopah (pop. 2,478), to ask whether I could observe for a few days. The staff told me to meet them before dawn at a spot on a lonely highway that shoots east of town, where a missile stands fixed to a pole by the roadside. The Stone Cabin Valley was miles away, but since there were no road signs, no manmade landmarks to go by, no buoy in the sea of sage to help navigate, the staff said the missile was a convenient landmark.

When I got there, early on a chilly but clear morning, the missile's tip pointed up at an angle, as if soaring off the launch toward an unseen target. A sign underneath the missile read TONOPAH TEST RANGE, DEPARTMENT OF ENERGY. It marked the northern edge of a vast section of southern Nevada cordoned off by the federal government in the 1950s. These hundreds of square miles were so rocky and hot and dry, so useless and deserted, that during the Cold War the federal government decided they were perfect for nuclear testing, missile experiments, and development of other classified weapons. Area 51, the desert valley where watchers theorize the government is hiding flying saucers, was just down the road. Naturally, a place so harsh, empty, and remote has plenty of wild horses.

The BLM regularly gets requests from the public to visit round-ups. Usually the observers are a mix of horse advocates, wildlife photographers, and local reporters who write the same story over and over about how roundups are controversial but necessary. It was going on long before I got involved, and the BLM has developed a cordial but grudging approach to it—the way some people feel about entertaining their least-favorite in-laws. But with the advent of social media, it has become more problematic for the bureau. One wild horse advocate standing in the sage can share what is happening to a worldwide audience of activists. A horse shot or whipped in the middle of nowhere can be seen by a hundred thousand eyes and spur outrage that could alert officials in the head office or members of Congress. Because of this, the BLM has become much more cautious. Public viewing areas are put farther from the trap. It was only after the rise of Facebook and Twitter that the agency began having armed guards at roundups and corralled viewers in small boxes marked off by pink plastic tape.

When the BLM's pickups pulled up a few minutes after I arrived, only one employee got out, standing at the side of my car just long enough to say, "Are you all set? Then let's go." Our convoy headed east on a straight highway that followed the rhythm of all highways that cross the Great Basin—bowing up to a distant mountain range, then cresting through dark and jagged rocks and dropping to the next valley, where the road stretches out again for ten or twenty straight miles to another crest.

The land here is exceptionally empty. The town of Tonopah, too small to have even a traffic light, is crowded compared to the stretches of desert on either side. Going east, the next gas is in the tiny town of Rachel, 110 miles away. In between, there is basically nothing. Nye County, which holds Stone Cabin Valley, is bigger than Maryland but has only about forty thousand inhabitants, and all of them live far from Stone Cabin. No one lives in the four-hundred-thousand-acre basin—at least not anyone I could see.

I followed the BLM pickups up over a jagged strand of rocks called the Monitor Mountains, and down into Stone Cabin, where we turned north onto a dirt road, then northwest onto a smaller dirt road that wriggled up into the hills, then finally turned again onto a rutted track. We finally ended near a broad arroyo that the BLM had chosen as a good place for a horse trap.

Stone Cabin, like a lot of Wild Horse Country, has a history straight out of a Zane Grey paperback. The herds here are thought to be the legacy of a valley resident named Jack Longstreet, a moonshiner who was rumored to have had his ear cut off as punishment for stealing cattle as a boy in Texas. He had killed two men in Nevada and taken shots at a fair number of others. After ranging around several mining boomtowns in the region, he married a Paiute woman and moved to the valley in 1906. He set up a horse ranch, where he introduced Thoroughbred stallions into the native herds and sold his half-wild horses to the US Army. The horses in Stone Cabin have a distinctive gray coat said to be left over from a gray stallion Longstreet brought from Texas. How much is truth or legend is too blurry ever to sort out.

I came to the Stone Cabin Valley to observe not so much the horses as the roundups. Roundups are all you hear about in the world of wild horses. Advocates have been fighting them since the 1970s. They say they are brutal and cruel. Hope Ryden blasted them for needlessly spreading panic and dust-borne pneumonia in the herds. Some horse advocates talk about roundups in language from the Holocaust. The BLM, in contrast, portrays helicopter roundups as the safest, most humane way to control horse herds—a gentle gathering. I wanted to see for myself whether roundups were really that bad.

Opposition has hardly softened since Velma Johnston stood here in 1975. In the months leading up to the roundup, a Los Angeles–based wild horse group was lobbying to shut down the operation, and the Nevada legislature introduced a bill favored by ranchers to change local water law to specifically prohibit wild horses and burros from drinking. Both were eventually unsuccessful, but they have not discouraged similar efforts since then.

Other things have changed a lot. The BLM now uses helicopters instead of water traps. It also has a long, legally required planning-and-comment process for roundups. It no longer relies much on "foster parents" to take wild horses, and instead it has developed a vast system for storing them. A Supreme Court ruling put an end to states' constitutional challenges of ownership.[2] But the fundamental approach has not changed much. It still follows a template created by mustangers a century before: Round 'em up and move 'em out.

For more that forty years the BLM has used roundups as its main and often only management tool for wild horses. It has had one goal in mind: Limit wild horses and burros to twenty-seven thousand on the range. The agency calls this number the Appropriate Management Level, or AML. That golden number—twenty-seven thousand—is what BLM range ecologists say can be sustained on the available land. Plenty of wild horse advocates disagree with this number, saying it is kept artificially low to serve cattle interests, but the BLM has stuck with more or less the same number for thirty years. Agree with it or not, it has steered policy.

The agency has never actually reached that golden number, though. One program director after another has sought to do so. If they could reach AML, they reasoned, then the roundup strategy that has not really been working for forty years would start to work. That is because at AML, the number of extra horses that need to be removed each year could reasonably be adopted out. By adopting horses out instead of storing them, the agency would keep costs down. That number would also keep peace with cattle and wildlife interests on the land. From the agency's perspective, all would be good.

The agency has been trying to reach AML since at least 1980, but never has. Every time it gets close to twenty-seven thousand, it is overwhelmed by the cost and controversy of the massive roundups needed to reach the number. Then it must give up, exhausted, and let the number of horses on the land begin to increase again. Nonetheless, that has not stopped the BLM from repeating the effort every decade or so.

In 2016, I toured one of the thirty ranches the agency rents to store wild horses it has gathered off the range. With me was the director of the BLM's Wild Horse and Burro Program. By that point, attempts to reach AML already had failed three times, wasting hundreds of millions of dollars. Despite the efforts, the wild horse population in the West was almost triple AML. I asked the director what he thought the program should do. "I really feel," he said, "if we could just get down to that number, reach AML, it would take care of a lot of our problems."

Here is what keeps tripping up the agency: Roundups produce thousands of captive horses for which the BLM has to find a place. It has an adoption program that trucks wild horses all over the country in an attempt to find homes. Nearly anyone can adopt a mustang for $125. But the number of adopters has never equaled the number of horses the agency removes from the range. The unwanted horses build up in storage, and storing horses costs a lot of money.

When I arrived at the trap site, I expected to spend most of the day alone, except for the armed guard at the pink-tape public viewing area that has become standard at all roundups. But when the BLM public affairs officer led me to the taped-off rectangle on a hillside of rocks, someone else was there.

Sitting on a cold chunk of basalt was a middle-aged woman with long, reddish blonde hair, camouflage pants, and an oversize Carhartt jacket. In the jumble of boulders, she had managed to set up two tripods, each topped with a small video camera recording the scene. She held a cigarette in one hand and a camera with a long lens in the other. When I scrambled up onto the rocks, she tucked the cigarette between her lips, held out her hand, and said, "Hi, I'm Laura."

Her full name was Laura Leigh—a name that invokes quick reaction in all corners of the wild horse world. To some advocates, she is a tireless hero, to others a grandstander or sellout. To ranchers, she is a persistent meddler, and to the BLM she is often seen as big trouble because lawsuits she files against the agency seem to arrive as dependably as summer and winter.

"I'm a pain in the ass, but that's kinda the point," she later told me. "I make them do their job."

The day I met her, she described herself with a sly smile as a "wild horse groupie"—one who tours from herd area to herd area and roundup to roundup, recording everything with the zeal of the most dedicated Deadhead bootlegger. I later learned she is much more than that. She has a detailed understanding of the law and a passionate desire to see horses treated humanely, and, because of this, she has dedicated her life to making sure the spirit of the Wild Horse Annie Law is carried out.

Just down from our pink-tape public viewing area, she had a beat-up green Ford Explorer with a tire lashed to the roof. She had bought the used Explorer with a hundred thousand miles on it, and within a few years she had put on a hundred thousand more while driving to the different herd areas. The dashboard was piled with papers and coffee cups. The back was a heap of clothes, tarps, sleeping bags, filing boxes—everything she needed for life on the road. The passenger seat was occupied by an aging Bernese mountain dog. Somewhere in the mess was a 9mm pistol she kept in case of trouble. The tire on the roof was not a spare but a seat—a perch where she could get a good look at the roundups when the BLM's pink-tape public viewing area was less than optimal.

"The road really has become my life," she said. "I've sold everything I have of value. I have no more jewelry left. I have nothing left except that truck and what's in it. It's frankly freeing. Possessions never created something of meaning for me. Interaction, conversation, making a difference. That has real value."

It was still cold in the early morning light. We could hear the whine and THWOP of a helicopter echoing off the distant hills, but we could not yet see it. Below us, about 150 meters away, was a big round corral with wings of canvas opening on one side like a broad beak.

With nothing to do yet but watch our breath condense in the crisp air, I started asking Leigh about where she came from and why she was here.

She had ended up in Wild Horse Country via a long and winding road. She had grown up a dozen miles west of Manhattan in Bloomfield, New Jersey, the daughter of a cop. She had lived a relatively footloose life as an adult—first in New York City, then Haiti, then Maine, then most recently in Puget Sound, where she bred dairy goats, made cheese, and rehabilitated orphaned wildlife.

Her love of animals led her to adopt an old, unwanted domestic horse bound for the slaughterhouse. That led her to learn about horse slaughter, which led her to learn about wild horses. After watching her first roundup, she was hooked. That and a failed marriage put her on the road in 2009. She has basically been there ever since, going from one roundup to another, trying to document the everyday operations of the BLM. She works alone, paid survival wages by a nonprofit she founded called Wild Horse Education, which relies on small donors, mostly other women who follow her journey on Facebook.

The wild-horse-advocate world does not have one unifying figure like Wild Horse Annie anymore, and hasn't since she died. In 1971, when the law passed, there was a more or less united front under Velma Johnston, and the willingness to unite behind her vision had helped push laws through Congress. But even before Johnston died of cancer in 1977, the movement had started to splinter. At the Stone Cabin roundup in 1975, Johnston was supporting the roundup and her main ally in the East, Joan Blue of the American Horse Protection Association, opposed it. Blue thought Johnston had become a caricature of herself and was too cozy with the BLM. Johnston thought Blue, who lived in the suburbs of Washington, DC, was too eager to bad-mouth ranchers and too quick to turn to the courts instead of compromise. By 1975, Johnston thought Blue was trying to undercut her support.

"I wouldn't slam an outhouse door the way Joan Blue slams me," Johnston once said.

Since then, the movement has only grown more Balkanized. Small advocacy groups pick their prize issues, and though they generally are united in bad-mouthing the BLM, they have rarely been in agreement on long-term solutions or presented a united front in a push to guide reforms. There is no broad strategy on when and why groups should take the bureau to court. The worst of the advocates are little more than equine Internet tolls who never set foot in Wild Horse Country. The best of them are good-hearted, hardworking groups who spend time on the ground and have detailed knowledge of specific herds. Most of them have a genuine desire to find workable solutions. But there is no larger, long-term vision of where they want to go and how they will get there. Many are as suspicious of each other as they are of the BLM, and afraid of having donors wooed away by a grandstanding competitor.

I have only met a few who spend as much time on the ground as Laura Leigh. As the sun rose at Stone Cabin, we heard the helicopter coming up over the gray sage. Leigh crushed out her cigarette on the chunk of basalt and slipped the butt into her coat pocket. She lifted her long lens and swept the sage with a practiced glide, then settled on a spot between two low hills where a flash of sun showed the helicopter's polished white flanks. Her shutter began to click. Just below, eight horses crashed through the sage. Some were mahogany, some light cream. Under the click of her camera, I could hear Leigh whispering, as if talking into a horse's ear. "Hey pretty girl," she said. "Hey pretty girl, I know you don't like it. I don't like it either."

The helicopter pushed the horses down into a shallow draw where the trap waited.

"It's OK, babies, it's OK," Leigh whispered. She kept her lens trained on the chase, clicking the shutter every few seconds as the horses were pushed into the trap.

We sat for hours, watching the helicopter bring in one band after another until that corner of the desert was almost swept clean.

In her lawsuits and in her documentation, Leigh has pushed for humane treatment. She is not against roundups per se, though she sees the BLM as biased toward cattle interests. But in her opinion, horses should not be run too long, too fast, or in weather that is too hot. Family bands should not be run when the mares are pregnant or the foals are too young. And horses should not be rounded up unless good science shows it's really necessary.

"I don't think that is too much to ask," she told me. "And I'm going to keep asking until they actually do it."

In 2009, when she watched her first roundup at the Calico Herd Management Area, just over the border in Oregon, she saw contractors using cattle prods and a helicopter chasing a foal over rough, rocky terrain for miles, until it was near exhaustion. She later tracked the foal to a BLM holding corral and saw that its hooves had

A HELICOPTER ROUNDS UP HORSES IN STONE CABIN VALLEY, NEVADA, 2011.

detached during the long chase. For days after seeing the foal's injuries, she kept asking BLM staff about its fate.

"They told me it was fine, that he had recovered. It was only when I kept digging that I found out they had put it down," she told me. "To me, that story is everything that is wrong with this agency. It is this old boy buddy system that will lie to your face if you let it. And the horse is the last priority."

She soon realized that photos and videos were the only way anyone would believe her, and she set about documenting every roundup abuse she saw. She posts the videos and photos to social media. At times, the BLM has tried to shut her out. In 2010, during a roundup of the Silver King Herd Management Area in Nevada, the agency put the pink-tape public viewing area fifteen miles from the trap site. Leigh left, figuring she could find the site on her own, and was stopped by a BLM law enforcement officer who told her the trap was on unmarked private land, and if she tried to approach it, she would be arrested.

Leigh sued, saying the bureau was infringing on her right to freely observe the government's activities. A federal appeals court agreed. She has sued the agency several times since, always pushing for the humane treatment of animals and access for the public. In 2011, a judge shut down a roundup in Nevada after she filmed a helicopter hitting an exhausted mare with its skid.

"To me, the horses are not just a number," she told me. "They are not an estimate or a spreadsheet, they are individuals. They live as part of a family. I push to make sure they are treated humanely. But I think the BLM guys just shake their heads and think we are a bunch of tree huggers." She paused and smiled. "That's fine, because we can take them to court."

As we sat in the pink-tape public viewing area, a helicopter brought in six more horses. We watched contractors in big black cowboy hats wave horsewhips tipped with white plastic shopping bags to urge the mustangs out of the corral and into waiting goose-neck trailers. It was as practiced and smooth as the roundup I'd seen in Sand Springs Valley. And just like at Sand Springs, I was struck with how the valley, which the BLM said was over its carrying capac-ity, seemed so empty. I mentioned this to Leigh and she nodded.

"The BLM keeps talking about how wild horses are so overpopu-lated and are destroying the range, but how can it be the horse's fault?" she said. "Horses are on 10 percent of the public land, cattle are on 65 percent. Cows outnumber horses out here by at least 100 to one."

The 1971 law stipulates that horses are to be the primary manage-ment focus in areas where they are found, she told me. "That never happens. Instead, the BLM creates these arbitrarily low numbers of horses that can be on range, then says there is a crisis when there get to be too many and rounds them up."

In the afternoon, after rounding up dozens of horses, the helicopter crew called it a day. Leigh and I followed trailers full of mustangs
in a long banner of dust as they rumbled down the desert valley
toward the highway. At the highway, our caravan stopped at an old
gravel pit, where the contractors backed up the trailers until they
clanged against large, square corrals. The doors opened and the
horses surged out into the pens. Wide-eyed, they turned and ran,
looking for an escape, but there was none, so they settled into slowly
milling around the enclosure.

Men with horsewhips and electric prods separated the bands by
sex: stallions in one corral, mares in another, colts in a third. Horses
reared and shrieked, kicked and jostled, trying to figure out where
they were and how to get out. The gravel pit echoed with the ring of
hooves against the metal corrals.

The sorting went on for the rest of the day. Near sunset, a long

A STALLION TRIES TO ESCAPE WHILE BEING SORTED FOR THE HOLDING SYSTEM AFTER A
ROUNDUP IN STONE CABIN VALLEY, NEVADA, 2011.

semi-trailer arrived. Three dozen mares were loaded up the ramp. The men in the black cowboy hats closed the big metal doors, and with a sigh the semi took off, going east. Another load of horses for the holding system.

"I understand the need for roundups," Leigh said as we stood on a mound of gravel and watched the semi disappear in the distance. "But the more I see it, the more I realize it's a racket. Those horses don't make anyone any money when they stay on the range. They begin to make money for someone as soon as they are taken off. Rounding up, processing, holding—it's people's livelihood and they will defend it. But who will defend the horses?"

During the weeks of the Stone Cabin Valley roundup, the BLM removed about five hundred horses. In the process, fourteen died. One broke its neck, one its leg, one old mare just gave out. The rest were shot because of deformities or because they looked too weak to survive the holding system. This is not unusual. Federal audits over the years have found that about 1.2 percent of wild horses rounded up are killed in the process—a number the BLM describes as acceptably low.

Are roundups so cruel and traumatic that we should end them, as many advocacy groups have argued? They clearly are not a threat to the survival of the wild herds. We've been using helicopters for decades, and there are more horses now on the land than at any point since the law protected them. Are the roundups traumatic and cruel for individual horses? No formal, independent scientific study of the effects of roundups has ever been done. But clearly, the practice frightens animals and severs long-held social bonds.

What is more worrisome than the impact on individual horses is the impact on the agency that oversees them. Roundups have become a crutch that has kept the BLM from finding a better way of doing things. But they've done more than that. They have encouraged waste that has bred resentment and begun to undermine what wild horses mean. In many places in Nevada, they are no longer symbols of individual freedom. They are symbols of federal mismanagement and waste.

After we watched the last of the horses drive away in a semi and I said good-bye to Laura Leigh, I drove back to Tonopah. I planned to sleep out in the desert, but I wanted to get a hot meal first, so I stopped at one of the few sit-down restaurants in town—a little, sun-bleached Mexican place. At the bar sat three men in big black cowboy hats, the felt brims covered in gray dust—the contractors from the roundups. They wore boots with spurs and weathered jeans covered in the same dust. And in front of each man was a tall, frosty-pink strawberry daiquiri in a fancy glass with a long green straw. A man with long silver hair and a droopy mustache passed by the backs of their stools, his belly preceding him. "You boys trying to round up all of Tonopah?" he said with a chuckle.

"No, rounding up wild horses for the BLM," said one of the contractors.

"Wild horses? Good. Get every one of those sons of bitches," the man growled.

After the first Stone Cabin Valley roundup in 1975, the BLM had the legal clearance to take the roundup policy to all of Wild Horse Country. The agency started by trying to chase mustangs the old-fashioned way, on horseback. That quickly proved to be impractical. "We spent hours on horseback, not only just walking along but when the chase was at close quarters, galloping through brush and over loose, jagged rocks the size of footballs," an author named Alden Robertson wrote, describing one of these early attempts. "That sort of riding was very hard on the horses, and if one got too tired or lamed up, its rider walked. Often a cowboy had to switch to his spare horse partway through the day. And sometimes he wore that one out as well." The group Robertson shadowed spent three days riding dawn to dusk and caught only ten horses.

The BLM quickly realized that if it wanted to round up horses efficiently, it needed to go back to its old ways. It began lobbying for a change to the law that would allow them to use aircraft. It got the approval in 1976, when Congress added a small amendment to the Federal Land Policy and Management Act, or FLPMA. The law, which nearly everyone calls "flipma," is basically the Magna Carta of the BLM—a wide-ranging law that gave the agency a new mission to manage lands sustainably for multiple uses, including mining, grazing, recreation, and wildlife.

The introduction of helicopters started a pattern that has continued until the present. Every year, the agency spends millions sending contractors with helicopters and corrals on a tour of the West, gathering up thousands of horses that are almost all shipped to the holding system. Often the same pilots who had captured horses for dog food before FLPMA were the pilots hired after the law to round up horses for the BLM.

The BLM has received steady criticism from horse advocates for continuing the pattern, but in many ways it had no choice. Public-land law requires the bureau to manage for multiple uses, which means keeping wild horse populations under control to maintain what it calls, "a thriving ecological balance and multiple use relationship." When herds got too big, ranchers sued, saying the excess horses were eating grass that under multiple-use doctrine had been allocated to cattle. The BLM's only ready solution was roundups.

The agency began removing thousands of horses every year: about two thousand in 1978, four thousand in 1979, and six thousand in 1980. But managers soon realized that this wasn't enough. The wild horse population in 1978 was at about sixty-two thousand. Just to break even, the agency would have to remove more than eighty-five hundred horses a year. To get to AML, they would have to remove far more, so BLM director Robert Burford decided in 1981 to double the roundups.

His staff came up with a plan. It was going to slowly chip its way down to twenty-seven thousand horses on the range. If the BLM could cut the wild herds to twenty-seven thousand, the remaining herds would only produce about forty-five hundred extra horses each year—a number the bureau thought it could realistically adopt out. Helicopters gathered 12,500 horses in 1981 and almost as many in 1982. But the huge removals had a quick and obvious consequence: Suddenly there were thousands of horses in BLM captivity. The bureau had never been able to find adopters for more than a few thousand horses a year. It suddenly had ten thousand horses on its hands and began paying to keep them in private feedlots. The bill in 1982 climbed to $4 million—more than the entire budget of the program.

Fiscally conservative Republicans who dominated the West were not pleased. Senator Ted Stevens of Alaska, who had worked for the Department of the Interior before entering politics, proposed an amendment to give the BLM authority to sell horses in storage to slaughter buyers. But he quickly withdrew his amendment after Idaho Senator James McClure, a longtime ally of ranchers and an advocate of roundups, sent him a letter warning that it was politically impossible: "Those who would protect the wild horses are zealous to a fault in their protection." McClure told Stevens that letting the BLM sell to slaughter buyers "is going to inflame their passions."[3]

The Reagan administration then made its own move to head off costs. Secretary of the Interior James Watt approved a directive stating that adoptions must pay for themselves. To meet the goal, the BLM announced it would raise the adoption fee for mustangs from

$25 to $200 and instituted a policy that horses that were not adopted in forty-five days would be destroyed. The 1971 Wild Horse Annie Law had not addressed overpopulation, but a 1978 amendment, requested by the BLM, gave the secretary the authority to euthanize "excess" horses humanely. Up to that point, no one had ever done it, but the agency began to draw up plans.

An internal memo estimated the BLM would have to kill about six thousand horses, probably by lethal injection, though some would be shot and their carcasses burned on the range. In July 1981, someone in the bureau leaked the memo to a reporter at the *Philadelphia Bulletin*, immediately sparking what a BLM spokesman at the time called "an emotional firestorm."

Velma Johnston had died of cancer in 1977, but Joan Blue, president of the American Horse Protection Association, took over as the main voice for wild horses.

"The ranchers have always wanted to get rid of all those wild horses, and now they've got the right administration," she said. "We're appalled by this and we're going to fight it."[4]

Director Burford tried to reason with horse advocates, saying the BLM was in a bind and lacked the cash to keep rounding up horses, which he said was necessary to protect the range. "If horses and burros are allowed to destroy the range, they destroy it for all," he told them in a meeting. "The wild horse and burro herds suffer, livestock suffers, as do bighorn sheep, antelope and the many other forms of wildlife that inhabit the public rangelands."

The bureau and the advocates met several times but were not able to find a compromise. So, just as the killing got started, Blue and two other horse-advocacy groups filed suit in federal court, saying the roundups violated the 1971 law. In all, only about fifty animals were killed before the BLM director, in January 1982, placed a three-month moratorium on euthanizing horses. It was seen as a temporary stay until a judge could rule on the case. It has never been lifted.

When the BLM backed down from euthanizing horses, it was still left with a growing problem of how to manage horse herds—a problem that became worse the longer the agency waited. By 1984, the number of horses on the range had grown to about sixty thousand again, and the BLM was facing lawsuits from ranchers. Once again, the agency pitched a familiar plan: Round up until the wild herds are down to twenty-seven thousand so the program could sustain itself. This time, though, the bureau added another piece: To achieve its goal, it would need more money. Way more.

In 1985, Congress agreed to more than triple the program's funding, raising the budget from $5 million to $17 million, with the understanding that the agency would round up twenty-seven thousand horses in twelve months. The bureau staged what was likely the largest roundup effort since the heyday of the Chappel Brothers canning plant. The helicopters launched all over the West. More than a thousand horses were removed from Stone Cabin Valley alone. In the end, the agency was only able to gather about eighteen thousand wild horses in 1985. It gathered ten thousand more in 1986 and eleven thousand in 1987. If the BLM had kept on that track, it eventually might have reached AML. But nearly every horse removed was a horse the agency had to house and feed. The agency tried adoptions, but many of the horses were what one BLM wild horse specialist once described to me as "too old, ugly, or ornery" for anyone to want. Instead, the agency was saddled with animals. By the end of 1985, it was spending $26,000 per day to feed and house them—more than $9 million annually. (Remember, in 1971 the BLM had said the whole program would cost about $3 million.)

What to do with all these extra horses? The obvious answer from a rancher's perspective was to treat them like any other livestock and sell them to the slaughterhouse. A horse could bring $150 to $250 at auction. It didn't make sense to house them, many ranchers argued, when you could recoup the taxpayers' roundup costs at the market. Idaho Senator McClure, who four years earlier had warned not to introduce a slaughter bill that would "inflame the passions" of the wild horse groups, now introduced his own slaughter bill, which would allow any wild horse to go to slaughter buyers if it was not adopted in forty-five days. It didn't go over well. Most of Congress had no reason to vote on a politically poisonous bill to kill wild horses. The bill died in committee.

That left the BLM on its own. Director Burford's moratorium against killing was still in place. So the agency tried something slightly left of euthanasia to achieve its goals—something that hinted at the corrupting influence of the roundup program that in later years would grow worse. They would give horses to slaughter buyers. They just wouldn't advertise that they were doing it. The agency created what it called the "fee waiver" adoption program. Anyone who agreed to adopt a hundred or more horses at a time could have them for free. Horse advocates said it was a fig leaf to hide the BLM's real intent. After all, who buys a hundred untrained horses unless they plan to sell them to a slaughterhouse? Animal welfare groups immediately took the bureau to court, but while the case was pending, the program kicked into high gear.

Later government reports showed the agency gave away twenty thousand wild horses between 1985 and 1988, counting them as "adoptions" when in fact they were sending truckloads to "kill buyers"—the middlemen who deal in unwanted horses and deliver them to the slaughterhouses. During those years, fee-waiver horses accounted for two-thirds of all adoptions.

It was about as ugly a system as you could design. The mustangers of yore were still making money from sending wild horses to the dog-food factory, but they no longer had to go out and catch them. Under the new system, the bureau was doing all of the work—kill buyers just had to haul away the horses. At the time, a thousand-pound horse could fetch $250, so during the program BLM gave away about $5 million worth of horses.

Regulations designed to protect horses from cruelty only added to their suffering. Fee-waiver buyers had to keep horses for a year before gaining the titles that would legally allow them to sell the horses to slaughter. It was a safeguard the agency had created to take away any incentive to the slaughter buyers bent on a quick profit, because buyers would have to feed and house horses for twelve months. But an investigation released by the Government Accountability Office found that this requirement often led to horses being kept under near-starvation conditions during the waiting period by kill buyers who wanted to maximize profit.[5]

In a number of cases, the BLM, desperate to get rid of the surplus horses that were dragging the program down, was aware of problems with the bulk adoptions but did nothing. At one location in Nebraska, a BLM inspection discovered six hundred horses living in a small lot without enough food or water. Thirty had died in the two months after they arrived at the lot. A veterinarian hired by the BLM said the remaining horses were facing death, too, if they were not given food, but the bureau did nothing. "Less than 1 month later, 40 more horses were reported dead," noted a later review by the Government Accountability Office. "But BLM took no action." In all, 150 horses died before the BLM arrived to reclaim them.[6]

In Oklahoma and South Dakota, investigators found the agency had given nearly 1,100 horses to groups that had then sent 687 to slaughter. Investigators warned the BLM about what the buyers had done, but the BLM issued titles for the remaining 394. They were quickly slaughtered. One buyer of 140 horses, who was contacted by suspicious Department of the Interior officials, wrote a letter to assure them that he did "not intend to use or exploit said horses for commercial purposes." Seven days after he gained title, he trucked his herd to slaughter. The BLM got a call from the local slaughterhouse, where the man's horses were waiting to go down the chute. The factory owner was concerned about so many wild horses in his stockyard and wanted to make sure killing them was legal. The BLM told the slaughterhouse owner to go ahead and kill them. No charges were ever brought against the buyer.

Technically, horses were not supposed to go to fee-waiver adopters if the BLM thought they might end up in slaughter, but the agency was so desperate to get rid of horses that it was willing to look the other way. In the end, the investigators said, the program was a "prescription for commercial exploitation of wild horses."[7]

In October 1988, after three years of legal battles, a federal judge sided with wild horse advocates, saying the fee-waiver program "renders the adoption process a farce" by failing to screen out kill buyers. The court barred the BLM from transferring title to anyone who planned to slaughter horses, and the agency officially ended the fee-waiver program a few weeks later.

The legal ordeal and public airing of its slaughter record that forced the BLM to cancel the fee-waiver program was not only an embarrassment, it also cut off the agency's only effective way of getting rid of excess horses and left the BLM stuck back where it started. The BLM was still required by public lands laws to control horse numbers on the range, and since it still relied on helicopter gathers, it still needed to do something with the horses it gathered.

Knowing that the fee-waiver program would likely lose in court, Interior Secretary Donald Hodel in 1987 had put together a citizen advisory board made up overwhelmingly of ranchers. In a report issued that year, they recommended euthanasia, stating, "Some 13 million dogs and cats are destroyed annually by humane organizations in this country. It is reasonable for the federal government to implement the legal provision for humane destruction when faced with a surplus of wild horses and burros."[8]

Robert Burford, still the director of the BLM after six years, considered lifting his five-year-old moratorium and instituting a policy that would allow unadopted horses to be euthanized. "When we're cutting programs for the poor in this country, should we be feeding excess wild horses?" he asked, when questioned about the program that year. "Someone needs to bite the bullet."[9]

There were about seven thousand horses in government holding pens in Nebraska, Nevada, and Texas in 1987. Caring for them cost $7 million annually. Burford was considering a plan to kill nearly all of them. He never got a chance. In the fall of 1988, the Democrat-controlled House of Representatives inserted a rider into its annual appropriations bill barring the BLM from spending any money to destroy healthy horses. Even if the BLM wanted to euthanize horses, and could somehow convince the public that it was a good idea, it no longer was allowed to spend the money to do it.

Pressure on the BLM mounted. It was still being squeezed by ranchers demanding that it remove horses, but now it had fewer ways to relieve pressure by getting rid of them. Instead of taking a step back and asking whether it was time to fundamentally change the roundup approach, though, the agency kept the helicopters flying and kept selling the horses to slaughter buyers. It just became less open about it.

After the fee-waiver program ended, people could only adopt four horses at a time. The limit was an attempt to keep would-be commercial kill buyers from acquiring enough mustangs to make a profit. But kill buyers soon found a loophole—one the BLM seemed to hold wide open. Regulations allowed an adopter to sign a power of attorney to have a proxy buyer adopt a horse for them. It was intended as a way to allow people who lived far from an adoption site or were unfamiliar with the process to be able to have a mustang. Kill buyers began obtaining dozens and dozens of these forms, asking friends, relatives, and sometimes complete strangers to sign them. Then they had hundreds of horses shipped to one proxy buyer. Once the horses were adopted, the kill buyer would often—though not always—hold them for the required year to obtain titles, take ownership of the whole herd, and ship them to slaughter.

Not only did the BLM allow this to go on, but many of the people who participated in the scheme were BLM employees. James Galloway was one of the regular buyers. For more than a decade, he had worked for the BLM, helping with roundups and arranging what the BLM said were adoptions for more than nine thousand horses and burros. In 1992, a tipster told BLM law enforcement that Galloway was fattening up a herd of horses to send to slaughter on a friend's ranch near Del Rio, Texas. These law enforcement agents were not part of the Wild Horse and Burro Program, and were not aware that this kind of scheme was tacitly allowed.

For the law enforcement agents, what at first seemed like a simple bust in Del Rio soon ballooned into an investigation that sprawled across the entire agency, drawing in the Department of Justice, a grand jury, and the interests of top officials in Washington. It shows the creeping corruption roundups have encouraged. People in wild horse circles familiar with the case still refer to it ominously as "Del Rio."

Very quickly, the law enforcement agents learned that Galloway had been tipped off by his BLM supervisor that investigators were arriving. They also learned that his supervisor had illegally killed horses and falsified documents. Galloway was fired by the BLM, and began cooperating with investigators, insisting that his superiors were aware that horses were going to slaughter. "It doesn't take a space scientist to realize that if a man adopts 100 head of horses, he's not going to feed them for the next 30 years," he later said.[10]

By the middle of 1993, investigators had uncovered what they said was widespread collusion among BLM employees, kill buyers, and middlemen. An internal memorandum by the agency's chief of law enforcement that year noted that the BLM was "promoting and organizing group adoptions for the intended purpose of selling the wild horses to slaughter plants," and that "the scope and complexity of the investigation also increased to include scores of individuals, including allegations against private citizens and middle and upper management of the B.L.M."

When I first started traveling to see roundups, I thought horse-advocate warnings of a BLM cover-up sounded too much like a classic conspiracy theory to be true. But what happened with Del Rio will have nearly anyone reaching for a tinfoil hat. The corrosive effects of the cover-up reached the highest levels. Much of what is known about it comes from BLM investigators who became whistleblowers against their own agency, and from the reporting of Martha Mendoza, a dogged young Associated Press journalist, based at the time in Albuquerque, who later won a Pulitzer Prize. Here's what unfolded.

As investigators realized that selling wild horses to slaughter went well beyond one rogue employee, they got in touch with the Department of Justice, which assigned the case to a young assistant US attorney named Alia Ludlum. Late in 1994, Ludlum convened a grand jury in Texas to look into widespread abuses that agents had found in the wild horse program.

But the BLM began trying to sabotage the investigation. In February 1995, BLM administrators ordered the seven law enforcement investigators who had been piecing together the case to stop working on it and not to assist the assistant US attorney. If they did help the attorney, they were told, they would be fired.

The lead investigator, Steve Sederwall, retired in frustration and became an outspoken critic of the bureau's cover-up, guiding reporters to facts the agency was hoping to bury. "In 23 years as a cop, I've never seen anything like the depth of corruption I've seen in the BLM," he later told a reporter from the *Christian Science Monitor*.[11]

Meanwhile, the assistant US attorney kept building a case for indictments. She showed the Del Rio grand jury evidence that BLM employees had placed more than five hundred horses with people, telling them they could sell them to slaughter after a year, and they tipped off people once the investigations started so they could get rid of evidence. BLM managers, she said, pressured employees not to talk to investigators and falsified adoption records to hide what had happened. The list of suspects grew steadily. The grand jury foreman believed there was probable cause for arrest, saying, "We want these charges filed."

An internal Department of Justice memo reported that the BLM had a "don't ask, don't tell" policy with wild horse adoptions. Employees, it said, "freely admit that everyone 'knows' as a general proposition that most of the horses adopted out go to slaughter eventually, [but] the agency tries to avoid finding out that this will happen in any given adoption."[12]

Then Washington got involved and the case began to unravel. Some attorneys in the Department of Justice were old colleagues of a woman who had become chief of staff at the Department of the Interior, which oversees the BLM. The deputy US attorney pushing for prosecutions in Texas began to suspect top-level people in the Departments of the Interior and Justice were having meetings in Washington without her to quietly bury the case. Then the

Department of Justice began interfering in her investigation. It sent another attorney to Del Rio, and he began his own investigation, directing the BLM to use only certain investigators.

The original attorney on the case, Alia Ludlum, subpoenaed records for the horses in BLM storage pastures, but the BLM refused to provide them. "Something smells fishy," she wrote in a memo to her boss in 1995. The memo, along with a thousand other pages of documents from the grand jury, was later obtained by the Associated Press. "I am sure that 'stuff' is happening in Washington concerning my case that I surely don't know and can never hope to know. I just don't understand how 36 horses could cause such overwhelming governmental distress unless there are lots of problems and we are not supposed to find out what the problems are or to solve the problems. I don't like what is happening."[13]

In May 1996, officials from the Departments of Justice and Interior eventually pressured the attorney in Del Rio to drop the charges. The original suspect, Galloway, his supervisor, all the people who profited from illegally selling wild horses to slaughter, and the BLM employees who orchestrated the cover-up were never charged.

"I believe that my investigation was obstructed all along by persons within the BLM because they did not want to be embarrassed," the attorney in Del Rio wrote in a memo around that time. "I think there is a terrible problem with the program and with government agents placing themselves above the law."[14]

Not everyone was ready to give up. A month after the case was closed, Sederwall, the BLM law enforcement officer who had led the investigation, and five former colleagues sent a nine-page letter to then–US Attorney General Janet Reno, detailing "an ever-growing list of felony criminal violations committed by the Bureau of Land Management." They detailed how BLM employees were selling wild horses to slaughterhouses and falsifying records to cover their tracks. And, they said, the BLM and the Department of Justice colluded to stop the grand jury investigation, writing that "investigations have come to a grinding halt under the pressure of the B.L.M. and the Department of Interior."

Major newspapers ran stories on the letter, but officials did nothing. The story went away. Six months later, Associated Press reporter Martha Mendoza ran a scathing series of articles about the cover-up, showing that scores of BLM employees had profited from slaughter schemes and that the cover-ups had gone all the way up to the Secretary of the Interior. Congress and the White House did not act. Mendoza asked Tom Pogacnik, the head of the Wild Horse and Burro Program at the time, if the program intended to protect a symbol of the Wild West had evolved into a supply system for horse meat? "I guess that's one way of looking at it," he responded. "Recognizing that we can't leave them out there, well, at some point the critters do have to come off the range."

The anger over the slaughter and the cover-up stoked the rage of a number of activists. In the months that followed, members of the Animal Liberation Front began burning down BLM corrals. Their message was clear: If you try to destroy horses, we will destroy your program.

The public revelations of slaughter in the 1990s had the same effect as public revelations of slaughter in the 1980s: The BLM tightened adoption rules, making it harder to sell horses to slaughter, and vowed once again not to give horses to anyone who intended to sell them to slaughter. The agency also got all the slaughterhouses in the United States to agree to alert the government when wild horses showed up in their lots. But the BLM did not make any serious efforts to change the roundup strategy, which had been the driving factor in sending so many horses to the dog-food factory. The helicopters kept flying.

Instead of changing the policy, managers changed what they did with horses after they caught them. Since the beginning of the program in the 1970s, the BLM had temporarily kept horses in what it called "short-term holding"—a system of feedlots located on the edges of Wild Horse Country where contractors fed tons of hay to newly rounded-up herds until they could be adopted or "adopted." Facing increased scrutiny over adoptions in the late 1990s, the BLM decided to turn to a second system, called "long-term holding." The bureau would contract with ranchers in the Midwest to put horses out to pasture. The agency would save money by letting horses graze on grass rather than eat hay in feedlots. The lower cost would at least buy time while the agency figured out a new plan.

It was a temporary measure the agency turned to more than twenty years ago. The BLM has yet to figure out a new plan.

In 2000, there were an estimated forty-eight thousand wild horses roaming the West—far more than the twenty-seven thousand the agency thought the land could sustain. A new administration with fresh confidence decided that through bold action it could solve the wild horse problem once and for all. It called the strategy "Living Legends in Balance with the Land." But the bold action was just the same plan from fifteen years earlier: Round up enough horses to get the population down to twenty-seven thousand, then sustain at that level through roundups. To get the plan done, the agency said it would just need one thing: a lot more money.

The Bush administration and Congress bought into the plan. The Department of the Interior increased the agency's budget in 2001 from $20 million to $34.4 million, then kept funding near that level until 2005.

With more money, the BLM started rounding up more horses. Helicopters swept up on average more than eleven thousand per year between 2001 and 2005. The agency almost reached AML. But someone forgot to tell them what happened in the 1980s, and the program soon fell into the same trap. The number of horses in storage skyrocketed: fourteen thousand in 2003, twenty-two thousand in 2005, thirty thousand in 2007.

The BLM had long relied on adoptions to draw down the population in its storage system, but with more stringent slaughter protections, fewer people were buying. Adoptions decreased from an average of seventy-five hundred horses per year in the 1990s to closer to five thousand in the 2000s. The economic crash of 2008 pushed adoptions even lower. In recent years, they have dropped to an average of twenty-five hundred horses.

As the number of horses in storage increased, the agency started calling around to ranchers in the Midwest, looking for more big ranches that could hold impounded horses. The BLM had tried this once before, after the fee-waiver program collapsed in 1988. That year the agency signed an agreement with Dayton Hyde, an Oregon rancher-turned-naturalist with a sun-creased face who had written books about wildlife-friendly ranching. He said he'd take 1,650 horses if the BLM agreed to pay $1 per horse per day for four years as startup money, until his sanctuary could become self-sustaining. Things didn't go as planned. Hyde kept needing more money, until the agency was paying him much more than the agreed amount. As the four-year deadline approached, the sanctuary was nowhere near self-sufficiency. In 1993, the BLM repossessed almost all the horses. It shipped them to a vast cattle ranch north of Tulsa, Oklahoma, where it created its first "long-term holding facility" on thirteen thousand acres owned by a family of longtime cattle ranchers named Hughes. The BLM planned to keep the horses on the Hughes Ranch until it could come up with a better plan. They are still there.[15]

I visited the Hughes Ranch in 2016. The owner, Robert Hughes, showed me around the gorgeous undulating grass hills of his mixed-grass prairie home, where more than four thousand horses grazed. He was welcoming and cheerful, and clearly proud of his meticulously cared-for land. As we rumbled up a road through the flinty hills in his pickup, a few hundred mares, tightly packed on the hilltop where they were socializing and swishing away flies on a sunny morning, perked up at our approach, then peeled off in a gallop down into the blond, knee-high grass.

"I just love to see them run," said Hughes.

The government was paying him around $2 million a year, a fee that included no vet care. He just had to provide food and water to the horses, keep them separated by sex so they don't breed, and haul away their carcasses to a pit when they finally died. Some horses had been on his ranch more than twenty years. I asked him what he thought of the policy of horses rounded up from the wild. His grin broadened and he put up his hands. "Hey, look, man, I'm a grass farmer. I don't have a damn thing to do with policy," he said. "If this deal ended, we'd go back into livestock in a big way."

As the Hughes pastures filled up, the BLM began contracting for more ranches. There are now more than thirty ranches, mostly in Kansas and Oklahoma, in the long-term holding system. Many of these contractors are already wealthy, and the program is making them more so. One was a former CEO of Koch Industries, another is a banker and oilman with a business degree from Stanford, a third made millions leasing his land to his brother-in-law, the founder of Walmart. One of the newest contractors bought his ranch with the proceeds of a $232 million Powerball ticket. Some are being paid more than $3 million per year.

This unlikely setup has become the story of the modern mustang. Taxpayers shell out millions to remove wild horses from desolate land in the West, then millions more to put them on rich prairie grass in the Midwest. In the process, they make an icon of freedom into a ward of the state. However you feel about wild horses, it's hard to be happy with what has developed.

In 2004, some in Congress tried to force the BLM to start selling excess horses to slaughter buyers, without success. That year, Senator Conrad Burns of Montana, a former cattle auctioneer, slipped an amendment into an omnibus budget bill that allowed the BLM to sell any horses to slaughter that were older than ten or had been offered unsuccessfully for adoption three times. He saw it as a fiscally responsible move to rid the program of its long-term holding costs. But the BLM never used its new power. Internal documents suggest managers feared that sending healthy horses to slaughter would stoke so much public anger that they would lose their jobs, and maybe face more firebombings.

The surge of roundups in the 2000s came close to achieving AML. In 2008, there were about twenty-eight thousand horses on the range. One more year would put the agency over the finish line. But right at the point when managers thought they would be in the clear, the roundup program started to collapse under its own weight. There were thirty-two thousand horses in the holding system. There was no fee-waiver program, as there was in the 1980s, to sneak horses out the back door to slaughter. Nor was there a "don't ask, don't tell" adoption program, as there was in the 1990s. The vast majority of the horses rounded up by the BLM stayed with the BLM, and by 2008 they were eating through two-thirds of the program's budget.

That year, the Government Accountability Office issued a scathing follow-up to its 1990 report. It warned that the cost of holding so many horses was not sustainable. "If not controlled," it concluded, "off-the-range holding costs will continue to overwhelm the program." The report urged the BLM to explore ways to limit horses in storage, including euthanasia. In a written statement, the BLM concurred, saying it was considering euthanizing about twenty-three hundred horses and developing other strategies to limit the growth. But ultimately the BLM once again backed away, saying in internal documents that agents feared violence from animal rights groups.[16]

A new administration took over that year. President Barack Obama named a new Secretary of the Interior, Ken Salazar, a Colorado rancher who promised more sensible, scientifically based, sustainable management. It never happened. Under Salazar, the BLM kept gathering and storing. Same with his successor, Sally Jewell, the former CEO of outdoor equipment retailer REI, who took over in 2013. By 2016, the BLM holding system had exploded in size to include sixty private ranches, corrals, and feedlots storing forty-six thousand wild horses at a cost of $49 million a year. So much money was going to ranchers that, after the bill was paid, little was left for anything else.

The scale of what the agency has done in a few decades is astounding. For generations, Nevada had the largest population of wild horses. But all of a sudden, the largest population was in the holding system. There is something ironic about turning over thousands and thousands of acres of lush mixed-grass prairie to a bunch of mustangs exiled from their home in the hardscrabble desert of Nevada. Who could imagine during the 1950s, when J. Frank Dobie published his great history of the life and lore of the vanishing mustang, or in the 1960s, when schoolkids mobilized to save the last remaining herds, that fifty thousand wild horses would return as exiles to the same prairies from which they were purged a century earlier?

These are the same golden swales where the painter George Catlin first spotted wild horses on his way up the Arkansas River in 1834. This is where he first heard around the campfire the tale of the White Stallion, which would be told and retold for a century. This is where endless acres of bluestem and Indian grass built the great Horse

Nations of the southern plains that held back the American army in running battles that lasted longer than any of the country's major wars. This is where, after the buffalo were gone, the hide hunters turned their big guns on horses. This is where armies of hired hands strung barbed wire along the land at right angles, fencing the last of the wild horses of the Great Plains into oblivion. Now they are back, refugees in their own land, growing fat and shiny on the good grass. It's a present no one in the past could have ever foreseen.

Drive the dirt roads of this area of Oklahoma and Kansas and you can easily spot these big ranches. They are mostly in the Flint Hills, where plows never broke the rocky soil and vast swaths of prairie remain. In the golden grass along the fence lines, you can see scores of horses swishing their tails, their heads down, munching on the lush forage. When I went to visit the Hughes Ranch, it was late September, and the grass in places was up to my belt. With me was Dean Bolstad, head of the BLM Wild Horse and Burro Program.

As we drove around the ranch on narrow dirt tracks that rose and fell through the hills, we talked about the long history of roundups, and the future the BLM faced. Bolstad had grown up in Montana, the son of a ranch hand, and had worked for the BLM since college. He was working in Burns, Oregon, when the Animal Liberation Front burned down the corrals. He was in Nevada in 2001, when the program made the big push to bring the herds down to AML. And he took over as head just as the cost of storing horses had paralyzed the program. Looking out at the hundreds of horses grazing on the ranch, he seemed happy to see that the creatures were healthy and well cared for, but he said the program was in crisis. The agency was spending about $49 million a year to warehouse horses, and looking at liabilities of more than $1 billion to care for the horses it had already gathered. There was no more money to gather more horses.

The holding system was, he said, "an absolute anchor around our neck."

"We are spending nearly everything we can on holding," he said. "We have almost no money for other programs."

That means range improvements and development of springs and wells that might improve the carrying capacity of range in Wild Horse Country can't be done. Building the adoption program to get more horses out of storage and into homes can't really be done either. Developing new ideas that might eliminate or at least limit the need for roundups can't be done. There is just no money.

By 2016, even roundups had basically ground to a halt. In 2013, the BLM cut its roundup numbers to only about twenty-five hundred animals a year—a third of its historic average. It rounded up only thirty-eight hundred animals in 2013, and twenty-four hundred in 2015. Basically, it now only rounds up horses on the range when horses in storage die or are adopted. There is no more room.

With roundups down, the population on the range has shot up. In 2016, it sat at seventy-seven thousand—about three times what the agency says the land can sustain. Just to keep the population at that level, the BLM would have to remove ten thousand horses per year. It can't afford to come even close. The agency has 270 Herd Management Areas where wild horses roam. Almost all of them are now way over the target population.

You can argue about what the sustainable number of horses on the range is, and plenty of people do. Is it twenty-seven thousand, as the BLM says? Is it fifty thousand, as some advocates claim? Is it one hundred thousand? Two hundred thousand? Whatever the correct number, horses will eventually exceed it. No matter the number, we need a better answer for what we should do when we reach it. Rounding up and storing horses has proved to be a failed approach. No one has been able to make a case to the public that slaughter is an acceptable fix—so, politically, that strategy is a non-starter. But you also can't just walk away from the problem. Horses on the land have shown in almost all cases that they will increase to destructive levels. If the herds are allowed to increase on the range long enough, all of Wild Horse Country suffers, not just ranchers and cattle, but also antelope, bighorn sheep, native plants, butterflies, toads and salamanders that live around springs, jackrabbits and kangaroo rats that depend on grass seeds. And the horses themselves. When the damage is done, it will take generations for the West's dry and delicate land to recover. Something needs to be done, and quickly.

Mismanagement could also do lasting damage to the legend. When a bureaucracy is trying to preserve a symbol of freedom by spending more than a billion taxpayer dollars to keep it in captivity, while benefiting a few wealthy ranchers, the story of the wild horse starts to change. Animals that once were the embodiment of grit and self-reliance begin instead to symbolize waste, fecklessness, and inept bureaucracy. How long before this damage affects the legend? The White Stallion must always run free. He can't exist in long-term holding. If the legend is undermined, how long before people question why the nation protected wild horses and burros in the first place?

Already mismanagement is shaping the wild horse's image. You can see it in the way people now talk about wild horses. In 2009, the ranking member of the House Natural Resources Committee, Republican Doc Hastings, called them "welfare" horses that were taking away resources from hardworking Americans. In 2015, a pair of biologists called wild horses a "scourge" that had no place on the land and didn't deserve the protection afforded by their romantic past. No doubt, if the holding system gets bigger and more expensive, criticism will only grow louder.

Weeks before I met Bolstad in the fall of 2016, the BLM's citizen advisory board—a nine-member volunteer group set up to have a balanced representation of horse advocates, the livestock industry, wildlife conservation, the scientific community, and other interests—voted eight-to-one to kill the forty-six thousand horses in the holding system. The BLM should either sell the animals to slaughter or humanely euthanize them, they said.

I spoke to a few of the board members. One of them, a cattle veterinarian, had been pushing for slaughter for some time. But the others had been against it until the cost of holding started to overwhelm all other functions of the program. Ben Masters was one of the youngest members of the board. An outdoor guide and filmmaker, a few years earlier he had adopted seven wild horses and made a movie called *Unbranded*, about riding them from Mexico to Canada. He told me it had been a hard decision, but something had to be done to protect the landscape. We talked on the phone while he was on a tour of a Nevada Herd Management Area he described as "severely overgrazed." "It kills me," he said. "I'd love for there to be another way out, but I just don't see it."

The BLM responded that it could not comply with the board's recommendation to kill horses: A congressional rider still prevented the bureau from spending a nickel on killing horses. But its leaders did not put forth any alternatives. "We're in a real pickle," Dean Bolstad told me as we drove through the Hughes Ranch. "We have huge challenges ahead of us, and we don't have the resources to respond."

We stopped the truck and got out in a field on the ranch to look at the mustangs grazing in the setting sun. Beyond them on the grassy swells were more horses, scattered almost as far as the eye could see. For a few moments, it was easy to imagine I was crossing the prairies with the painter George Catlin 185 years ago, when everything from horizon to horizon was still wild and open and free, standing on a rise with a few Osage braves just before the chase.

The horses swished their tails and munched grass in apparent delight. But it was hard to feel excited about it. This was not the wild. In long-term holding, the horses are separated by sex. There are no more family bands, no more fights for dominance, no natural selection. The horses are by no means tame, but they are not really wild, either. It is a purgatory of sorts where animals wait, year after year, alive but not living, until they finally die. Watching darkness fall on the herds, I didn't feel the excitement I had many times before encountering wild horses in the West. A crucial element was missing. Taking wild horses out of the West was like dipping a cup of water out of a river. The physical thing was still there, but its wildness was gone.

CHAPTER 7

RANGE WARS

After I left the Stone Cabin Valley roundup, I headed east on US 6. The road is a straight, lonely ribbon of asphalt that climbs out of Stone Cabin to a gap in a long, empty chain of mountains that form a pleat in the undulating cloth of the Great Basin. In the summer, groves of piñon and juniper trees make the mountaintops look chalkboard black from a distance, but as I drove through in February, they were glowing white. As my car neared the top of the pass, I realized that the long mountain range was actually two sister ranges—the Hot Creek Mountains to the north and the Kawich Mountains to the south, with a little notch where the highway squeezed through like a lizard.

Below the mountain summits, the land was brown as usual. Just past the break between the two ranges, a hot spring rushes out of the foot of the Hot Creek Mountains, spitting out such a generous gush of scalding water that it cascades down into the desert, creating a small oasis called Warm Springs. When I came through not long after dawn, the entire line of the creek running down from the mountains and under the highway was steaming like a cauldron in the winter air. During the gold rush of the 1860s, the springs served as a stagecoach stop, where weary travelers could bathe and horses could recharge on good grass growing along the mineral-caked white banks of the creek. A few doorless and saddle-backed shacks still stand from those days, all but petrified by the desert air. There is also a cinderblock roadhouse, the Warm Springs Bar and Café, built in some optimistic era after the advent of motoring, but long before the interstates sucked all the traffic off of blue highways like this one. It was closed when I arrived. Boards tacked over the café's doors and windows were faded and buckling. Salt brush grew waist-high in the front walk. It had been a long time since anyone had gotten a drink there. To the side was a concrete pool—deep and sparkling aqua blue. But whoever boarded up the café also fenced the spring. A rusty lock hung on the rusty gate.

There was no one around, so I stripped down in the frigid air and took a hot bath in the overflow water splashing out into the desert, then got back in my car to cross the valley on my way to visit the Twin Springs Ranch, one of the largest ranches in Nevada.

Twin Springs is a small family operation, but, like many things in the West, geographically there is nothing small about it. It covers 660,000 acres—an area almost exactly the same size as Rhode Island. It stretches from one mountain range to the next and encompasses everything in between. The population is ten or fewer, depending on the time of year and how many buckaroos the family has hired to work on the ranch, and how many family members have come in from out of town to help with branding. There are no other residents in the valley, and there haven't been for decades. It is just the ranch owner, Joe Fallini, his wife, their daughter, her husband, their children, and usually a few men from the nearby Paiute reservation who help out with the cattle.

I was headed to pay them a visit because you can't understand the predicament of wild horses without understanding western ranching. The ranchers helped create the herds of wild horses in the century before the Wild Free-Roaming Horses and Burros Act was passed in 1971, and the ranchers were most responsible for trying to eradicate them. Since the law, ranchers have been a reliable and a united voice of criticism, pushing for the reduction of wild horse numbers. They say locals, and not the federal government, could manage the population best. Often ranchers are painted by wild horse supporters as classic villains—greedy fat cats wrenching their hands as they connive with the BLM about how to kill innocent horses. But they are usually also the people with the closest connection to the herds, and the most nuanced understanding of the land—a relationship forged over generations of earning a living on the grudging desert.

Wild horse advocates perpetually accuse the BLM of doing the bidding of ranchers. But spend much time with ranchers and you soon realize that, far from being in cahoots with the agency, ranchers often see the BLM, which controls many of their grazing rights, as an incompetent and wasteful nuisance. Some even see it as an enemy agent of the coastal elites, bent on destroying their traditional way of life. Most blame the bureau for unleashing wild horses upon them like so many locusts.

The Twin Springs Ranch has been at the heart of the fight over wild horses for almost as long as the 1971 law has existed, so I wanted to see for myself what the world looked like from the rancher's front porch. I drove across a wide, empty valley dotted with sagebrush and turned onto an unmarked dirt road that led to a small nest of bedraggled trees in the vast bowl of golden desert. I passed through an outer ring of rusted pickups, irrigation pipes, and other farming equipment set out to pasture by generations of stockmen, then through a clutch of old sheds and bunkhouses. At the center was a ranch house surrounded by shade trees, raspberry bushes, and fruit trees, creating a small oasis. In the harsh Nevada atmosphere, I later learned, the trees never gave any fruit.

Two ranch dogs came out barking, and in time a man in worn jeans emerged from the house to assess the racket. The man was about fifty. His broad, barrel chest was stuffed into a snap-button shirt, and both chest pockets were crammed with small notebooks, folded papers, pencils, and pens—the mobile office of a rancher rarely at his desk. This was Joe Fallini.

He had a thick thatch of dark brown hair and skin tanned and creased by the desert sun. His mouth was nearly hidden by a push-broom mustache. He saw me walking up to the house flanked by the barking dogs, but he made no move. Like many people who've spent their lives outdoors, he was slow to speak—not only comfortable with silence but generous with it. I had called ahead, and expected him to raise a hand in welcome, but he just stood, watching me approach.

When I finally reached the front step and introduced myself, he nodded slowly, then said, "I guess you found the place OK then."

He invited me in and led me to a long, polished dining-room table where we sat down. An old pump organ stood against the wall. Above it hung sepia-toned photographs of family members who had worked this land long before he was born. In the living room, hundreds of delicate stone arrowheads, some not much bigger than a dime, were arranged in frames— the heirlooms of earlier inhabitants collected near the valley's springs by the family over the decades.

"It started with my grandfather a long time ago," Mr. Fallini said of the ranch.

Giovanni Fallini, who started the ranch, grew up near Milan and arrived in New York by boat in the 1870s. He arrived in the silver-mining boomtown of Eureka, Nevada, about a hundred miles north of the ranch, in 1874. The twenty-year-old immigrant was saving up to bring over from Italy the woman he had fallen in love with, so they could get married, and he did anything he could to make money. One of his jobs was to haul freight with a pair of oxen between Eureka and another small mining outpost to the south. On his trips, he began stopping at springs, like the one gushing out of the Hot Creek Mountains, and planting vegetables.

"He'd pick the vegetables on the way back on his rounds and sell 'em in town, and I guess he did pretty well," Fallini said.

As Fallini explained the history of his grandfather, he seemed to warm up to the idea of talking to a writer from the city, because he knew I would hear the whole story, not just the account of the latest roundup. Too often, people who write about wild horses don't bother to understand the past, and with many ranch families, the past is as present and real as the photos hanging above the organ. Memory is long here. What men did a generation ago, or two, still matters. For the rest of the day, Fallini was welcoming, generous, and open.

Slowly, over the years, he said, his grandfather saved money and bought control of many of the springs along his supply route. "Water," Fallini said. "That has always been the key. He realized it then, it's just as true now. This is good land, but you need to have the water."

That lesson—that water is the key—was embraced by the whole West, and it helped create ranches like Twin Springs. Twin Springs is like few other ranches in the United States, but it is like nearly all ranches in the arid West. It is made up almost entirely of land the ranchers don't own.

Settlers moving into the West figured out that anyone who controlled the water could control grazing on public land far beyond the property line. After all, no one could graze animals if there was no place to drink. This was a particularly powerful strategy in Nevada, where springs may gush from the foot of a mountain, only to disappear a hundred yards later into the porous sands of the valley bottom. There are few true creeks and rivers. A homesteader could fence off ten acres around a spring and potentially own the only water in a hundred square miles. Even though the homesteader didn't own the grass on the public land surrounding his spring, he commanded it all by fencing off the water.

That is just what the Fallini family and every other successful rancher in the Great Basin has done. They own a relatively small spread of land around key water sources that allow them to have exclusive grazing on a vast spread of public land. The Fallinis have only about two thousand acres, all of it around small springs on the flat valley floors where they can irrigate hay, but their grazing stretches for miles beyond in all directions.

During Giovanni Fallini's life, Nevada was changing. Many of the mines closed, workers left, local markets died out. Ranchers went bust, often because they tried to run too many animals on too little grass, and when a bad drought year came around, and there was nothing for the animals to eat, families had to sell. Over the decades, Fallini's grandfather saved up to buy out other ranchers and add new springs. A small ranch became a larger ranch. Giovanni's son Joseph, born in 1904, did the same. By the 1950s, the family controlled the sprawling ranch it has today.

"I guess over the years we've put together a pretty good spread," Joe Fallini said with a chuckle.

He grew up working cattle on the ranch on horseback, then went to the University of Nevada. He learned to fly a plane and got into skydiving. In his office upstairs in the ranch house hangs an old picture of him free falling while dressed in a black witch's cloak and trying to put a broom between his legs.

"That broom was like a rudder that flipped me all over the place," he said, grinning. "I never did get it to work."

After college, Fallini taught himself to drill for water in the desert. He bought a used drill truck and added dozens of new wells to the ranch. He fell in love with his college roommate's sister, Susan, and persuaded her to marry him and move out to the ranch.

Living miles and miles from anyone, Fallini and his wife, who grew up near Los Angeles, have learned to do a lot for themselves. When it was going to cost too much to bring electricity to the ranch, they strung miles of power lines on their own. They drilled wells for water. An old stone cabin next to the ranch house had once been a stage stop—Susan turned it into a school and taught her three daughters and a scattering of ranch-hand kids. The daughters, now all grown, learned to rope and brand steers and all have graduate degrees. One of their daughters and her husband run the family hay farm a few miles up the valley. Their grandson, Giovanni, the fifth generation, grew up in the saddle and may one day inherit the entire operation.

"The most fun time around here is branding," Susan said. She had wandered in to sit with us at the table. "It's work from dawn until way past dusk, but the whole family gets together and we do what we always used to do."

She pulled out pictures of her kids herding cows and her grandson asleep in the back of a pickup after a long day. "It really is a good life we've made here," she said, "and we are glad they like it enough to keep it going."

There have been a few changes over the years. In the 1990s, Joe Fallini learned to fly an old Bell 47 helicopter, which he now uses to round up his cattle. Doing it on horseback used to take more than a month and often meant sleeping out on the range. He laughed as he told me this, adding, "I know how long it takes because I used to do it when I was a kid."

We walked out to a barnlike hangar across from the house, and he showed me his helicopter. I asked whether he did the maintenance himself. "Nope," he said quickly, then, with a wry smile, added, "Lot of moving parts in that thing. All very important."

With the long family tradition in this valley in mind, Fallini said, he tries to operate the ranch in a way that will sustain the land for his grandchildren and their grandchildren. He runs about eighteen hundred cattle, and he said he tries to keep about two years' worth of grass in reserve on the land in case of drought.

"Dad made sure we always took care of the land," he said, "and I've tried to, too. But these horses, these goddamned horses." His face grew dark, he shook his head in disgust, and his words trailed off.

If the notebooks stuffed in Fallini's shirt pockets kept a list of existential threats to his ranching operation, wild horses would probably be at the top. The Bureau of Land Management would probably be second. He will tell you in no uncertain terms, with a long string of expletives attached, that he hates the goddamned horses and he hates the goddamned BLM even more.

"You can't trust them—you just can't," he said, his voice rising and his eyes narrowed to slits. "They're a bunch of rotten bastards."

At first, the sudden anger can seem offbeat for an otherwise placid, friendly man who has worked hard his whole life, loves what he does, has done well, and brims with pride when talking about how his children and grandchildren are following after him. But one mention of horses and there it is. To understand it, you have to go back a hundred years to when wild horses roamed the land unprotected.

The Twin Springs Ranch is not just older than the Wild Free-Roaming Horses and Burros Act of 1971, it is older than the BLM, and older than the BLM's predecessor agency, the US Grazing Service. Though almost all of the land on the ranch is legally public land, the public rarely makes an appearance, and there is no one who knows the land as closely as the Fallinis—certainly not the BLM, which often has employees cycle through the region every few years. So, if you have lived and worked and occasionally slept in a bedroll on the land for more than half a century, just as your ancestors did, it is understandable that, while technically the land is federal, it can start to feel like it belongs to you. And you start to care very deeply about what happens to it.

Wild horses have been in the area as long as anyone can remember— whether they came from Jack Longstreet's herds on the other side of the mountains, or from the miners abandoning the area or the Paiute tribes, or escaped centuries earlier from Cortés himself, no one has any idea. Like most ranchers in the area, the Fallinis treated wild horses as part of the bounty of the land. They gathered mustangs to ride in the same way they gathered wood from the local hills to burn and stone from the local quarry to build. Anyone who needed a horse, they were there for the catching. The family tried to keep the number roaming the ranch at about 120, and occasionally they added domestic stallions to the mix to try to improve the bloodlines.

As a kid, before the 1971 law, Joe remembers the family setting up a water trap with a big corral fence around a spring and a door that swung shut. Then he or one of his brothers, or maybe his dad, would wait out there for the right horses to wander in. "We liked the horses," he said. "We liked seeing them out there. Every once in a while, there got to be too many and we would need to get rid of them. So we would go get a permit."

At the time, there was no federal law controlling wild horses. County commissioners gave permission for roundups in Nevada, regulating them much the same way building permits are regulated today. This is the system Velma Johnston encountered when she successfully shut down a roundup in Storey County in 1952.

After the horses were trapped, Fallini said, the buckaroos who needed a horse to ride could pick out the one they wanted, rope it, and break it. The family would also tell other folks in the county to come take a look.

"If anyone wanted a horse to ride, they could come look them over and pick them out," Fallini said. "And we would chicken feed whatever nobody wanted. That was just normal. It's how everybody did it."

Over the years, members of the Fallini family have depended on good mustangs for ranch horses. It was sustainable, he said, it was well managed, and "it didn't cost anybody anything." That was the way things were when he was growing up, and to him it was so typical that, as a young man, he didn't give it much thought. Then the Wild Free-Roaming Horses and Burros Act passed in 1971, the BLM got involved, and everything changed.

The law allowed ranchers a limited time to claim horses on public land that were private—domestic horses that had been put out to graze without a permit. For each one gathered, ranchers would have to pay a trespass fee. The idea was to give everyone a chance to take what was theirs before new regulations took effect, but the regulations didn't make much sense to ranchers in Nevada. For decades they had added domestic studs to wild herds and gathered the wild offspring for ranch work. In their view, almost all of the domestic horses were wild and almost all of the wild horses were domestic. The lines were so blurred that ranchers could easily make a claim that all the horses were theirs or none at all.

Many ranchers at the time simply decided to pay the fee and get rid of the horses, rather than cede control of the resource to the feds. In Montana, they got rid of nearly every wild horse. Only a small herd remains in the Pryor Mountains near Bighorn Basin. The same is true in the Elko District of Nevada and the Lakeview District in Oregon. In both cases, the local BLM district chief, sensing problems with the wild horse law, encouraged local ranchers to round up the horses, assuring them he would charge a low trespass fee that in the long run would be worth it. Lakeview ranchers claimed and removed sixteen hundred horses. Elko got rid of at least thirty-five hundred. In the mid-1970s, when the BLM got around to doing a formal inventory of wild horses, Lakeview and Elko had none left. On maps of Nevada today, you can still see a large void. The whole state is covered with Herd Management Areas except in the northeast corner. That corner is the Elko District.

When it came time for the Fallinis to decide what to do about the new law, Joe and his father disagreed. His father was all for getting rid of the wild horses on the ranch. It would be expensive to pay the trespass fees, he said, but he didn't trust the federal government, and he didn't want it interfering on the ranch. He had learned to mistrust the government in large part by ranching land directly north of the Nevada Test Site (now the Nevada National Security Site) during the nuclear tests of the 1950s. Clouds of fallout from the tests drifted over the ranch. Cattle started dying, as did a few of the dogs, but officials from the Atomic Energy Commission denied there was any danger. In Joe's office is a full-page framed black-and-white photograph of his father. He is crouched down on his land, fingering a fist of dirt. The photo ran in *Life* magazine in 1957, in an article in which the Atomic Energy Commission said nuclear testing was safe. It quoted his father saying, "Until proven different, we view radiation as a threat."

His father took the same approach with the wild horse law. The government might be saying it would be OK, but he would assume it was dangerous.

Joe, who was thirty at the time, had more faith in a good outcome. He remembers telling his father that he liked the horses and didn't want to get rid of them. He eventually persuaded the family to keep the mustangs around. "Stupidest thing I've ever done," he said when we met years later. "They've cost me well over a million dollars, and damn near ruined the ranch."

The problem with horses on his ranch is simple, he said. The BLM has not done what it said it would do. It did not do what the law said it had to do. And it has never faced consequences for its actions.

In the 1970s, he said, the BLM estimated that the area where wild horses roamed on his ranch could reasonably sustain between 150 and 250 horses. Fallini went into a drawer in a bank of file cabinets and pulled out a stack of photos and papers. He keeps meticulous detailed accounts of his ranch, including how the horse herds increased. He began flipping through the photos, all taken in roughly the same spot over time. As he flipped, he read off figures from his annual horse counts. In 1971, when the law passed, his notes show there were 126 horses. By 1974, there were 480. By 1977, there were 703. By 1983, there were nearly 2,000 horses.

This was during the time when the BLM was scrambling to figure out what to do with all the horses captured in its roundup program. Fallini repeatedly wrote to the bureau, demanding they remove the excess horses, but his ranch, so far from everything, was pushed to a back burner.

The photos he held showed the impact. He started out with one taken in the early 1970s, an image of sagebrush intermingled with the platinum-blond tufts of rice grass and other native grasses. As he flipped through the photos, all showing the same general spot, the grasses grew sparser, then began to disappear. Spots of bare earth started to increase, then dominated. By the end, even the sagebrush—a hardy, woody shrub that is barely palatable to most animals—was mangled, and the grass was completely gone.

"Nothing but a moonscape and horseshit," Fallini said.

According to Nevada Department of Wildlife surveys, deer and antelope herds nearly disappeared from the area during the same period. Horses were also playing havoc with the system of water troughs Fallini had created for his cattle. Horse herds jostling to get water would often break the tanks with their kicks, he said. They drank twice as much as the cattle, and soon the extra money spent on pumping water was running around $50,000 a year.

Laws controlling wild horses require the BLM to set a population for each Herd Management Area that maintains a "thriving natural ecological balance" and immediately remove horses when they exceed that level. But the BLM would not gather the horses in the Herd Management Area at Twin Springs, despite repeated pleas from Fallini. The bureau was too busy dealing with the costs of warehousing already gathered horses and the protests of wild horse groups. Apparently the problems of one rancher in one of the emptiest corners of the country could be ignored.

Desperate to protect the grass on the ranch, Fallini offered to remove the horses himself. The agency told him that if he touched the animals, he would be violating the law.

For Fallini, the BLM's new role as a protector of horses was an ironic reversal. For decades, the bureau's main role had been to gather up stray animals and encourage the livestock industry to be efficient and sustainable—at least from a beef and wool production perspective. Wild horses were like tumbleweed to the agency. They were unwanted, unproductive invasives. Getting rid of them was seen as being in the national interest. During World War II, Secretary of the Interior Harold Ickes proclaimed, "The removal of wild horses would protect the range in the interest of legitimate cattle and sheep production to win the war." The agency fought horse protection efforts, like those of Velma Johnston, for twenty years before the 1971 law passed. It was making plans to kill horses right up until the 1971 law passed.

Fallini pulled out a two-page mimeographed planning document that the local BLM office had printed in 1971, just a few months before the law passed. He had kept it for decades as a reminder of the agency's sudden shift in roles. The document was a plan to kill thousands of wild horses in central Nevada. The faint purple type showed that the BLM had listed tools needed: an asphyxiation chamber, a D9 bulldozer to cover the thousands of carcasses, and sharpshooters to take down the animals that couldn't be caught in the roundup.

"Can you believe this?" he said, shaking the papers. "They were going to annihilate damn near every horse in the country, and a few months later they're in charge of saving the damn things."

The Fallini family was careful always to rotate its cattle from place to place, giving pastures plenty of rest so grass could grow back. But the wild horse herds stayed on the land year-round. Legally, the Fallinis were not allowed to herd them out of overused pastures or even shoo them away from water tanks. Slowly, the grass the family had banked for emergencies was eaten away.

In 1983, when the horse population in the West was around fifty thousand—twice the government's goal—Fallini went to testify before the Senate Committee on Energy and Natural Resources at a hearing held in Rock Springs, Wyoming. The BLM had about ten thousand horses in the holding system at the time. The committee was discussing a bill that would allow the horses to be sold for slaughter. It was an idea many ranchers saw as common sense. Several ranchers spoke that day, all basically echoing the same concern: They had no problem with wild horses, but the herds were not being managed and their numbers were out of control.

"Our ranch has been completely devastated by these wild horses, and we're footing the expense," Fallini told the committee. "We have not turned a profit on this ranch for three years on account of the horses." He warned that if the herds were not brought under control, it would put many ranchers like him out of business.

A sheep rancher from Colorado, John Prulis, was grazing his herds in Wyoming on the morning of the hearing when he heard about the meeting on the radio and hurried over. "I want to tell you for sure that us sheep ranchers and cattlemen are not rapists of the land that we have been accused to be," he told the committee. "We believe in the conservation of our lands for production of food and fiber, which to me I think is a very essential contribution to this country. . . . And we have horses, we use horses, we like horses. We do not advocate for the eradication of wild horses, but we sure need to control them. . . . If it continues this way, it's going to run not only us out of business, it's going to ruin our public lands."

Both the BLM and the ranchers told the committee they supported the bill to sell horses to slaughter. A number of representatives of animal welfare groups testified in opposition, saying it was the cattle that were overpopulated and needed to be reduced. A spokesman for The Fund for Animals, based in Manhattan, told the committee that its thousands of members would fight any move to slaughter horses. The bill didn't make it out of committee. However dire things looked to western ranchers like Joe Fallini, politicians outside the Great Basin could see little upside to voting to condemn wild horses to slaughter. They could probably imagine the bags of mail flooding in from heartbroken children.

The wild horse herds on the Twin Springs Ranch continued to increase. Hundreds milled around water tanks, pounding the surrounding range to dust. At the peak of the population in the early 1980s, an anthropologist and author named Richard Symanski, who wrote a very thorough book called *Wild Horses and Sacred Cows*, spent a day touring the ranch with Fallini. Though wild horses had once been found in only one area, they had spread across the whole ranch. Symanski reported seeing "scores and scores of horses kick up dust and take flight at our approach." Watching the fleeing horses, he later wrote he felt like it was the closest thing in modern times to early reports of the teeming grass sea of horses on the Wild Horse Desert of Texas two centuries earlier. "I was stunned," he said, "by the number of horses I had seen."[1]

Wild horse advocates often blame ranchers for the BLM's roundup policy. If cattle weren't eating all the forage, they say, horses would have plenty. Some have suggested it would be cheaper and more humane to buy out ranchers.

There is no doubt that cattle get most of the forage in many areas. But simply getting rid of cows won't solve the problem. Horses, if unmanaged, will still proliferate until there are huge die-offs. There is a rarely mentioned example of this just south of the Fallini ranch on the missile testing grounds of Nellis Air Force Base. The base was the site of the first-ever wild horse preserve, created by the federal government in 1962. Since there were no cattle or other residents, and no mustangers could legally enter the place anyway, it wasn't politically contentious to suggest that mustangs could have the run of the place. The next thirty years saw no management, no round-ups, and no competition from cattle. Horses got what many advocates often wish for: They were left alone. The herds steadily increased until there were more than sixty-two hundred of them. In the late 1980s, a drought came and they began to die off. In 1990 and 1991, an estimated two thousand horses perished. Bleached carcasses dotted the sage. In an effort to try to save the horses from cruel deaths, the BLM began a roundup, removing 1,862 horses over the summer of 1991. Witnesses at the scene described hundreds of gaunt animals trying to drink from a spring no bigger than a puddle, while coyotes circled, ready to feast on those too weak to fight back.

"It was the kind of thing you don't ever forget," Dawn Lappin, a close friend of Velma Johnston who helped with the rescue, later told a reporter. "These animals were in a complete state of panic, dying of thirst and hunger."[2] That kind of disaster doesn't just affect the horses. The whole ecosystem is thrown for a loop and it can take generations to recover.

After years of asking the government to remove horses, Joe Fallini finally sued. In 1984, a judge ruled the BLM was violating the law by not keeping the wild horses contained to the area where they were originally found when the law was passed, and ordered the BLM to limit the herd to around 140 horses. The agency is now required to round up horses in the valley every few years. Since then, Fallini has sued thirty times over smaller points—his right to build hefty steel barriers to keep horses out of his springs, for example—and has won every time but once. But he doesn't see these as victories. All told, he said, he has spent about $1 million on legal costs and another $1 million fixing damage done to his ranch by horses.

When we had been discussing Fallini's family history, and how his grandson, named after his grandfather, was now learning to herd cattle, he had nearly glowed. But as we talked about his long battle with the BLM, he started to sound defeated, even despondent, and seemed to be struggling with whether his family should keep up the fight, or just light out for new territory. "Jesus, you put your whole life into trying to make something work," he said, shaking his head, "and they just keep trying to put you out of business. I'm so damned bitter. This whole stupid law never should have happened."

The Wild Free-Roaming Horses and Burros Act was a striking reversal of the status quo. For more than a century in the West, ranchers and farmers had worked to get rid of the wild, and the feds had backed them. By 1970, they had made monumental progress. They had eradicated wolves, killed off most of the grizzlies, driven back mountain lions, and were making good progress on coyotes. The federal government had formally organized grazing rights to keep out speculators and nomad sheepherders. The Homestead Act had ended; the public land that was left would stay public land forever. Ranchers had drilled wells and installed gas engines to bring water up into the desert. Public land ranching had finally beaten back most of the uncertainties of wildness that it had battled for generations. Then the wild horse law came along as part of a wave of laws, including the Endangered Species Act (1973) and the Wilderness Act (1964), which sought to bring an end to the Great Barbecue and save some of the wild scraps of the nation that were left. Those laws, though widely popular, often contradicted the traditions relied on by many western ranchers.

Wild horses were a threat to the bottom line, but, just as important, they were also a troubling sign for ranchers of changing times. They were a sign that the federal government would no longer always be on their side. For ranchers, the horses eventually became a symbol of galling mismanagement that was clear evidence, for anybody who cared to look, of the federal government's inability to manage the land properly.

Because the wild horse has become a symbol of broken trust and mismanagement, the legend of the wild horse as companion to the cowboy has started to disappear in Wild Horse Country. Hatred of wild horses is not hard to find. Mention mustangs in almost any small-town bar or café and prepare for an earful. "They're just trash horses, not even wild," one man told me in a café in the remote Nevada town of Ely. "People think they saved the mustangs. Well, if you want 'em so bad, come out and take 'em."

After the Wild Free-Roaming Horses and Burros Act passed in 1971, the anger festered until some locals started shooting horses. In 1988, in central Nevada's Lander County, an estimated five hundred were shot by a high-powered rifle, their bones left to be scattered by scavengers. Was it frustrated ranchers? Local beer-drinking yahoos? Or just a statement about local disdain of federal intrusion? The culprit was never found. In 1989, in Nevada's Antelope Valley, near the Utah border, another hundred were found dead. Though federal agents combed the area and banged on doors to question locals, no one said they saw anything and no one was ever charged. Since then, a steady stream of horses have turned up dead, often in lonely, empty valleys far from witnesses. Sometimes just one or two, sometimes a few dozen.

Often horses are shot far from any witnesses and drop into the sage, only to have their bones found months later, if at all. But even in cases where suspects are identified, local US attorneys have rarely filed charges. When they have, juries in the Great Basin have again and again voted for acquittal. Dawn Lappin, who took over Velma Johnston's organization, told a Nevada newspaper in 1988, after hundreds of horses had turned up dead, that the BLM only takes about a fourth of all cases to court, and juries rarely vote to convict. "There is such anti-Bureau, anti-government feelings," she said. "I think they felt the government had set them up."[3]

Successful prosecutions under the Wild Free-Roaming Horses and Burros Act have been few. The penalties often amount to small fines and probation. And the BLM has misrepresented how successful its enforcement is. In the 1990s, when the bureau was facing broad criticism for allowing horses to be sold to slaughter, it told Congress it successfully prosecuted 125 people between 1985 and 1996. In fact, the Associated Press later found, the real number was just three. Since then, there have been only a handful of successful cases.[4]

Shooting leaves bodies, which could eventually lead to prosecution. Some locals instead preferred to make horses disappear by sending them secretly to slaughterhouses, which got rid of the evidence while providing the rancher with cash. In 1977, the BLM caught a longtime Nevada mustanger named Max Allred using a traditional water trap to catch mustangs. Allred had been working as a ranch hand in the area for decades, putting out domestic horses in his spare time and selling the offspring, as well as whatever else he happened to catch. When caught, he claimed the horses he was gathering were not wild, but domestic. A jury acquitted him. He later wrote a letter to the local paper, lambasting the BLM for mismanagement. "Why don't the BLM give up their horse control, admit that their whole program is comparable to some wino's dream and let the people of Nevada handle their own overpopulation of wild horses as they did before this thing reached its present Idiotic proportions?" he said. "When there is an overpopulation of cattle you don't let people adopt them, you don't shoot them, you sell them. . . . The people of Nevada have been paying for the grass these animals eat, sometimes at the expense of their own cows, sheep and horses. So they should be permitted to gather and sell some of the horses instead of having the ranges littered with dead horses."[5]

In 1981, a BLM ranger came across another water trap holding four mustangs near Fire Lake in Nevada. Fresh tire tracks suggested several loads of horses had already been taken from the trap. The ranger staked out the trap and caught a rancher and his son returning with an empty trailer. The rancher said he was just trying to catch his own stray domestic horses. He was never charged.

In 1990, a rancher named George Parman, who lived not too far north of the Fallinis' ranch, was caught with 117 wild horses. He also said they were domestic horses. A jury found him not guilty. In 1997, when contacted by the Associated Press, Parman was not afraid to call himself a mustanger. "I'm proud of the fact that my family, whenever we needed money, we made our money off the mustangs," he said.[6]

In a 2010 letter Parman posted on the Web, he longed for the good old days:

What we need to do, is to let the ranchers and the mustangers take care of the problem, just as they did in the old days, back when, along in the Fall a handful of cowboys would take their saddle horses—throw a bunch of grub and their bedrolls in the back of a pickup—and off they'd go to do a little mustanging. It was a perfect system. . . . It cost the taxpayer nothing. The best of the horses were put on the market for people to use and enjoy. The remainders of the older and less desirable animals were euthanized via a facility that made good use of the end product. Rangelands were not overstocked. Springs were kept open and maintained by the ranchers. The cattle had plenty to eat. The horses had plenty to eat. Wildlife did well. Everything was better.[7]

Frustration over the current situation on the range is easy to understand. Ranchers like the Fallinis see the way the BLM manages horses as an egregious double standard. Using range science to calculate sustainable grazing, the agency sets the number of cattle each rancher can graze on public land. Ranchers caught running more cattle can be fined, or, in extreme cases, lose their permits. The BLM also sets the number of horses that are sustainable in a region. The agency has almost never met its own numbers, but there is no penalty for the agency like there is on ranchers. In fact, the penalty for BLM mismanagement is often visited on the rancher. When horse herds grow to double or triple the management levels, and grass is depleted, the agency often orders ranchers to reduce their cattle count to limit damage to the range.

A few years ago, I talked to a rancher named Mark Winch in the Wah Wah Valley, on the Utah/Nevada line. There was a drought, and little grass had grown. Horses in the valley were way over the agency's goal, but it had no money to remove them, so it ordered him to reduce his cattle herd by half. "I don't understand it," he said to me as we looked at a muddy spring that he said had been trampled by too many horses. "If we have to play by their rules, why don't they?"

Not only is the BLM not penalized when horses exceed management goals, it often comes out ahead. When the population mushrooms, the bureau is given a larger and larger budget to tackle the problem. Though the budget hikes have never led to progress, no one in the agency leadership has ever been fired or even formally admonished for failing to meet goals. Instead, the agency has only gotten more money. Practices that would put a ranch out of business have actually allowed the agency to add staff.

If there is a sentiment nearly all ranchers share, it's that wild horse numbers need to be managed at the level set by the BLM. They often preface their statements by saying they like horses, and want them around. But, they say, if the BLM can't manage herds because it is spending all its money on the holding system, then it should sell the horses to slaughter.

"I would not want to see all horses eliminated," the president of the Nevada Cattlemen's Association told the *New York Times* in 1989, echoing a sentiment ranchers have shared many times since. "But how many do we need for scenic and historical purposes? Do we want to sacrifice food and fiber for wild horses?"[8]

Ranchers chafe against money misspent on wild horses, and look back longingly on the days when they could harvest the herds. And certainly, the BLM's practices of paying to round up horses and store them, only to quietly sell them to slaughter buyers at great expense, makes no fiscal sense. But the wild horse budget pales in comparison to federal subsidies spent on public land ranchers.

While ranchers often think of themselves as rugged individuals and independent businessmen, and scoff at the inefficiency of the wild horse program, they too benefit from government subsidies. They pay just $2.11 per month to graze a cow on BLM land—less than a third of the average cost for grazing on private land in the West. The BLM raised about $15 million in grazing fees in 2015. But it spent more than $36 million to run its grazing program. Almost any way you look at it, this is a losing proposition for the American public.

At the hearing in Rock Springs in 1983, when Joe Fallini testified before senators, one of the senators harangued the director of the BLM for losing millions on the wild horse adoption program, to which the director replied, "We run a money-losing program with western ranching too."

The federal government provides other subsidies, including about $9 million a year in predator control. Then there are farm and drought subsidies. The Fallinis have received nearly $50,000 in farm subsidies over the years.

How much do we as a nation really need ranchers like the Fallinis? Very few jobs are tied to these vast, arid ranches. Though cattle cover much of Nevada, the whole industry employs fewer people than a single large casino in Las Vegas. Repeated studies have determined that even though the federal lands in the West where cattle are run cover the same number of square miles as all the states along the East Coast, those ranchers only make up three percent of all cattle growers. And because it can take fifty acres to sustain one cow in the arid West, versus just a few acres in the East, they produce less than one percent of all beef. If all public-land ranching west of the Rockies were ended, many studies have suggested, the industry would hardly notice. As George Wuerthner, the author and ecologist, concluded in an essay on the subject, western public-land ranching "is insignificant to all but the individual rancher."[9]

Horse advocates say ranchers should not complain about the glut of wild horses since there are vastly more cattle in Wild Horse Country. In 2016, when the wild horse population was at its highest since the law passed, the West had about seventy-seven thousand wild horses. At the same time, there were about seven hundred thousand cattle on BLM land. If there is a shortage of grass, muddy springs, invasive weeds, and deteriorating range in the West, horses can hardly take all the blame, or even most of it.

Both environmentalists and horse advocates have called for an end to government support of public-land ranching. Better, they say, to turn federal land in places like Nevada over to wildlife. Let elk, antelope, and mountain lions be free of competition with cattle. Let jackrabbits, coyotes, rice grass, desert marigolds, shovel-nosed snakes, collared lizards, desert tortoises, and sage grouse reclaim the land.

The arguments seem compelling from afar, but they are less convincing if you have spent a day with a family like the Fallinis. Walking down the long gravel drive of the Fallinis' ranch after talking with them for several hours, I listened to the crunch of stones under my feet and then looked up at the wild crest of the Hot Creek Mountains, with their distant snow. The shadows showed uncounted, unvisited canyons that flowed down. My eyes scanned the smoke-colored hills below as a warm wind whisked up from the south, bringing the sweet scent of sage from the nearby atomic testing grounds. I thought about all the fall evenings Fallini had spent out there, bringing in cattle. To one side of me stood an old shack, where generations of branding irons hammered out by hand were hanging from weathered wooden pegs.

My journey there had started with a flight to Las Vegas. In the city, there are statues and murals of wild horses everywhere, but the city is mostly about tearing down the past. I drove north through old mining towns, thrown up by eastern capitalists and abandoned as soon as the pay dirt ran out. I drove past the nuclear testing grounds, where the United States tested ever-bigger bombs to try to ensure its safety. Standing on that gravel road, I felt for the first time in a while that I was in a place that made sense.

When I started out exploring Wild Horse Country, I thought that, after learning enough about ranchers and mustangs, it would become obvious which had the proper claim to western lands. As I walked back to my car, I realized what an impoverished place the West would be without the two. What we need most is balanced land use—leaving space for horses and other wildlife, and for ranchers.

It's not that we need horses or ranchers materially. We don't need public-land ranchers for the beef any more than we need mustangs for saddle horses. But we need them both because, in order for America to work, in order for the story we tell ourselves about our country to be real, we need space for both free-ranging animals and free-ranging people. Both are part of our story. Get rid of one and you are likely to lose the other. Man never catches the White Stallion, but he is always there in the picture, chasing him.

CHAPTER 8

ALL THE
MISSING HORSES

"You ever wonder where these horses end up?" Laura Leigh said as she looked through her view-finder to reframe her shot.

We were crouched in the pink-tape public viewing area on the winter morning I visited the Stone Cabin Valley. A helicopter had just come over a hill, driving a band of about eight horses into the steel corral of the trap. As it headed off again, a handful of cowboys waved whips to drive the mustangs into a trailer. The doors clanged shut and the trailer rumbled off down the rutted dirt road toward the highway.

"I can tell you where they end up," I said. "Long-term holding."

"Yeah, but after that?"

As far as I knew, there was no "after that" in long-term holding. It was a life sentence. "Heaven?" I said.

She chuckled. "I'm sure that's true," she said, "but before that?" She got up and rearranged one of the tripods holding the camcorders she had fixed on the corral.

"You have me out here watching the roundups," she said. "No one ever watches the holding system. You could get rid of a lot of horses there and no one would know."

She lifted a long Canon lens to her eye and scanned across the sage, waiting for the return of the chopper. "I wouldn't be surprised if a lot of them end up going to slaughter."

I held my tongue. Wild horse advocates are constantly theorizing about how wild horses are going to slaughter in the way some gun owners constantly fret that the government is coming to get them. By the time I had been touring Wild Horse Country for a few months, I had heard all sorts of theories but had seen nothing that resembled credible evidence.

I had no doubt the BLM had looked the other way as tens of thousands of horses were slaughtered in the 1980s and 1990s, but because the agency had been caught each time, flogged in the press, investigated by the Department of Justice, and firebombed by environmental radicals, I figured they had learned their lesson. Plus, after each scandal, safeguards had been added to make it nearly impossible to sell horses to slaughter without being caught. By the time Leigh and I met in Stone Cabin Valley, the BLM was so emphatic that no wild horses ever went to slaughter that at the top of a list of "myths about Wild Horses" it published on its website was a bold proclamation: "Myth: It is the BLM's policy to sell or send wild horses to slaughter."

I figured the agency's slaughtering days were in the past. So when advocates started in on slaughter conspiracy theories, I tried just to nod politely and hope that the subject changed. Maybe it was because we were sitting alone amid hundreds of miles of desert with no horses in view yet, or because I had learned to respect Leigh, but this time I didn't just brush her off.

"You don't really think that stuff is still going on?" I asked.

"Well, those horses are worth a lot of money, and that money is going somewhere," Leigh continued.

"I don't buy it," I said. "No one at the BLM would be stupid enough to let that happen."

She smiled and said, "There's an easy way to find out." Forget the adoption program, she said, and look at something called "sale authority" horses. A sale authority horse is any horse that was either older than ten years or passed over for adoption more than three times. They are essentially government surplus—bargain-basement horses. The BLM quietly created the sale authority program in 2004. Anyone could buy one of these horses for $10 each. And the BLM would deliver them for free.

The BLM assured the public that the sale authority program was not a clandestine slaughter scheme like the fee-waiver program set up in the 1980s, pointing to the fact that it made buyers sign a contract swearing they wouldn't sell horses to slaughter. Anyone who broke the contract faced federal felony charges. But, unlike the adoption program, where the BLM holds a horse's title for a year to take away the financial incentives of slaughter buyers, sale authority horse titles transferred at the time of sale. Once people bought a sale authority horse, they could immediately do what they wanted with it.

The BLM doesn't talk about the sale program, Leigh said, but there are hundreds of horses sold each year. "Maybe someone could request the sales records, see who is buying those horses and what they are doing with them."

"If it's so easy," I asked, "why don't you do it?"

"I did," she replied, smiling as she looked at me. "But for some reason the BLM doesn't want to give them to anyone."

Two months later, there was a knock on my door and a mailman handed me a certified manila envelope from the BLM. Right after the roundup, I had sent a formal request under the Freedom of Information Act (FOIA) to the BLM, asking for all wild horse sales records. I'd been a journalist long enough to know that FOIA, which requires the federal government to share documents with the public, doesn't always get you what you want. Agencies can drag their feet for years. They can obfuscate or omit. They can illegally deny requests, knowing the likelihood of legal challenges is slim. They can censor with abandon. Once I got a sixty-page response from the US Air Force with every line dutifully blacked out. There are other requests I'm still waiting for, years later. But with routine data easily pulled from a spreadsheet, sometimes you get lucky.

I opened the envelope and pulled out page after page of spreadsheets that detailed years of sale authority purchases. I ran my eyes across the column labels at the top: Date of sale, buyer, buyer's address (this whole column was blacked out), holding facility where horses were purchased, number of horses bought. Then I ran down the rows, knowing within minutes that I'd be able to tell if Leigh's theory was just another activist fantasy. For a while, the data went like this:

Jessica Rue, one horse, Burns, Oregon
Jolene Pavelka, one horse, Cañon City, Colorado
Cinnamon Guller, one horse, Palomino Valley, Nevada

There were pages like this—bargain shoppers who were unable to visit a BLM holding facility without taking home a mustang. Leigh fit in this category. She had adopted three horses. But then the entries changed.

Tom Davis, 28 horses, Litchfield, California
Tom Davis, 31 horses, Fallon, Nevada
Tom Davis, 174 horses, Teterville, Kansas

All told, a guy named Tom Davis had purchased more than seventeen hundred horses in four years. The median number of horses most people purchased from the sale authority program was two, but Davis always bought at least a truckload at a time, and sometimes up to five truckloads. His purchases made up 70 percent of all sales. He wasn't just the biggest buyer in the sale authority program—he basically *was* the sale program.

I figured anyone doing something legitimate with that many horses would be well known to wild horse advocates and easy to find, but Google turned up no trace of a Tom Davis associated with wild horses. None of the big wild horse organizations had heard of him either. Who was this guy? Where was he? And how was I going to find him?

He had a common name and could be in any state—though I suspected I would find him in the West. As I searched for any Tom Davis associated with horses or the BLM, I found two promising suspects. One was an old rancher who had a big property in Oregon's Wild Horse Country. The other was a horse trainer and rodeo rider with a spread in Texas called the TNT Ranch. But which one was it, and how could I find out without tipping them off that I was snooping?

I called Leigh to talk through the problem. As a horse owner, she came up with a solution in about thirty seconds. In the cattle-rustling and horse-thieving days of the Wild West, most western states passed laws requiring any livestock being moved out of their home county to get a brand inspection first, to make sure the animals weren't stolen. Those laws are still active today. Every time the BLM shipped out a truckload of horses, it would have had to get them inspected, Leigh said, and the inspection for every truck the BLM sent to Tom Davis would have his address. "It won't tell you what he's doing with them, but at least then we'll know which Tom Davis we are dealing with."

It was brilliant, because I wasn't just worried about tipping off

Tom Davis. I was also worried about the BLM. The brand inspectors were state employees. I could dig through their files without the feds knowing.

It turned out that neither of the men I had identified was the right Tom Davis. Brand inspection records I requested came back with a delivery address in a tiny town in Colorado called La Jara. I had been through the town a few times. It was near the New Mexico border, in a remote spot called the San Luis Valley.

A search of the address on a satellite image showed a small house surrounded by corrals and holding pens. Two long, silver stock trailers were parked by the barn. It was the home of a sixty-four-year-old man with a cattle trucking business. He had the equipment, he had a knowledge of buyers and markets. This was our guy.

Everything I could find out about Tom Davis suggested he had lived in the San Luis Valley his whole life. It is a high, dry, flat valley rimmed by snow-crested mountains. Hours away from any city, large or small, it has a slow way of life that has resisted change. Many farmers still use traditional practices passed down from Spanish settlers who came generations earlier, during the mustang era. Some in the valley still practice a folk Catholicism that has changed little since medieval times.

Looking at the records, I realized that though Davis had lived in the valley his whole life, his wild horse purchases were from corrals throughout the BLM holding system: Colorado, California, Nevada, Oregon, Wyoming, Kansas, Utah. Everywhere the BLM was selling horses, he was buying. This was a telling detail. It suggested that he hadn't just worked out a quiet deal with one crooked BLM holding-facility manager or one state director willing to look the other way. He was getting the same deal everywhere. Which meant that whomever he had made the agreement with was in the central office in Washington, DC.

I would have to explore that link. But first I had to try to figure out what he was doing with the horses, without letting him know he was being watched. Here again, brand inspections became key. I had all the documents showing what was shipped *to* Davis's house. Next I requested all inspections of horses being shipped *away* from Davis's house. They showed that he was shipping horses out within a day or two of receiving them, and he was almost always writing on the inspection forms that they were going to a tiny town on the Texas border called Spofford. Why he picked Spofford, I never found out, but I couldn't help thinking it was a reference to the past. Right next door was the town that became notorious for the BLM's 1990s slaughter cover-up: Del Rio.

It didn't take long to establish that the Spofford story was a lie. The town has fewer than a hundred people. A few phone calls showed none of them knew anything about any big shipments of horses coming through on the single paved street.

The United States shut down its last horse slaughterhouses in 2007, after Democrats in Congress defunded the federal inspection program needed to process the meat. Since then, all horses bound for slaughter had been trucked over the border. Tens of thousands a year went to Mexico, where two massive, modern slaughterhouses produced a steady line of shipping containers full of frozen meat bound for Europe. Hides were made into mattress stuffing bound for Norway. Manes were made into hair weaves bound for Asia. I was willing to bet that the wild horses Davis said were bound for Spofford were actually ending up at those plants.

The motivation was clear. A guy could buy BLM horses at $10 a head, delivered free by the BLM to his door. Slaughter buyers were paying anywhere from $200 to $400 per horse in the Southwest. Anyone selling contraband wild horses to an exporter probably had to take a lower price, but even at half the market rate, he would still make a huge profit. I guessed he was shipping them to a border state, selling to a middleman, and then ordering more. The only thing that didn't fit my theory was how he was getting away with it.

Sure, the BLM wild horse program had repeatedly sold horses over the years to people who quietly found ways to get around regulations and profit from horses going to slaughter. But Tom Davis wasn't doing it that quietly. When you buy 240 horses, someone will notice. It didn't seem that he could get away with his racket unless someone at the BLM wanted him to. I hesitated to make that leap, because by doing so I knew I was entering the wild horse advocate world of conspiracy theories. True, as a journalist, I would be in good company. Martha Mendoza, the Associated Press reporter who dug into the Del Rio scandal in the 1990s, and who concluded that "a multimillion-dollar federal program created to save the lives of wild horses is instead channeling them by the thousands to slaughterhouses, where they are chopped into cuts of meat," not only turned out to be correct but also later won a Pulitzer Prize for other work. And her conspiracy theory was not just that the BLM was covering up the slaughter, but so were the Departments of Justice and Interior.[1]

Certainly the BLM had been courted by a steady parade of disingenuous suitors over the years, wanting to take wild horses off their hands. But it had usually refused. One of the more flagrant ones was in 2002, when a Montana rancher named Merle Edsall and his business partner, Johannes von Trapp, offered to care for ten thousand mustangs in Mexico, conveniently just out of reach of US law, under a program they called the Sonora Wild Horse Repatriation Project. When wild horse advocates howled that it was a thinly veiled slaughter program, the BLM passed on the offer.

Even though I was hesitant, I started believing in my own conspiracy theory. Something bugged me about Tom Davis's purchases. The BLM was busting other people for buying sale authority horses, but not Davis. In 2011, two Utah men, Robert Capson and Dennis Kunz, were arrested with a truckload of sixty-four wild horses bound for Texas. According to a federal indictment, they planned to sell the animals to an exporter for slaughter. Capson, an itinerant ranch hand with multiple bankruptcies in his past, owned no land to hold wild horses and no hay to feed them. He had bought the herd from a short-term holding corral near Salt Lake City, saying he planned to sell them as rodeo stock. He had the BLM deliver the truckloads to his friend Kunz, who was in the business of buying horses for slaughter. Within a few days, Kunz was on his way to Mexico with the whole lot.

Unbeknownst to both of them, the BLM was watching. Two hundred miles into the journey, federal agents closed in. They had set up a sting and had invited the local nightly news team, complete with helicopter video crews to document the highway patrol pulling over the truck and saving the mustangs. The two men were arrested and charged with wire fraud and making false statements. Both pled guilty and faced fines of almost $10,000.

This may seem like an honorable law enforcement action, but to me it only made the BLM seem more suspicious. Why was a guy who had bought one truckload of horses being paraded in front of the cameras in handcuffs when another guy who had bought dozens was counting his money at home? It would be one thing if the agency was just too overworked or inept to enforce its own rules. But that was not the case. They were enforcing the rules. They just weren't enforcing them against Tom Davis.

I talked to Kunz by phone right before he entered his guilty plea in 2012. He was angry, and he felt he had been tricked by the BLM. "The whole thing was a setup," he said. He had talked to top BLM employees in Utah who had explained the sale system to him months earlier. They told him that once the sale was made, the horses were owned free and clear. Kunz said he felt they were encouraging him to buy horses for slaughter.

"They knew who I was, and what they were trying to tell me," he said.

He said his partner, Capson, clearly had no way to care for a truck-load of horses, but the BLM sold them anyway. "If they didn't want us to have the horses, then why did they sell them to us?" Kunz asked. "And then they had all the cameras ready to make an arrest and make themselves look good."

The arrests made headlines and showed that the BLM was protecting wild horses. At the same time, though, they were selling hundreds and hundreds to Tom Davis, no questions asked.

As I thought about this, something kept popping up in the back of my head: Tom Davis's address. I grew up in Colorado and had visited the San Luis Valley dozens of times over the years, so I knew that Davis lived just down the road from the family ranch of Ken Salazar—a local boy who had grown up running cattle but had gone to college, then law school. He was elected Colorado's attorney general and then US senator. He campaigned for Barack Obama in 2008, bringing in crucial Hispanic votes in the swing state of Colorado, and was subsequently named Secretary of the Interior.

Salazar had been a steady critic of the Wild Horse and Burro Program since becoming secretary, calling the program, in a letter to the Senate, "not sustainable for the animals, the environment, or the taxpayer." He said rules for selling wild horses to private parties needed to be "more flexible where appropriate."[2]

The advocates hated him for it. He was a rancher, so they immediately saw him as a stooge for livestock interests. And they interpreted his comments as a call to loosen safeguards against slaughter. As a Colorado voter, I had always seen Salazar as a likable and fairly harmless centrist. But as soon as he was in charge of the BLM's Wild Horse and Burro Program, one of his longtime neighbors started buying truckloads of horses for slaughter from the bureau without anyone batting an eye. What was going on? I intended to try to find out.

First I had to find out more about Tom Davis. I didn't even have proof that the horses he bought were going to slaughter. I called the US Customs and Border Patrol in Texas, where most horses were exported to Mexico. On paper, both the US Department of Agriculture and its Mexican counterpart are supposed to keep records of each slaughter horse exported through Border Patrol corrals—a system set up to catch diseases in food products. But after I called, I learned that in practice the paperwork is often incomplete or not filed at all, so I had no way of tracing Tom Davis's horses once his trucks pulled away from his property.

The only person who truly knew the extent of what Tom Davis was doing and who was helping him was Tom Davis. Since I had exhausted the options for tracking him behind his back, I decided it was time to go talk to him face-to-face.

I found a pretext for visiting that gave me at least a little cover. In 1984, Tom Davis had self-published a memoir about a six-month ride he took from Texas to Alaska in 1976. The book was called *Be Tough or Be Gone: The Adventures of a Modern Day Cowboy*. It was a painful read, and long out of print (Sample passage: "I swear this little gal could charm the lard off a hog"), but it gave me an excuse to talk to him. I called him up and introduced myself as a writer and asked if I could talk to him about his adventures. He invited me to come on down.

I pulled up in front of his house about a week later and parked my car pointed out toward the road so, if I needed to, I could get out fast. It was a three-hour drive to reach his collection of corrals in the San Luis Valley, and the whole way down I'd been playing scenarios in my head of how the interview would go. None of them ended well. He had been making a comfy living off selling horses, and I was about to ruin it. And I'd be calling him a cheat and a liar to boot. I was pretty sure he would throw me off his property. When I arrived, the corrals were still muddy from a heavy rain the previous day, and a half-dozen horses and a burro nibbled at a bale of hay. A battered brown pickup sat next to a small, white ranch house. I knocked on the door, but no one answered. I walked around to the back and eventually found Davis by a tractor-trailer, winding up thick yellow straps he had used to deliver a load of hay the previous night.

He was a big man, a bit doughy in his old age, but strong. He had on black overalls that were new but slicked with mud. A thumb-softened notebook was stuffed into the chest pocket. Shaggy brown hair curled from under a sun-faded ball cap with the logo of his trucking company on the crest. His eyes squinted from beneath deep, drooping brows, making him look perpetually skeptical and a little sad. His face, like the rest of him, showed years out in the weather. He looked like a man who had lived hard his whole life.

I shook his enormous bear paw of a hand. He was friendly in an "aw, shucks" way, and he had a slow way of talking that you often find in the San Luis Valley.

I sat on the deck of his trailer, my legs dangling over the mud, and made small talk as he wound up the long, yellow straps. I hoped to steer our conversation toward the wild horses eventually, but not at first.

He had just gotten back from delivering a load of hay to Aspen, he said. He cut costs by taking the load up a winding, precipitous mountain shortcut called Independence Pass. "You're not supposed to take a trailer over 35 feet on that road but I ran it after midnight when no one was there," he said with a knowing grin.

What would happen when the Department of Transportation caught on, I asked.

"Fuck DOT, and the horses they rode in on," he said. "They're a bunch of educated idiots that have no idea what it takes to make a truck run. I don't have much use for 'em."

So began a two-hour rambling conversation well seasoned with swearing and racial slurs, in which, when it came to abiding by the law, Davis lurched between being coy and being jarringly honest. He'd worked with horses his whole life, except for a stint in Vietnam, he said. He'd hauled racehorses in Arizona and worked at a track, he had worked on ranches in Montana. He had even helped round up wild horses in that state right after the federal law took effect in the 1970s, during the claiming period when ranchers could take free-roaming horses as their own.

"These ranchers was hollering about the wild horses coming in and eating their hay stacks, so they declared there were no wild horses in that area and just shot a bunch of 'em," he said. "Well, me and another old boy we got us a case of wine and built traps and gathered a bunch of horses and trucked them off. They can't put you in jail for catching something that don't exist."

He paused, maybe sensing he had said too much.

"Don't get me wrong, I'm a supporter of wild horses, believe me, I love wild horses to death," he said. "It's like an addiction. I can't get enough. For some it's drugs, for me it's horses."

I asked him how well he knew Ken Salazar.

He had known him all his life, he said. When he was young, his father had farmed the Salazar land. Since then, he said, he had done "quite a bit of trucking for Ken."

"'Course, Ken's off in Washington, his boy runs the ranch now," he said.

Davis said he made his living hauling cattle, but recently he had been buying "lots and lots" of wild horses from the BLM.

"What do you do with them all?" I asked.

He paused, then said he kept about two hundred on a nearby pasture that he leased, and used them to breed bucking horses for the rodeo. He added that he had hundreds more that he leased to gas and oil landowners in West Texas, where the grazing kept down the grass for fire protection. He said he leased some to movie production companies in Mexico to use in films. And, he said, he had a thriving business selling horses to wealthy landowners throughout the southeastern United States.

"Lots of folks want to own a genuine piece of American heritage, a true mustang," he said. "I get the BLM to give me flashy, photographical horses. Ones that will look good in front of million dollar homes."

When I checked later, I couldn't find any evidence that these stories were true. There were no movie companies and no oil leases. The number of horses he said he was selling rich southerners were vast. If you added all of the nonprofit adoption groups that try to find homes for horses together, they were not moving as many mustangs. Yet no one in the close-knit wild horse advocacy world had ever heard of him.

Davis told me he'd like to buy more wild horses, but the BLM will only give him so many. "The tree-huggers will give them hell if they sell too many to me," he said. "The BLM gal in Washington who sells all the horses to me, she is always asking where I'm selling them."

"What do you tell her?" I asked.

"I tell her, 'None of your damned business,' that's what I tell her," he said. "They never question me too hard. It makes 'em look good if they're movin' these horses, see? Every horse I take from them saves them a lot of money. I'm doing them a favor. Hell, I'm doing the American people a favor."

The woman who ran sales in Washington later told me on the phone that all buyers are carefully screened, and there was no indication Davis was doing anything wrong. When I pressed her about what a man like Davis could be doing with so many horses, she hung up.

He shook his head and mentioned the holding system.

"More than 50,000 just sitting there and I can't get them," he said.

I pressed him to tell me who leased his horses, so I could follow up.

"No way in hell," he said. "You could cut me out of this deal, too."

I started to worry he was getting suspicious of me. Maybe the BLM had warned him I had requested the records. Maybe he suspected I was talking with wild horse advocates.

I cast my eyes around, looking for a way to change the subject, and spotted two long, silver trailers by his house—one single-decker for shipping horses, and one double-decker with lower ceilings, known as a "pot," for shipping cattle. I asked how he shipped his horses.

"I use that trailer right there," he said, gesturing to the single-deck trailer.

"The law says you can't take them to the kill plants in pots, so they all have to go in singles," he said. "But that's a pretty wide-open law. There is no kill plant in the US, so how are you going to haul horses to the kill plant when we ain't got any?" He raised his eyebrows for effect. "So you can haul them in any fuckin' thing you want to."

So much for him being suspicious.

"Besides," he continued, "horses spend their whole lives with their head on the ground eating. It ain't going to hurt them to be in this double trailer with their head at least level with their back. I mean, what's eight or ten hours?"

I mentioned how the BLM had been unable to control the wild horse population, and now had more horses than it knew what to do with.

"If the BLM and the tree huggers would get off their asses, they could go out there with a rifle and eliminate about three-quarters of their studs and then they would not have so many colts," he said.

Prices for slaughter were low now, because horses had to be shipped to Mexico, he said. For two years, he had been trying to start his own slaughter plant. He'd even asked Ken Salazar's brother, John Salazar, who was head of the Colorado Department of Agriculture, for help: "He said, 'I'd love to see it, but politically I can't go near it.'" Davis said he hoped the government eventually would lift the ban on slaughter.

"Why, hell, some of the finest meat you'll ever eat is a fat yearling colt," he said. "What's wrong with taking these BLM horses that they got fat and shiny and setting up a kill plant?"

I asked flat out if he had ever sold a horse to slaughter.

He became very gentle and quiet.

"No," he said, calmly. "I love horses. I find them good homes."

Where were those good homes? I told him I wanted to see the horses.

He laughed. "I'm not tellin' nobody nothin' on where they are going, because once they're mine, they're mine. And I make a living off of them."

He took a pebble and flung it at a burro that was chewing on one of his fence posts. "I'm doing them a favor by taking the horses to where we are not having to pay to keep them. They are spending a lot of money on that wild horse deal. And I am helping them eliminate some of it. Am I not doing the country a service?"

I insisted that it sounded to me like he was sending the horses to slaughter, and I asked if he had been lying.

"No. No. I'm not sending nothing to slaughter," he said. "But what a waste. Wouldn't it be better to be processing these sons of bitches into dog food? I talked to the Purina people about it and they said they couldn't do it. People wouldn't buy dog food with horse meat because the tree huggers would raise so much hell."

He said Ken Salazar had the authority to sell every wild horse in long-term holding to slaughter. "If they give me a hand, I would sell every one they got," he said. "And what I couldn't sell I would sell to the kill buyers because they'd be mine."

But if you sell a wild horse to slaughter, I said, you'd be prosecuted.

He said he wasn't so sure. Every batch of horses he bought, he got a bill of sale. That meant the horses were legally his property. They were no longer protected wild horses, they were private horses, and he could do what he wanted with them.

"I think there's loopholes," he said. "Lawyers are what runs this country and they put loopholes in laws for other lawyers. I've had several DUIs over the years and I've learned something: It's money. If you're accusing me of something, and I have enough money to hire a good lawyer, I can get out of it like—who's that nigger ballplayer that killed his wife?"

In all the time I talked to him, Davis never overtly admitted to selling horses to slaughter, even when I asked flat out and pointed out all the evidence. He remained cordial, and I left an hour later.

A few months later, I published a story about Tom Davis, funded by the nonprofit investigative news organization ProPublica, called "All the Missing Horses." I had tried contacting top BLM officials and Ken Salazar multiple times for comment, but neither responded. Salazar must have decided I wasn't worth the time.

Within days of the article, the BLM announced it was stopping all horse sales to Davis and opening an investigation. The state of Colorado, too, opened an investigation into breach of brand inspection laws. Davis's career as a covert kill buyer was over. But it bothered me that I still didn't know Salazar's involvement.

Several weeks after the story came out, I heard Salazar was coming to Colorado Springs, where I lived, to campaign for Barack Obama again. Politics had brought him out from behind the ramparts of the Department of the Interior building in Washington and forced him to mix with the common folk. It was my chance to question him. I rushed out to see him and introduced myself as a local journalist who had some questions about his department. He nodded, smiled, and said he would be happy to do an interview. I started asking him questions about the campaign, then shifted to questions about wild horses, and then specifically to Tom Davis.

When I mentioned the horse trader, I saw his face suddenly shift, as though realizing that he was now talking to the reporter he had been avoiding for months. I had caught him off guard, on a day when he wanted to talk about anything but wild horses. He then said the interview was over. He smiled and nodded, then walked up to me, got right in my face, inches from my nose, tipped back his white cowboy hat, and hissed through gritted teeth, "You set me up. Don't you ever. . . . You know what, you do that again . . . I'll punch you out."

I stepped back, a little shocked. I don't want to make it sound scarier than it was. Salazar was never really a physically imposing man, and by the time he threatened me, he was a grandfather. Over the years, I've interviewed smugglers, drug dealers, and murderers. People have threatened to do far worse. More than anything, I was confused. And as I watched him turn and quickly walk off to a waiting black SUV, I was disappointed that the interview ended without my knowing anything about Salazar's involvement with Tom Davis.

While I was ready to brush it off, not everyone was. Ginger Kathrens, a wild horse advocate who was in the room and saw the exchange, put out a press release the next day to all the major news outlets. It got picked up by the Associated Press and ran in dozens of papers, including the *New York Times*.

Salazar was forced to apologize. In a meeting with me a few weeks later in his grand office in Washington, he smiled, shook my hand, and swore he didn't even know who Tom Davis was. He was ready for the meeting with an array of new safeguards he had put in place after my reporting. The BLM changed its regulations so that no one could buy truckloads of $10 horses anymore. People could only buy six at a time, he said. Salazar admitted the program faced problems, but he said they were working on it. The most important goal, he said, was to keep doing roundups so the BLM could get down to twenty-seven thousand horses.

If shutting down Tom Davis's racket sounds like a satisfying ending, it is not. I didn't expect convictions for anyone in the BLM or for Salazar, but I did think the hammer would come down on Davis. His paper trail was so long and so blatant that it would be easy to gain a conviction. If not jail time, then at least a fine. It never happened.

The BLM spent months investigating. Other federal law enforcement agents got involved, too. One afternoon after the inquiry was completed, I received a phone call from a Department of Justice investigator. He confirmed what I had suspected: Davis had shipped all his horses to New Mexico. He sold them to an old friend named Dennis Chavez, who had an exporter's license. The horses were mixed in with trucks of other horses and shipped through a border crossing near El Paso. They went to the big, European-owned meat-packing plants in Mexico, where they were cut into steaks, frozen, and loaded into shipping containers bound for the other side of the Atlantic. In bistros in Antwerp, diners ended up unwittingly feasting on wild, free-range, organic American mustang.

Davis was not charged. The feds decided that by selling to an intermediary, he had protected himself from prosecution because he could plausibly say he had no idea the horses were going to slaughter.

Davis had broken state brand laws hundreds of times by shipping horses out of Colorado without a brand inspection. But the local district attorney in the San Luis Valley decided not to prosecute. Last I knew, Davis was still hauling cattle for a living and buying domestic horses for slaughter when he could find them cheap.

Investigators never looked into BLM involvement, the connection to Salazar, the complete breakdown in safeguards in Washington.

No one that I know of was fired or even admonished. When I talked to the head of the program, Dean Bolstad, in 2016, he said that the whole ordeal was extremely embarrassing for the BLM, but that they honestly had no idea Davis was doing anything wrong.

What happened with Davis shows the danger of sticking with a policy like roundups. I've already outlined many problems. Rounding up horses and storing them is going to cost us more than $1 billion over the next several years. It traumatizes horses and breaks up family bands. It erodes a symbol we as a republic have imbued with some of our most heartfelt ideals. But it also literally sows corruption. It happened in the 1980s. It happened in the 1990s. It happened with Davis. As long as there are horses with value, there will be unscrupulous people trying to get around the rules and pocket the profits, and cornered bureaucrats trying to throw a rug over the whole thing. But it gets worse. The policy gives otherwise law-abiding public employees an incentive to make deals with unscrupulous people or look the other way. The corroding influence of trying to cover up those deals ripples through not just the Department of the Interior but also the Department of Justice, and the rule of law. It has happened more than once. If we let it continue, it will almost certainly happen again.

CHAPTER 9

DISAPPOINTMENT VALLEY

After traveling all over Wild Horse Country, I'd come to believe that just stopping the roundups would lead to disaster on the land. At the same time, continuing roundups would lead to continued corruption and mismanagement in the BLM. I began casting around for another answer, and eventually I found myself crouching in the chalky dirt of an arroyo in far western Colorado, far from any town, in a place called Disappointment Valley, shoulder to shoulder with a woman holding a long rifle.

For early settlers riding into the area in search of places to plant or graze, Disappointment Valley was just that: disappointing. It is a broken country of mesas and valleys. The rising Rocky Mountains to the east eons ago pushed up layers of old sedimentary stone laid down by a moist coast environment about the time Hyracotherium was wandering through. A soft, bone-colored shale left by the lazy waters of a muddy coast eroded into the basin now called Disappointment Valley. The fine silt crumbles easily. It has formed steep, bare hills and badlands with furrows of earth that pleat the hillsides and fill the air as whirlwinds cut across the land in the midday heat. There is no running water in most of the valley. The soil is too alkaline to farm. Generations of overgrazing by cattle whittled the once-full bunchgrasses down to cheatgrass and greasewood. It is searing and shadeless in the summer, and whipped by icy winds in the winter. It is a forbidding, leftover place. Naturally, this is Wild Horse Country.

There is a BLM Herd Management Area here called Spring Creek Basin.

One morning, on the edge of the basin, I met up with one of the few human residents of the valley, a cheerful, athletic woman named TJ Holmes. There is a small house on the southern edge of the valley where she has lived as the caretaker for years. She has adopted several mustangs but only rides occasionally. She prefers getting around in a dust-covered Jeep, or, just as often, on her own two feet.

Holmes was tall, with curly red hair unfurling under a sun-bleached visor, and had the wiry build of a mountain-bike racer, which, by the way, she was for years. She had the friendly but skeptical nature of a small-town journalist, which she also was for a time. But she also wore dangling mustang earrings that pranced as she walked, and scuffed hiking boots, white with the chalk of the valley, that showed her current occupation: guardian of Spring Creek Basin's wild horses.

"I'm glad you could come see what we do here," she told me when we met. "I think it could finally end the roundups."

She had the guarded excitement of a true believer eager to share a discovery and also aware that it would strike the unacquainted as bizarre. We drove down a long, dirt track into the basin, passing miles of scrubby salt brush and bounding down into dry creek beds—there are no bridges here because there is rarely any water.

Finally we parked in a flat spread of land at the bottom of the basin, where brush dotted the plain in all directions. She opened her hatch and removed a long, green gun with a spotting scope clamped to the barrel. She checked that she had her binoculars and plenty of ammunition in her backpack, then she led me quietly down into an arroyo.

Like many wild horse advocates, Holmes first learned about the animals by watching a helicopter roundup. Early on, her activism focused on trying to stop roundups in Disappointment Valley. But as she spent season after season tracking the horses of the area, watching them breed and forage on the forbidding hills, she began to realize that simply opposing the BLM's roundups was not a solution. It would lead to overpopulation and disaster. So she searched for another way to control the population—something more selective, more efficient, and, she hoped, more humane.

"That's how I got started in this," she said with an exasperated chuckle. "If you had told me I'd be carrying a gun around . . ." She shook her head without finishing her thought.

We padded quietly up the bends of the dry arroyo. The walls, which were well above our heads, hid us as we wove deep into the salt brush. Holmes stopped at a spot where the banks were six feet high, and she set down her pack. She slipped her gun from her shoulder.

About sixty wild horses live in Disappointment Valley—more than the BLM says it can sustain. It's a small number, but they have significant impact in a valley with limited forage. Like most horse advocates, Holmes had come to regard BLM roundups as costly and needlessly traumatic to horses. But, unlike many others, she long ago sided with the BLM on one point: The populations needed to be controlled.

"At first I was against population control," she told me, "but it is better for the land, better for the horses. I realized it was the only way."

She edged up the dirt bank and looked over the rim. Three mares stood swishing their tails in the sage. She spotted a flea-bitten gray she had named Corona—her target for that morning.

"I have never missed," she whispered with a wry smile. "They call me Annie Oakley."

She stepped up over the rim, steadied herself on one knee, leveled her gun, and fired. The mare jumped. A spring-loaded dart about the size of a small syringe barreled from the gun and hit her in the rump. It stuck for a few seconds as the mare galloped away, then fell into the sage.

"Got her," Holmes said. She beamed as she stood up. She went to collect the dropped dart, then pulled out her phone, which contains records of every horse in the valley, and recorded the date in Corona's file. Corona was good for another year. Instead of bullets, Holmes's gun fired darts filled with a substance called PZP, which makes mares infertile for about a year. It's basically a birth-control pill for horses.

In the conundrum of how to manage wild horses—where managers must limit herd growth but cannot, politically, send them to slaughter, PZP has emerged as a promising alternative. The substance can slow or stop the growth of herds, it is cheap, and it is relatively simple to administer. It appears to have no harmful effect on the health or behavior of the horses, and it doesn't linger chemically in the environment. Most important, unlike helicopter roundups, it doesn't result in tens of thousands of horses living for decades in government storage, or quietly being shipped off to slaughter. One would think something that promises to ease the pressure on roundups would have the BLM chomping at the bit. Not so.

The bureau knows all about PZP. It has studied it, deemed it effective, and for twenty years has said that it is excited about the potential of PZP. It has repeatedly announced plans to roll it out.

But it never really has. Funding has been halting and inconsistent. Effective pilot projects have not been expanded. Its use has been so limited that on a broad scale it has made little difference.

In an ironic twist, the more horses that the BLM puts in the holding system, the less money it has for alternatives like PZP that could keep horses out of the system. The agency that now needs PZP more than ever, uses far less PZP than it did in the past. It can no longer afford it. But that does not mean PZP has been a failure. In the absence of BLM leadership, citizens like TJ Holmes have stepped forward. She is part of a grassroots movement trying to end the need for roundups through smart, efficient use of the drug. Volunteers are now darting in Montana, Wyoming, Nevada, Utah, Colorado, Idaho, Arizona, California, and New Mexico. Their work has eliminated or drastically reduced the need for roundups in almost a dozen herds. Their efforts are coordinated not by BLM agents, university biologists, or environmental groups, but by motivated citizens.

Holmes first came to Disappointment Valley in 2002 when she was working as a copy editor for a newspaper in the town of Durango, about two hours away. An editor, knowing that she had grown up around horses, mentioned there was a roundup going on. She was intrigued by the idea that wild horses still roamed the West, so she drove out to the basin to see for herself.

The local BLM manager had warned her not to expect too much of the Disappointment Valley herd. The wild horses in Colorado, he said, were not the regal Spanish steeds of old, but a bunch of malnourished mongrel misfits that weren't much to look at. "I was expecting pig-eyed, hammerheaded inbreds," she told me. But when she arrived at the roundup, the horses she saw running before the helicopter were stunning.

She went back to Durango, but the horses stuck in her mind. The idea of them captivated her. While she was back at work, or riding her bike, or lying awake on a stormy winter night, they were out there, unsheltered, making their own way, with no one's permission. Wildness. It was beautiful just knowing it was there.

"They don't need us, they don't want us, they are just there," she told me when we met. Her voice cracked, and for a moment she was on the verge of tears. "There is just something about that that is really amazing."

Holmes started going back to Disappointment Valley. A few times a year grew to a few times a month. Usually, she was the only one there. She trekked the hills and gullies, following the herds. She got to see how they lived when helicopters weren't chasing them—how the family bands interacted and how individual horses expressed distinct quirks.

In 2007 the BLM scheduled another roundup. By that time Holmes was editor of a nearby weekly newspaper called the *Dolores Star*. Holmes, notepad in hand, went to cover the roundup, and watched the horses running terrified into the trap, from which they were later trucked away.

"Why do you have to use helicopters?" she remembers asking the BLM employees.

"No other way, really," came the reply.

After the roundup, she grew even closer to the herd. She took her lunch and ate with them. She stretched out in the sun and slept with them. At first they were skittish, but eventually some let her approach within a dozen meters.

Soon she had a name for each horse. She carried a long-lens camera and started snapping hundreds of photos. She began jokingly referring to herself as a "wild horse paparazzi." You realize, after meeting her, that this is not far off base. She posts her pictures online in a blog she created called "Spring Creek Basin Mustangs," along with gossipy bits of horse news. "Comanche has taken to hanging with Hollywood, and David has added Kestrel, Juniper, and Madison to his family, which previously included just Shadow. No pix yet," she said in a typical post. She often refers to the constant horse drama she covers on her blog as "As the Basin Turns."

In 2011, a few years after she started the blog, the BLM brought in a helicopter for another roundup. The day of the roundup, the normally abandoned valley suddenly was transformed. About twenty protesters showed up from Telluride—a wealthy ski resort town two hours away. They waved signs and chanted slogans, saying the BLM was in the pocket of ranchers. They filed a lawsuit saying the roundup violated the Wild Free-Roaming Horses and Burros Act and a number of other federal laws. They brought along a documentary filmmaker in a leather vest to record the injustice. A small plane buzzed the area, at one point getting so close to the helicopter that the roundup was suspended for the day.

In the end, the roundup went forward, despite the protests. During a four-day operation, which netted fifty horses, Holmes watched the helicopter sweep indiscriminately through the valley, breaking up family bands. One stallion trying to escape broke his neck and was shot.

"It was brutal, horrible," said Holmes, remembering the scene. "And all those horse people had come out here and screamed and sued and it had done no good."

She became determined to avoid another roundup. She connected with two wild horse activists at the Pryor Mountains in Montana and in the nearby town of Grand Junction, where a few volunteers cared for a small herd in a desert rimrock area called the Little Book Cliffs Wild Horse Area.

In the Book Cliffs, volunteers had worked with the BLM to get rid of helicopter roundups. Instead, they used dart guns loaded with PZP to slow reproduction. The Book Cliffs herd only produced a handful of extra horses every few years, so instead of an expensive helicopter, they used a water trap to gather extras. This allowed the BLM to take only the horses it wanted— young, adoptable ones. No horses were going into the holding system from Little Book Cliffs. "It just made so much sense," Holmes said. "I didn't want to be just another advocate screaming that I hated what the BLM was doing. I wanted to change something."

She decided she would teach herself to shoot a dart gun and learn how this thing called PZP works. The decision led her in 2011 to the back lot of the zoo in Billings, Montana, where the reigning expert on PZP, Dr. Jay Kirkpatrick, offered classes on using the vaccine.

That is where I eventually went to learn about PZP, too.

A few weeks later, I was waiting outside Kirkpatrick's office in Billings when he pulled up, driving an ancient blue Subaru hatchback with a faded Cornell sticker on the back. In his early seventies, he was wearing a khaki uniform like a man on safari. He opened the door and pushed back the front seat to let out an equally ancient sheepdog that followed him into the building.

Kirkpatrick had short, gray hair parted neatly to the side, wire-framed glasses, and a number of one-liners well polished by having told the story of PZP to dozens of classes over the years. After shaking my hand, he put on his best fake sinister smile and told me, "I want you to become an emissary of PZP. Let the indoctrination begin."

Kirkpatrick is the accidental Johnny Appleseed of PZP. He is not a horse person, but he was motivated by his belief in wildness. In his decades of work with the substance, he has trained hundreds of people with a three-day course that explains the biology, politics, and practical application of PZP. It includes plenty of dart-gun practice.

On the morning I arrived, Kirkpatrick led me down a small hall in his lab to a room where his latest class was waiting. In a room filled with various models of dart guns sat three other students: a regional BLM wild horse manager Holmes had persuaded to take the class; a wildlife director at the Humane Society of the United States, which was using PZP on horses and urban deer; and a twenty-year-old woman with a baseball cap pulled down low over her eyes and camouflage fleece zipped up to her chin. Her mother, like TJ Holmes, had started darting a local herd. This one was in the McCullough Peaks, in the Bighorn Basin, near Cody, Wyoming.

"I really like to hunt," the woman said. "Since I like to shoot things, my mom said I should try doing it for good instead of just killing them."

"What do you like to hunt?" Kirkpatrick asked. The girl shrugged as she weighed how to word what could be a very long answer, then she smiled and said, "Food."

Next it was the BLM manager's turn. He had just moved from the Midwest to take over range management in the region that includes Disappointment Valley. The first person to show him around the wild horse herd was TJ Holmes. "So of course she told me all about PZP," he said, "and it makes sense. Right now, with these roundups we are just filling buckets and no one has turned off the spigot."

The woman from the Humane Society of the United States said her group saw PZP as extremely promising and planned to expand its efforts with the vaccine.

When it was Kirkpatrick's turn, he settled in for a long yarn that told the whole history of PZP. "I've been doing this for more than forty years," he said. "There is a lot to catch up on. It started in 1971, the same year the Wild Free-Roaming Horses and Burros Act was passed. I was a wet-behind-the-ears reproductive biologist, just a few years out of Cornell, and I had a job at Montana State University. One summer afternoon two BLM cowboys with sweaty hat bands and shit on their boots walked in."

One of the men was the manager of the Pryor Mountain Wild Horse Range, which roamed a windswept ridge not too far from Billings. The Pryor Mountain Range was created by a separate decree in 1968, before the 1971 law. The herd was starting to grow, and managers doubted they could find adopters for all the horses they wanted to remove. The manager asked Kirkpatrick whether there was any way to stop horses from reproducing.

For the reproductive biologist, it was an odd question. People had studied animal reproduction for centuries, but nearly all of their focus had been on how to increase reproduction, not how to put on the brakes. Kirkpatrick thought for a minute. He had grown up during the introduction of the birth control pill, so obviously he knew there was no physiological reason something couldn't be done. That no one had done it yet did not mean no one could. Not realizing that his answer would dominate his life for the rest of his career, he casually told the cowboys, "Yeah, I guess so."

Kirkpatrick and his good friend from grad school, John Turner, started working on the problem. First, they realized they had to learn something about how wild horse herds reproduce. The closest wild horse area was in the Pryor Mountains, about forty miles southwest of Billings, on an eighty-eight-hundred-foot windswept collision of mesas and ridges. Lewis and Clark had passed by the mountains in 1804, on their exploration of the West, and named the area after Nathaniel Pryor, a sergeant in the expedition who had gone south toward the mountains trying to recover horses stolen by the local Horse Nations. Wild horses have been living up in the Pryor Mountains—isolated from other herds—for as long as anyone could remember.

To Kirkpatrick and Turner, it seemed like the perfect place to understand the horse's reproductive dynamics. With his wife and Turner, he began spending summers in a one-room cabin in the

Pryors, studying behavior and reproduction rates. During the winters, they tried to come up with a practical strategy for birth control.

Their first attempt at controlling reproduction was to try vasectomies for dominant stallions—something Velma Johnston had suggested as an option in 1976, shortly before her death.[1] Their theory was that the snipped stallions would retain their harems of females but not reproduce. While the procedure worked, doing the surgeries in the field was too costly and controversial to be practical. Vasectomies were also less than ideal because they were not reversible. If a natural disaster wiped out too many horses, there was no way to reverse the fertility control.

Next they tried to make stallions infertile with high levels of testosterone. Horses tranquilized by dart from a helicopter were then given a huge dose of slow-release testosterone in a hip. It also worked. But the steroid was expensive and the use of the helicopter pushed the price beyond what the BLM could afford. The team also soon realized that focusing on one dominant stallion had little effect, because there is a lot of hanky-panky among the herds, and mares became pregnant anyway. "It was a pharmacological success and a practical failure," Kirkpatrick said.

After that, they turned to trying to control mares, testing different hormone treatments that worked much like human birth control pills. Still they ran into problems. Natural hormones, like the ones millions of women take daily, broke down quickly after being injected, providing only a few weeks' worth of contraception. Synthetics lingered in the food chain too long, meaning the effects could get passed on to other animals. One hormone they tried actually made the birth rate go up. "We tried so many things, but none of them really were acceptable," Kirkpatrick said.

In 1985, after years of work, Kirkpatrick and Turner were still trying to perfect hormone treatments when another researcher discovered a different approach—one that used a horse's own immune system as a contraceptive. Irwin Liu, an immunologist at the University of California at Davis, was working with a slaughterhouse byproduct called porcine zona pellucida, or PZP. Zona pellucida is a naturally occurring sticky protein that coats all mammal eggs and allows sperm to bind to the egg. It has a unique molecular structure that acts like locks that only sperm can fit. *Porcine* zona pellucida comes specifically from pigs' eggs. Dr. Liu found that the zona pellucida from pigs is different enough from a female horse's zona pellucida that, when injected into the horse's bloodstream, the horse immune system flags it as an outside pathogen. The immune system then begins producing antibodies to fight the foreign zona pellucida. The antibodies are designed to bind to the pathogen and neutralize it. But pig and horse zona pellucida are similar enough that the antibodies designed to bind to pig protein also bind to horse protein. The antibodies essentially jam the locks on the horse's eggs so no sperm can enter. No sperm, no foals.

To get a reaction, it takes only a small amount of PZP—a few drops that can easily be loaded into a small dart. The antibodies stay in the horse's system for about a year, after which the effects wear off, so PZP is reversible in case there is a sudden drop in population, but it lasts long enough that it can be applied with an annual dart.

To determine whether PZP could really work in a wild herd, Kirkpatrick and Turner needed an isolated test population. They found it in an unlikely spot, far from the wild horses of the West. Along the coast of Maryland and Virginia is a long, narrow strip of sand called Assateague Island. For as long as anyone can remember, wild horses have roamed the island's marshes. Locals say the horses—which records show have lived on the island since before the Revolutionary War—were marooned when a Spanish warship bound for Cuba was dashed on the beach by a storm. The National Park Service, which runs the thirty-seven-mile-long island as a national seashore, says the horses more likely are strays from early settlers. But, like most mustangs, they are both. Tests have found Spanish and domestic genes in the herd. Either way, they have lived wild for a very long time.

The Assateague horses became famous in 1947, when Marguerite Henry—the author who later wrote *Mustang: Wild Spirit of the West*, about Wild Horse Annie—published a book called *Misty of Chincoteague*, about a wild foal that grows up wild on the island and is captured by a pair of kids who befriend her, then eventually let her go because they see her yearning to be free. It's a simple story that sold more than two million copies and was made into a movie in 1961. No doubt it influenced many young people who later pushed for the 1971 law.

The wild horses on Assateague were protected by the National Park Service in the 1970s, but with no plan in place to limit population. By the late 1980s, the narrow island had 175 horses—more than the Park Service thought the sandy spit could handle. Kirkpatrick got a call from a ranger on the island, asking whether he could do anything to control the horse population.

"I didn't even know there were horses out there," Kirkpatrick said, recalling the conversation, but he said he would give it a try. An isolated island was the perfect test for PZP. In February 1988, he and Turner arrived on the island with a gun and a box of darts. The plan was to bring the population of 175 horses gradually down over several years to 100 and hold it there through annual darting. Each horse would get shots for three seasons, then be allowed to have a foal. That would allow the genetics to be passed down, while limiting growth of the herd.

Kirkpatrick and other researchers began sloshing through the marshes and crashing through the brush. At first it was easy. The horses were so used to tourists that the researchers could walk within ten yards, load a dart, and fire. But as the team started going back spring after spring, the horses got smarter. They started to recognize the men and remember the sting of his dart. They kept a wider and wider distance. The darters learned too, though. They began to feign a lack of interest. Kirkpatrick pretended to be a tourist clamming or bird-watching. He ambled toward each mare in a series of tangential sashays, until he was close enough to hit his mark. The team learned to recognize each horse, keeping a folder with the markings and age of each, and the date when they were darted. The herd stopped growing and gradually started to shrink. The data showed the drug was about 90 percent effective, and, just as important, a small group of people, or even one individual, could deliver it by dart. The cost was far lower than any other alternative, including roundups. The project continues to this day.

"It was the shot heard around the world," Kirkpatrick told the small class. "The first time anyone had controlled fertility in a wild population."

Kirkpatrick and his colleagues published their findings in the *Wildlife Society Bulletin* in 1990. Soon, he was getting calls from around the world from people who wanted to use PZP on elephants, elk, zebras, tapirs, bison, bongos, giraffes, and hippos, even bats. The need for controlling wild populations in the field stretched well beyond horses. He traveled the globe doing tests. "With cats it doesn't work," said Kirkpatrick "but with bats it works. And anything with a hoof, it seems to work."

Kirkpatrick founded The Science and Conservation Center in a back lot of the zoo in Billings to produce PZP from discarded pig ovaries and teach people how to use it. He invited wildlife managers from around the world to take his classes. Today, PZP is used in zoos,

African game parks, suburban deer herds, and a bison herd on California's Catalina Island.

For years, there was pushback from wild horse advocates who viewed PZP as potentially harmful to the wild herds. Research shows that PZP does have some impacts, but, on balance, negative effects seem negligible, and PZP may actually benefit herds. Kirkpatrick and other independent academic researchers found that mares that did not give birth every year because of PZP were in better condition and lived longer. They also found that mares treated with the vaccine generally spent their days the same way as untreated mares, though, as might be expected with no one pregnant, there was more time spent on what reports call "reproductive behavior."

Scientists also looked at whether the drug would destabilize bands as mares looking to get pregnant went to find new stallions, or stallions might be becoming more stressed and aggressive. Results have been mixed, with some researchers reporting more instability and others not. But even in studies where researchers did find some disruption in social structure among the herds, mares were healthier and lived longer.

Of course, it is wrong to claim that there are no effects from PZP. Whenever you interrupt a population in a way as profound as limiting reproduction, there will be broad consequences. But there are already consequences now imposed by years of helicopter roundups. Which method is less disruptive? Kirkpatrick bet on PZP. And so did a growing number of wild horse advocates.

Despite its widespread success, however, PZP has largely missed its intended target—the mustangs of Wild Horse Country. It's not that wild horse tests weren't promising. Turner and Liu gave PZP to several dozen mares captured by a BLM helicopter roundup in Nevada in 1992. Only five percent of the mares got pregnant in the next twelve months, compared to 50 percent of untreated mares.

The BLM knew for decades that rounding up horses and putting them in storage was a losing strategy. Its own advisory committees warned against storing horses and urged development of alternatives. In 1980 and again in 1985, a National Research Council study recommended using fertility control. It produced reports that showed treating a horse with PZP costs about $110 per year, and rounding up a horse and putting it in storage for the rest of its life costs about $50,000. In 2001, when the BLM persuaded Congress to double its budget so it could round up more horses to reach the elusive goal of twenty-seven thousand horses on the range, it did so in part by saying it planned to start aggressive use of PZP. BLM directors have repeatedly said they are changing their old ways and moving to PZP. But they never have—at least in any meaningful way.

The number of horses darted has always been too small to make a real difference. A herd might be darted one year, but not the next. Sometimes supplies of PZP weren't refrigerated, and became useless by the time they were injected. And the expertise to manage a herd over time was hard to maintain as federal employees came and went.

After years of having little luck with the BLM, a partial solution came knocking at Kirkpatrick's door. Certain herds were watched by admirers like TJ Holmes who were determined to end helicopter roundups. Those advocates had the will to push local managers and the knowledge to recognize individual horses as they were darted, so they could be recorded. A few of them came to Kirkpatrick asking for help. When their efforts proved successful, more came.

At the Little Book Cliffs Wild Horse Range in western Colorado in 2002, the US Geological Survey Biological Resources Division funded a small study of PZP. It started with injecting mares that had been rounded up by helicopter. Then two longtime wild horse watchers from nearby Grand Junction stepped forward and offered to start treating the mares with a dart gun. Reproduction rates in treated horses were soon cut by 75 percent. Volunteers have been darting the herd ever since. "We knew that area better than the BLM did," said Marty Felix, a retired elementary teacher who taught herself to shoot a dart gun, told me. "So we taught ourselves how to do it, and I think we've done pretty well."

Also in 2002, volunteers in the Pryor Mountains, led by a local man named Matt Dillon, began darting horses—though the program has attracted some controversy and it has not happened every year. From there, the use of PZP spread as people began to see results. In 2008, the Humane Society of the United States funded a test of a new slow-release version of PZP, called PZP-22, which would last two years. They darted horses in the Sand Wash Basin in Colorado—an effort volunteers continued even after the study concluded in 2012.

In 2011, a small group of citizens calling themselves Friends of a Legacy, or FOAL, who advocate for horses in the McCullough Peaks Herd Management Area of Wyoming, started pushing for PZP. They convinced their local BLM office that PZP would be cheaper than helicopter roundups, which, even in its small herd of about 140 horses, cost about $120,000 per roundup. Two women from the group trained with Kirkpatrick and started a program.

The same year, TJ Holmes posted this on her blog: "Read carefully: The Little Book Cliffs roundup this fall has been canceled. Canceled. Now ask 'why?'—and why am I doing a victory dance?" The reason, she said, was PZP. She was so impressed that she immediately began planning a similar program for the horses in Spring Creek Basin.

Volunteer groups inspired by the success of areas like Little Book Cliffs have continued to adopt PZP.

With the holding system near bursting, the Department of the Interior requested a review of its management program from the National Academy of Sciences to find an alternative that would help solve the problem. In 2013, the group published a 383-page report called *Using Science to Improve the BLM Wild Horse and Burro Program: A Way Forward.*

Its panel of experts, which studied the problem for two years, began the report with a quote from Lao-tzu: "A journey of a thousand miles begins with a single step." The report went on to say:

> It is clear that the status quo of continually removing free-ranging horses and then maintaining them in long-term holding facilities, with no foreseeable end in sight, is both economically unsustainable and discordant with public expectations. It is equally evident that the consequences of simply letting horse populations, which increase at a mean annual rate approaching 20 percent, expand to the level of "self-limitation"—bringing suffering and death due to disease, dehydration, and starvation accompanied by degradation of the land—are also unacceptable.

The report recommended the BLM start a fertility-control program immediately. (It's worth noting that the panel was not allowed to explore euthanizing horses.) Nearly all of the major wild horse advocacy groups backed the proposal, calling PZP "a cost-effective alternative to roundups and removals of wild horses from the range."

The BLM issued a statement, saying it "welcomed" the recommendations and planned to act. "The report will help the BLM build on the reforms that the agency has taken over the past several years to improve program effectiveness, such as the stepped-up use of fertility control," it said.

Then . . . it did nothing.

Grassroots groups kept expanding their efforts. In 2014, volunteers with Wild Love Preserve began darting horses in the Challis Herd Management Area in Idaho. In 2015, volunteers started darting horses in the Onaqui Herd Management Area in Utah. In 2016, the American Wild Horse Preservation Campaign and the Humane Society of the United States announced a five-year program focused on Nevada's Virginia Mountains—the same region where Velma Johnston got her start.

But the BLM actually decreased its use of PZP. In 2012, the BLM said it would inject a record two thousand mares. Instead, it treated only about 1,015. In 2013, it planned to treat far fewer: about nine hundred. But it only treated about five hundred. In 2014, it treated about 380. In 2015, it treated about four hundred. Just to hold population growth steady, the program would need to treat about thirteen thousand mares a year.

Why did the BLM do so little? Largely because it was stuck in a cycle of roundups. By 2013, when the report was released, there were forty-seven thousand horses in the holding system, eating up most of the budget that would be needed to scale up a big fertility-control program. Making problems worse, the BLM views the use of dart guns as impossible in large herd areas where there is little cover. To apply PZP, it says, it must still round up horses with helicopters and inject them by hand. That cuts the savings of using PZP.

There were also potential legal challenges in herd areas where horses were already over the prescribed population. In 2015, ranchers took the BLM to court for planning to release horses it had just treated with PZP. Try telling a rancher in a valley where the horse population is six hundred horses over the limit that you are not going to round up horses and instead are going to start a darting program that could take a decade. A rancher like Joe Fallini might say, "I'll see you in court."

When I met with Dean Bolstad, the director of the BLM's Wild Horse and Burro Program, in 2016, he said he wanted to use more PZP or other fertility-control drugs—a lot more. But they were still impractical. Darting mares every year was too much work. They needed a drug that lasted five years, not one. Kirkpatrick's longtime colleague, John Turner, was trying to make a longer-lasting version of PZP that would meet the need, but it had not yet been proven effective enough to fit BLM goals.

That could soon change. In recent years John Turner has been working on making a long-lasting PZP vaccine, and found that darting horses with PZP-22, then regular PZP a few years later, offered a longer period of infertility. The combination produced about four years of contraception in a six-year period.

More than anything, though, the BLM was getting pressure from ranchers.

"We can't leave horses on the land, they are overpopulated," Bolstad told me. "We have to gather."

He also didn't think shooting horses with darts was practical in most of Wild Horse Country. "You might be able to sneak up on a horse in Colorado," he said, "but try doing it in Nevada. You can't get within 200 yards."

I actually have my doubts about that, especially since horses have to come to a few places in the desert to drink. It would be possible to set up blinds near springs and dart the horses as they came to drink.

Sitting in his office after teaching the class how to shoot a dart gun, Kirkpatrick looked back at the twenty-five years of inaction by the BLM that followed his successful application of PZP at Assateague. He shook his head. "The BLM is still staffed by cowboys," he said. "And cowboys have a certain way of doing things. They want to round things up. Practically, PZP was a success. Politically, it has been a total failure."

In December 2015, Jay Kirkpatrick died of cancer. He was seventy-five. The last time I met him, a few years before his death, he was pessimistic about the future of wild horses and wild animals in general. I asked him for predictions about the years ahead. Human populations would continue to grow, he said. Resources would become increasingly scarce. Wide-open spaces for large animals would disappear.

"I just don't see how the horse can win in all that," he said. But then he grinned and added, "But we can try."

That seems to be the strategy of the grassroots groups on the ground now. They are scraping together funds and training volunteers to fire darts. They have had successes persuading the BLM to give them a hand in management. But increasingly, they are facing an unexpected obstacle: other wild horse advocates.

A number of people oppose management of wild horses in almost all forms, and refuse to support PZP. A Connecticut-based group called Friends of Animals has become the leader of the opposition, teaming up with a small but vocal organization out of Berkeley called Protect Mustangs. Friends of Animals had not been involved in wild horse advocacy before, but in 2015 it went all in.

That year it sued the BLM over a proposal to use PZP in Nevada's Pine Nut Mountains Herd Management Area. The project had the backing of all the major wild horse groups, and had volunteers lined up, but Friends of Animals successfully argued in court that the BLM had not done its planning paperwork properly. The BLM canceled plans to dart, and instead in 2016 asked the volunteers to dart the horses in the nearby Fish Springs area. Friends of Animals sued again. In court, its lawyer argued that allowing private citizens to dart mares with guns constituted "harassment," which is forbidden by the 1971 law. It was also ready to argue that the behavior changes seen among mares darted with PZP violated the management guidelines of the law. Rather than fight a precedent-setting legal battle that could end all use of PZP, the bureau suspended the Fish Springs project. In the summer of 2016, Friends of Animals sued again, this time to revoke regulatory approval for PZP, which it calls a "restricted use pesticide," ending all PZP projects in Fish Springs.

Friends of Animals also lambasted the BLM at public meetings. At a Wild Horse and Burro Program advisory board meeting in Nevada in 2016, the group's "campaign director," a willowy young vegetarian from Manhattan, stood up and laid into the agency. "We are disgusted with sitting in these meetings year after year and hearing this nonsense," she said. "We will continue fighting legally to challenge roundups, to challenge [the] PZP Frankenstein monster show and we will continue and continue and continue to show up and we will not be silenced. . . . We are not here to beg or plead for the BLM to do the right thing, because we already know it is a hopelessly corrupt agency that acts as an extension of the meat industry."

Men in the audience yelled for her to sit down. Someone yelled, "Cut off her mic!" An armed officer escorted her out as she yelled, "BLM lies! Horses die!"

For TJ Holmes, PZP was an attempt to avoid the type of controversy now being stoked by Friends of Animals. Protest is easy, she acknowledged, but finding policy that works is a lot harder. PZP is far from perfect, but right now, she said, it is the best option, and she sees tracking and darting horses in Disappointment Valley as an act of love and dedication, not harassment.

Holmes hoped to end the pointless protests and wasted money that roundups created so that the local BLM could focus on managing the land. It seemed to be working. Before she started darting in Spring Creek Basin in 2011, the local herd had thirteen surviving foals. The next year, they had nine foals. The next year, three foals. She hopes she never again sees a helicopter in the area.

The boundaries of the Spring Creek Herd Management Area are outlined with barbed wire and natural barriers. Forage is limited.

Water is scarce. But if Holmes and a few other volunteers can keep the population stable, life will be a little easier for the herd.

"In the beginning, I said I'd never dart my horses. They know me, they trust me, I'm their friend," she said. We stood watching a band of seven mustangs grazing a hundred meters away. "But it is the only way. These guys have so little here. If it is destroyed, they're gone. People like to think we can just let them run wild. But I don't think we live in that world anymore. I don't think we have a choice."

There is no doubt PZP works. And no doubt that small groups of people can use it effectively to manage wild horse herds. Or that doing so can save millions of dollars. But after learning about how it is used to control wild horses, I was left uninspired. Other longtime voices in the wild horse world that I talked to agreed. Almost everyone thought it was the best option, but no one really liked it. The vaccine may be practical, but it is not beautiful. It relies too much on human interference. The wild horse of myth must be independent. But the real wild horse is equal parts animal and myth, both flesh and legend. That has been the tension since the 1971 law was passed. How can you protect the myth but still manage the flesh? PZP takes care of the flesh, but in the process it contaminates our notion of what is wild and free. We love wild horses because they are not managed, not controlled, not tainted. We love them because the White Stallion can't be caught. Take that away and the wild horse is just livestock.

CHAPTER 10

A WILD SOLUTION

O n a sweltering June afternoon, I walked off the jet bridge at the airport in Las Vegas on the hunt for a solution for wild horses that did not involve helicopters or slaughter or sticking them with PZP—something that could limit the herds without poisoning the legend. A huge mural running along the wall of the terminal showed a desert tableau of red cliffs and distant lavender mountains. On a rise stood three wild horses, their ears up, their eyes fixed on the horizon, as if scanning for predators. Just below, methodical retirees, as pale and pudgy as bread dough, plunked quarters into banks of slot machines. Some of those quarters, too, likely had images of wild horses on them. Nevada's official state quarter, released in 2006, has three mustangs galloping across a mountainscape. As I drove out of the airport onto I-15, more wild horses galloped past in the form of public sculpture along the highway.

The legend of the wild horse was not dead yet, I thought.

Urbanites in Nevada love wild horses. The state is a microcosm of the country. Residents of Las Vegas and Reno—people who for the most part grew up somewhere else and moved here recently—see mustangs as a symbol of freedom and a proud and unique mascot for the state. Residents of the state's rural counties hate the horses. They overwhelmingly see them—and the people in Las Vegas, for that matter—as pests, and they would sooner put a pack rat on the state quarter.

I drove north through downtown into a landscape that aptly traced the stark polarity of this divide. On the north end of Las Vegas, as I crept through stop-and-go traffic, an armada of billboards and fast-food logos sailed above swells of suburban stucco. Then the city suddenly ended. One block was dense humanity, the next nothing but creosote and Joshua trees spilling out into the distance. The traffic was gone. I was hemmed in only by rough, dark, roadless mountains and a timeless desert.

I was on my way north to a lonely ridge on the border between California and Nevada, where I hoped to find an answer to the wild horse question. The place was called Montgomery Pass. From what I could tell, it offered a promising solution—or at least the seed of one. It wasn't PZP. It wasn't selling to slaughter buyers. It seemed to have the potential to make both horse advocates and the BLM happy. It would cost almost nothing, and the means to make it happen was already there. Best of all, it would preserve the legend that prompted us to save wild horses in the first place. Despite all this, no one seemed to be paying any attention to it. In fact, if anything, it was something the country was actively working to undermine.

The solution is mountain lions.

Just saying that, I know, has cost me the attention of nearly everyone who has ever been involved in wild horse management, either on the citizen side or the government. To anyone who has been around awhile, it sounds laughably naive. For decades, the BLM has said the wild horse has "no natural predators." The big National Academy of Sciences report that came out in 2013 con-

WILD HORSES NEAR ELKO, NEVADA.

cluded that "the potential for predators to affect free-ranging horse populations is limited by the absence of abundance of such predators as mountain lions and wolves" in Herd Management Areas. It is something newcomers to the issue almost invariably suggest, and it has become a reliable indication of ignorance of the issue. The idea has been proposed to the BLM by citizens and dismissed outright so many times that even mentioning it causes an almost reflexive eye roll. If a panel of top scientists has dismissed it, why give it more thought?

But the same people who have long dismissed using predators to control horses as impossible have never made an attempt to understand it. They have likely been too busy rounding up and storing horses. If they took the time to look into the idea of mountain lions, they would soon see that research on the ground contradicts the conventional wisdom.

The road out of Las Vegas took me into the heart of Wild Horse

Country, past repeated signs warning that the next gas was 50 miles, 80 miles, 110 miles away. The thermometer in the car reached 109 degrees. I drove for hours, getting deeper into the nothing. Here and there, a few boarded-up bordellos sat in the wind in empty valleys where it's a wonder anyone ever found the staff, let alone customers. I crossed a few mountain ranges where small towns once had sprung up around silver mines. Time and the desert had reduced them to stone foundations in the sage. As I passed one, a gang of three coyote pups darted across the road, jumping and grinning, as if they had won. Maybe no other place in the United States has so often shrugged off the attempts of civilization and remained its wild self.

Near dusk, I drove around the north shoulder of Boundary Peak, on the California border. The sun was low, and though it was June, thick robes of snow still hung on steep shoulders of the summit, glowing pink in the fading light. As I came around its side, I dropped into a broad bowl of sage and grass with high hills hemming in all sides. This was Montgomery Pass. The road was lonely. There was no traffic—a single ribbon of asphalt that cut through a valley with no houses, no ranches, no trees, no nothing. Wild Horse Country. I slowed my car and scanned the brush. I was searching for a dirt track cutting off to the south toward a cluster of sandstone cliffs. I had been told that if I found it, I would find a scientist I was looking for named Dr. John Turner.

Turner had been studying wild horses and their interactions with mountain lions in the region for thirty years. He knew more than anyone about whether predators could really be part of the solution for wild horses. When I called him at his office in Ohio, he had invited me to visit his summer field camp and see for myself.

Just before it got too dark to see the side of the road, I spotted a ramshackle 1970s trailer off in the sage. I swung off the paved road and bumped my little rental car gingerly up a two-track path, scraping more times than I'd like to admit. At the base of the cliffs, a man came out from behind the trailer wearing dirty blue surgical scrubs and a sun-bleached old dress shirt that was unbuttoned and flapping in the evening breeze. He had a wild beard, a faded bandanna, and a single gold ring in his ear. The whole getup made him look a bit like a pirate who had escaped from a psychiatric hospital. Maybe I had the wrong place, I thought.

"We were getting worried that you wouldn't find it," the man said.

I had found Dr. John Turner.

The name may sound familiar. John Turner was the longtime friend and colleague of Jay Kirkpatrick, the Johnny Appleseed of PZP. He spends the cold months in a lab trying to refine the fertility drugs and the warm months trying to understand the natural relationship of predator and prey in the hills that could make fertility drugs less necessary.

The John Turner I encountered in hospital scrubs and a faded bandanna was John Turner in field-biology mode. He spends most of the year teaching physiology and sexual reproduction at the University of Toledo's medical school. There, he wears crisp ties and ironed shirts. But every summer since 1987, he has ditched the tie, said good-bye to the med school, and headed west to study horses, camping out under the stars near Montgomery Pass.

Over the years, he adopted a number of practical desert-rat habits. The lightweight cotton scrubs and old, threadbare shirts were ideal, he found, for warding off the sun and the biting insects that are a constant presence in Wild Horse Country. They also keep him cool. The bandanna was good for sopping up sweat and keeping his hair from going too feral between showers. The gold hoop earring he wore year-round. "Keeps me from becoming an administrator," he said with a grin.

Not becoming an administrator kept his summers free to come

back to Montgomery Pass, something high on his priority list. "This is a special place," he said as he welcomed me into his small camp, where we settled into lawn chairs.

We looked out from a parapet of sandstone cliffs into a broad, empty valley. Nighthawks floated like kites in the last lavender of dusk. Beyond the valley, low mountains cloaked in juniper and piñon looked like dark swells rising from the sea. Beyond them was the jagged tooth of Boundary Peak, its ridges and couloirs clear in their details, though it was nearly twenty miles away. A high cloud stood like a banner ten thousand feet over the summit, catching the fiery light of sunset long after we were in shadow.

"It's so massive," Turner said as he looked at the sweep of desert and mountains. "It's so separated from the human effort." He is not a horse person, but a person who treasures wildness.

As we sat, Turner told me a little about how he ended up spending a good part of his life in the valley. It started in a bar in Idaho in 1971, where Turner and Kirkpatrick had stopped to get a cold drink after a backpacking trip. As they drank their beers, they heard a group of ranchers at the bar complaining about the numbers of wild horses, about how they weren't allowed to gather them anymore, and about what they should do. It was a fascinating puzzle for two reproductive biologists out of Cornell.

"We didn't start work on it until about 1973, but it got us thinking about the issue," he told me. In the years afterward, Turner and Kirkpatrick worked together on the long string of failures in Montana before discovering PZP and testing it on Assateague Island.

"It was an interesting time," he said. "No one had really ever thought of trying to use fertility control on wildlife."

When Turner first came to Montgomery Pass in the 1980s, he thought it would be to continue the fertility-control research that he and Kirkpatrick had been doing for a decade. He had been presenting at a wildlife conference in Australia when a veterinarian (who oddly enough lived near Montgomery Pass) pulled him aside. The veterinarian's family led pack trips into the mountains of Montgomery Pass to watch wild horses. There were about 190 horses in the region, and the BLM was fixing to round up much of the herd, leaving only about seventy-five animals. The veterinarian wanted to know whether there was any way to avoid it.

"Could you see if you can use fertility control in our area?" the veterinarian asked.

Turner was eager to find a new place to test fertility control, and he said he would take a look. He came to Montgomery Pass in the summer of 1985. His plan was to begin by just studying the population dynamics of the herd. He had to learn how the horses lived and how fast the population was growing before he could design a program to try to slow their reproduction.

He got to know the place by going out into the hills with some of the area's longtime buckaroos, who had worked the region for decades and even done a bit of mustanging before the Wild Free-Roaming Horses and Burros Act was passed.

On one of his first nights there, he and his guide, a particularly leathery old fellow, threw their sleeping bags down under the stars near a spring in the hills above the pass. It was a remote place, hours up a rough Jeep road. "There's a lot of mountain lions in these hills," the old buckaroo said as they bedded down. Before a slightly startled Turner could respond, the buckaroo added, "There's some people who'll say you have to be afraid of them, but they're real shy. You'd have to sleep naked wrapped in bacon to have any trouble."

The buckaroo grinned and looked sideways to see the city-slicker scientist's face. Then he continued on a more serious note. "Don't worry. We hardly ever even see a lion. Once in a while, you'll find a mustang colt that looks like it was a lion kill, but that's about it."

Turner nestled into his sleeping bag and looked out at the dark trees and stars, not yet realizing that the cowboy had just mentioned something that would occupy him for decades. Over the next few years, he returned each summer to study the population so he could design a management regime. But he soon stumbled on something he had not seen before. There was no population growth. The wild population in the region was actually holding steady. And it appeared that mountain lions were keeping the population in check.

"The BLM was saying there was overpopulation and there was actually underpopulation, because the mountain lions were just going crazy. This was something totally new," he told me. "The old timers around here knew cats were hunting horses, but no one in the scientific community really realized it was happening, or that it *could* happen."

The morning after I arrived, Turner took me out to the place that had long maintained a steady herd with no interference at all. We started in a level expanse aptly called Adobe Flats. It was broad valley penned in on all sides by empty mountains. The rose-colored soil was dry and powdery, but you could easily imagine that, when wet, it would turn to a slick clay that could eventually dry as hard as adobe brick. Tufts of sage dotted the flats and feathery rice grass grew in sheltered nooks.

We stopped the car along a small dirt road and got out. In front of us was a stone corral, built by hand. It was about fifty feet across and perfectly round, with thick, strong walls high enough that a tall man could just peek over them. Compared to the standard wood-slat corral, this was a fortress. No ranch hand would bother building something so time-consuming for cattle. It was an old mustangers' trap—not a relic of the dog-food era, when mustangers would truck animals off to slaughter, but one from the days when the divide between man and wild was not so wide, and residents of the Great

Basin depended on the bounty of the land for what went under their saddle. Just like the gathering traps of today, the corral had no corners where horses could pile up and be trampled. In the middle was a snubbing post used to saddle break horses.

"Look at this," Turner said, motioning to me as he walked through the sage. He stopped at a swift creek, maybe a yard across, pulsing through the sage. "There is water here, there is good grass, it's a perfect place for horses. The old-timers must have known that."

Two miles to the north, the flat weft of sage warped upward into a dark range of mountains that rose nearly two thousand feet above the valley. The geologic brow was covered with small evergreens and creased with canyons and crags. That was Montgomery Pass. There were no lions in Adobe Flats. The plain offered them nowhere to hide and nowhere to hunt, but the mountains above provided uncounted ambush sites, and often when horses went in, a few didn't come out.

We got in the car and headed up through the sage toward the hills.

Mountain lions are perhaps the most adaptive big predators the world has ever produced. Among mammals in the Americas, their range and flexibility are probably exceeded only by humans. In part because of this, they have more names than almost any other animal: cougar, panther, painter, mountain lion, wildcat, catamount, puma. In Wild Horse Country, people most familiar with mountain lions usually call them simply lions—a fitting nickname, because mountain lions are found not only in the mountains but also in thorny desert canyons, rain forests, steamy swamps, and snowy subarctic forests. Before the settlement of the United States, they lived in every state from Florida to Maine to California. In recent years, one has even taken up residence in a park in Los Angeles.

They now remain in about fifteen states, but they appear to be expanding back into parts of the East. As is obvious as soon as you spot one licking its paws or switching its tail, they are more closely related to house cats than to lions and tigers. They also are easily America's most stunning hunter. One study found they consume about ten thousand pounds of prey a year. They are able and willing to kill almost anything: deer, of course, but also elk and moose, coyotes, raccoons, rabbits, birds, even porcupines. The Los Angeles lion stands accused of killing one of the local zoo's koalas.

They range in weight from 100 to about 180 pounds. Though they are about the same mass as humans, their heart rate is twice as high and their lung capacity is much smaller. They are sprinters, not marathoners, made for a quick lunge. At a dead run, deer can easily outpace them, so they rely on ambush. They crouch, a silent coiled trap of tooth and bone ready to spring. Their haunches are piled with muscle for an explosive forward dash. A lion can jump twenty feet in a single bound.

Once they close the distance, their technique is simple and time-tested: Jump on the back, anchor in with hooklike claws, bite the neck. A lion has daggerlike canines more than an inch long. Behind them is a gap allowing each tooth to sink to the bone. The teeth act as wedges, finding the gaps between the top few vertebrae and forcing them apart. The spine is severed and the prey goes limp. The whole operation can last mere seconds.

For me, the most powerful testament to the lion's stealth is this: In the decades I've spent roaming the West, I have probably clocked thousands of days in remote mountains and deserts, on lonely trails at dusk and dawn, often by myself. I live on a steep road on the edge of the Rockies, where a number of mountain lions prowl the neighborhood. A neighbor's infrared game camera sometimes catches them at night. Over the years, I've stumbled upon lynx, bobcats, wolves, ringtails, and all manner of other elusive critters. I have seen the torn and bloody deer limbs that lions have left after kills in the hills. I have stopped in my tracks at the strong scent males use to mark their territory. I've even awakened in a remote red-rock canyon after a rainy night to find a cat's broad tracks pressed into the damp, red sand all around my camp. No doubt lions have seen me. But I have never seen them—not even a shadow disappearing into the brush.

Mountain lions are just as invisible in the world of wild horse management. They are prowling all around and through it, but no one seems to be able to see them. The Bureau of Land Management is in a curious position when it comes to the animals on its land. It controls livestock, but not wildlife. Wildlife is overseen either by states or by the US Fish and Wildlife Service. The bureau controls the management of the wild horses, but not the management of the predators stalking them. So, in the management of wild horses, the influence of lions has never been considered. The bureaucratic divide keeps it from happening. In the beginning, the BLM was largely staffed by ranchers, not wildlife biologists, and they have always taken a ranchmen's approach to management. Study mountain lions? For generations, they had been trying to ensure the only thing they studied in mountain lions was bullet holes. Because of this, when John Turner showed up at Montgomery Pass, almost nothing was known about how mountain lions and wild horses interact.

"It was just a total disconnect between wildlife and wild horses," Turner told me, as we drove along the mountains. It isn't just a bias on the part of the BLM, he said. Wildlife biologists who study wildlife often view feral horses as a corruption to the natural system that is more likely to disrupt an ecosystem than become a part of it. They avoid studying them, too. So the amount of research on the relationship between wild horses and predators is very thin. "People don't really see them as part of anything," Turner said.

Since the 1970s, when the BLM realized that wild horse herds were increasing, it has said the same thing over and over: "The wild horse has no natural predators."

"The lack of natural predators is the reason for the growth spurt," a BLM range conservationist told the Associated Press in 1976, when the bureau was first starting to look at population control. "Only the mountain lion attacks the horses, but it is not believed to kill many." What he forgot to tell the reporter is that he actually had no data to support his assertion.

The BLM is still saying basically the same thing today, with the same lack of data. I've heard it from at least three BLM wild horse specialists in the field: The wild horse has no natural predators. Sure, occasionally a lion might take down a horse in Colorado or Utah, they say, but most horses are too big, and in the desert, where most of them live, the land is too open for lions to hunt.

What Turner and his team of researchers found totally upends this thinking. In 1987, Turner hired lion hunters with dogs to go out tracking in the hills of Montgomery Pass at dawn, looking for fresh lion signs. When the dogs hit on a scent, they would race off after a lion, eventually cornering it in a tree. Once a lion is treed, hunters generally finish it off with a large handgun. Instead, Turner shimmied up into the branches close enough to jab the lion in the haunch with a tranquilizer.

Each lion then got a radio collar. For five years, Turner's team tracked their movements, plotting where they went and what they killed. A clear pattern emerged that showed the BLM's basic assumption was wrong: Horses *do* have natural predators, and mountain lions can have a significant impact on horse populations. True, as the BLM says, horses are generally too big for a mountain lion to take down, and lions stand little chance of catching a horse in the open. But by tracking their collars, Turner discovered a secret strategy that lions had known for eons. Every spring, the horses of Montgomery

Pass would move from Adobe Flats up into the hills, in search of green grass, cooler temperatures, and reliable water.

Water is rare in much of the West, especially in the dusty corners into which the wild horses have been swept. You can forget lakes and rivers, or even ponds and streams. In much of Wild Horse Country, water appears only as springs that bubble up and trickle a few feet before being sucked up by the sand. The hills of Montgomery Pass had seven permanent springs. Though the region comprises more than 100,000 acres, the springs, when combined, would maybe cover only a single acre. Nearly all of the region's wildlife had to pass through this tiny bottleneck. That is where the lions waited.

Turner and I drove up as far as we could get onto the pass. On either side, the rolling hills held a jumble of boulders and pines, with feathery grass growing in between.

"This is good lion country," said Turner. "The horses don't like to come up here if they don't have to. They would rather be out in the open. But to get grass and water, they will come."

On average during the study, five lions lived in the hills, both males and females. Turner found that they would crouch along the trails leading into the springs, then pounce. But the lions did not go for just any horse—they waited for the foals. Just as the herd moved up from wintering grounds in the valley in April through June, mares began to have their babies. The foals were smaller, weaker, slower. Examining kills, Turner's crew found the same pattern over and over: foals killed within a few hundred yards of water. Some years, nearly two-thirds of the young were eaten.

"You would have some lions eating a foal every other week or so," Turner said.

The pattern continued every summer until the fall, when the foals got too big for most lions to tackle and the horse herds retreated to their winter grounds in the valley below. After that, the lions would switch prey, going after deer during the winter and spring. When summer came, they would switch back again.

In more than five thousand hours of fieldwork, Turner and his team tracked the mountain lion population and the horse population. The horse herd started at about 140 horses and rose to almost 160 horses over five years (a 4 percent annual increase, versus the 15 to 20 percent annual increase typically seen in herds without predators). Then, over the next five years, the population decreased 37 percent, to about a hundred animals. Then it began slowly to climb again. The mountain lion population mirrored the horse population.

None of this would have been obvious without rigorous research. Mountain lions are so stealthy that even when they bring down a horse, people rarely see any evidence of them unless they are actively searching. In all his years tracking lions, Turner only saw one of the lions he collared after their initial capture. Though his team was carefully watching the springs, they only witnessed one lion attack on a horse.

"We were totally caught off guard," he said. "The thinking was that lions might catch a horse once in a while, but that it was unusual. We found the lions really relied on horses. Mothers were teaching their kittens to hunt horses. And it was having a real, lasting impact on the population."

That mountain lions hunt horses shouldn't really come as a surprise. Before Clovis hunters showed up about fifteen thousand years ago, horses were part of North America's prehistoric Serengeti—that crowd of mammoths, mastodons, giant sloths, and strange ancient also-rans like giant beavers and car-size armadillos. The continent's herbivores were hunted by just as varied a troupe of carnivores: 150-pound wolves, saber-toothed cats, two-thousand-pound short-faced bears. In that group of meat-eaters was *Puma concolor*, the cat of one color, the American mountain lion. Fossils of big cats are notoriously scant, making it hard to reconstruct the lions of ancient times, but DNA analysis suggests mountain lion ancestors came over the Bering Land Bridge about eight million years ago and settled into life in North America right when horse species, large and small, proliferated in the plains and forests of the continent.

Like species of the horse family before it, the mountain lion family evolved to fill North America's varied landscapes. On the open grasslands, it formed the genus *Miracinonyx*, which was long and lean, with a shortened face and sprinters' legs that made it look very similar to the modern cheetah. They likely hunted horses, just as modern cheetahs hunt zebras on the Serengeti. That cheetahlike lion went extinct with North American horses about ten thousand years ago. The mountain lion that is still with us stuck to forests and canyons where it could rely on ambush. What mountain lions hunted millions of years ago is lost to the fossil record, but it's not a stretch to assume that, over the last eight million years, they ate a lot of horses. It's also not a stretch to assume that a predator–prey relationship evolved, so that predation by the mountain lion shaped the horse and the horse shaped the mountain lion. More than a dozen mountain lions have been found preserved, along with horses and hundreds of other beasts, in the La Brea Tar Pits in Southern California. Researchers who analyzed microscopic variations in their teeth theorized that the reason the mountain lion survived extinction, when most prehistoric North American big cats did not, is because it was a generalist. It could switch prey easily and often did. When the horse became extinct, it switched to deer. It is no surprise that when horses returned, so did the lion's appetite for them.

You might think that a government agency with a horse population problem would be pounding on researchers' doors to find out more about how mountain lions control horses. But since John Turner published his first findings in 1992, the BLM has showed almost no interest. It has neither spent its own money researching predators nor encouraged independent researchers to do so. The agency does not even know how many of the West's wild horse Herd Management Areas have mountain lions, let alone how many horses lions kill each year.

To be sure, the BLM has been busy rounding up and storing horses. So it is hardly surprising that it has failed to seek out a hard-to-see management potential of lions. But the BLM also repeatedly ignored evidence when others stumbled across it. In one study after another, researchers tracking wild horses in the Great Basin have come across significant numbers of lion kills. Each time, the impact was significant enough that scientists trying to study other aspects of horses were astounded.

For nine years, two researchers tracked a herd at the weapons-testing range south of the Fallinis' Twin Springs Ranch to determine population growth. As with Montgomery Pass, the horses migrated up into rugged, treed country in the summer. The team saw a steady decline in the herd size over the years, driven by deaths of foals. During their studies, they saw three injured foals and two confirmed kills by lions, but mostly foals just tended to disappear. The researchers theorized that lions had the main impact on population growth.[1]

The BLM took no interest.

In 2005, a University of Nevada graduate student started tracking horses in the Virginia Mountains near the California border to document the effects of PZP on horses. She soon noticed that often when she went out into the field, she found the remains of foals near water holes. She eventually trapped a 130-pound female mountain lion, fitted it with a radio collar, and tracked it for ten months. She found that horses made up 77 percent of the lion's diet. Mule deer made up just 13 percent. The lion also appeared to be actively training her kittens to hunt horses.[2]

The BLM did nothing with the findings.

In 2004, in Montana's Pryor Mountains, the BLM was just a year into a program to control the horse population with PZP when darting had to be suspended because mountain lions had apparently eaten all of that year's foals. The bureau eventually resumed darting a few years later, but it did nothing to study how to encourage mountain lions to limit the herd. In fact, just the opposite happened. The state of Montana encouraged lion hunting in the area to protect a nearby bighorn sheep herd it had introduced in the 1970s. Private hunters shot an average of two lions in the area each year. After 2004, when the wild horse population began increasing again, the BLM did nothing to encourage the return of lions. In a 2006 report on environmental factors affecting the herd, the agency flatly stated: "The BLM is not responsible for managing predators through hunting."

In 2012, a research team at the University of Nevada at Reno—motivated by the fact that most mountain lion information available in the state was limited to how many lions had been shot—began studying the habits of mountain lions statewide. "Our preliminary results indicate that wild horses are an important source of food for cougars in Nevada, and being taken in proportion to mule deer," they concluded.[3]

In northern Arizona, just a few miles outside of Kingman, on historic Route 66, is a chain of scrubby desert ridges known as the Cerbat Mountains, which rise three thousand feet above the valley floor. For as long as anyone can remember, about seventy horses have grazed the thorny slopes in small family bands. The mustangs are small and stocky, usually less than fifteen hands high. They are genetically the most purely Spanish herd in any wild horse area in America, according to tests done by Texas A&M geneticist Gus

Cothran. Over the generations, the population has stayed stable. It expands and contracts, depending on drought and other factors, but there has not been the unchecked growth seen in many herds. The BLM has never done a roundup in the Cerbat.

The BLM says the steady population is probably kept in check by a healthy mountain lion population, but that is about the extent of the understanding. The BLM has never done any formal counts of the herd. The BLM has never studied the predator–prey dynamics here, nor has anyone else. They can't explain why the Cerbat herd holds steady when other herds in desert areas have growing populations. In a way, places such as the Cerbat are like the good children ignored while parents are consumed with the bad ones. The BLM is too focused on removing horses to pay attention to places that don't need removals. But ignoring places like the Cerbat, or the Virginia Mountains, or Montgomery Pass, is a mistake, because these places likely have important lessons for the management of Wild Horse Country.

And good management is critical. If we can move away from roundups, we can move away from storing horses. If we can move away from storing horses, we can move away from the corrosive effects it has had on the integrity of the BLM and the rule of law. If we can find a way to manage in balance, we can protect the animals, the ranchers, and the legend.

And understanding how to manage for mountain lions is vital. Small decisions can change the balance and have broad consequences. John Turner has seen it happen in the last few years at Montgomery Pass. For years, when Turner was studying the herd, the best grassland in Adobe Flats in the winter range below the mountains was fenced off, because it was being leased from the BLM to graze cattle. It is flat, open, and fed by permanent streams and springs that nourish a lush, eighteen-hundred-acre emerald carpet of grasses and forbs. Wild horses likely gazed longingly at this forage, but it was out of bounds to them. So as summer came, they headed into the hills.

In 2006, the rancher with the lease stopped using the Adobe Flats pasture, and the fence fell into disrepair. Horses that had been nibbling on scraggly grass from between sagebrush outside of the fence moved in. Because they now had year-round water and grass, the herds no longer had to go up into the hills in the summer. And because they didn't go up into the hills, they didn't face predation by mountain lions. The lion population decreased and the horse population started growing—from 43 in the valley in 2005 to 180 in 2011.

In 2016, when I arrived at the spot with John Turner, bands of horses dotted the broad lawn of the cattle lease, grazing and swishing their tails. Young studs gamboled and fought, stallions herded their mares with heads down and ears back. Turner lifted his binoculars and scanned. His mouth moved as he counted silently: 353 horses.

"That's a huge increase. I can't blame them for being here. There is everything a horse could want," he said. "But you can see how one little change can have a big impact."

He had tried to talk the BLM into managing the horses in a way that would move them back up to the mountains in the summers, but the response had been tepid. Turner tried asking a rancher in the area to try to move the horses by turning on and off a series of water sources that would encourage horses over time to move from the flats up to the hills. The rancher, he said, did not want wild horses at his troughs. Now, the herds are continuing to grow, and there are only one or two mountain lions left in the hills. The balance Turner had documented for decades has faded away for want of a little barbed wire.

"They are probably going to start roundups here again," he said. "I wish they would just try to realize what is going on."

Clearly the predation happening at Montgomery Pass is not happening all over Wild Horse Country. If it were, there would be no need for roundups. But why are the interactions between lions and mustangs not more common? One reason is that the same group of stock raisers and government agencies that tried to exterminate the mustang during the dog-food era also did their best to wipe out the mountain lion. Predators were a threat to sheep and cattle. The ranchers wanted them gone in the name of progress, and the Departments of Agriculture and Interior were happy to help. As with horses, the eradication effort started with local bounties offered by ranchers, then grew to state programs. The first efforts started in the 1870s, and the value steadily grew. In 1888, Utah labeled the lion an "obnoxious animal" and set a $5 bounty. In 1915, a Denver newspaper was offering $25 per lion. The state later raised it to $50. By 1920, the Colorado Stock Growers Association publicly announced its goal of hunting mountain lions to extinction.

Just as the wild horse became the "range robber," eating grass that should be given to livestock, the mountain lion was seen as a drain on the system, an impediment to progress, or, as the Arizona Territorial Legislature called it, an "undesirable predator." What was wild was deemed inherently disruptive for stock raising and needed to be purged. Wolves, grizzly bears, mountain lions, coyotes, bobcats, eagles, even prairie dogs were considered varmints and were slated for destruction.

Amid this thinking, in 1914 Congress created the quaintly misnamed Bureau of Biological Survey, a federal effort to get rid of predators. The bureau hired trappers and coordinated eradication campaigns. It used poisoned meat and snares, guns, and steel traps.

One early critic called it "the most destructive organized agency that has ever menaced so many species of our native fauna."[4]

This may seem like just another abuse of the Great Barbecue, and it was. But here is the shocking thing: We are still doing it. The Bureau of Biological Survey over the generations has often provoked public outcry, but it has never gone away. It has only changed its name, becoming an agency called Predatory Animals and Rodent Control, and then Animal Damage Control. Now, as part of the Department of Agriculture, it is called Wildlife Services. Its mission, though, when it comes to lions, has remained relatively unchanged: It kills them. In 2014, Wildlife Services killed 305.

State wildlife agencies, often subsidized by the federal Wildlife Services program, also still kill hundreds of lions. Then there are the hunters regulated by the states. In 2014, in the eleven western states that make up Wild Horse Country, they killed almost 2,800 mountain lions. So, in the West, in 2014, we wiped out at least 3,105 lions.

That number in itself is alarming, but this is the craziest part: The places where the federal government is spending hundreds of millions to round up and store wild horses are often the same places where the federal government is spending piles of tax dollars to kill the lions that would likely eat them. I'm not talking about "the same places" in general, regional terms. I'm talking about the exact same places. Lay out the maps and the two overlap to a surprising degree: Colorado, Utah, Wyoming, Oregon, Idaho, Nevada, and New Mexico all fit the pattern. Only California, where voters outlawed mountain lion hunting, is different.

Not only are government agencies removing lions from wild horse areas, private hunters are also overwhelmingly hunting them there. In many states, the highest number of lion kills come from hunting zones that overlap overpopulated wild horse Herd Management Areas.

Here is what the Nevada Division of Wildlife spent to kill lions in recent years: $70,000 to bait and trap lions in Washoe County, an area that is home to half a dozen wild horse areas; $30,000 to kill lions in the Gabbs Valley and Black Mountain—both wild horse areas. And $50,000 to pay trappers to kill lions as needed in other parts of the state. In 2017, the state proposed to ramp up its lion hunting, spending more than $200,000 on trapping, hunting, and shooting mountain lions from helicopters.

The federal Wildlife Services program had a $121 million budget in 2016, about $30 million of which goes to predator control. It doesn't break out the details of what is spent on killing mountain lions, but it helps fund lion kills across the West.

The economic tangle of killing predators while storing horses is mind-boggling. The Bureau of Land Management warehouses thousands of horses each year. Each of those horses costs on average $50,000 to capture, house, and feed over its lifetime. At the same time, we are spending millions to kill mountain lions in the West. It is fairly safe to say that every dollar spent taking out mountain lions in Wild Horse Country drives up the cost of storing wild horses.

Consider this: If just a fraction of the roughly three thousand mountain lions killed by the government and hunters every year— say, a hundred—were active horse hunters, and each of them killed five foals a summer that would otherwise end up in the storage system, the savings over a lifetime of those horses would be more than $23 million. That is a third of the wild horse program's annual budget. Obviously, the BLM would not see all the savings immediately, but if you repeat that reduction with just a hundred mountain lions every year, pretty soon you are talking about real money.

How many herd management areas could integrate mountain lions into their management plans? It's a great question that has never been asked. The BLM wild horse program has about 160 employees, but not a single biologist who specializes in predators. The BLM has never done a formal survey of what Herd Management Areas might include the necessary criteria for lion predation. It hasn't even asked what those criteria are. BLM wild horse specialists with whom I've talked have repeatedly told me that there are probably almost no places in the West where setting up Montgomery Pass—style wild horse predation is practical. I don't doubt their sincerity, but I think the real answer is that they don't know.

What the work of John Turner and other researchers suggests is that we don't need mountain lions everywhere in the West to make a big difference. A few hundred lions in a third of the wild horse area could fundamentally change the program and save the public hundreds of millions of dollars. We would likely still need some round-ups. We would likely still need PZP. In the short term, we would definitely need both. But we could set a long-term goal of maximizing the predator management wherever possible.

How would we do it? That's far from clear. Managers can start by building on the knowledge that lions hunt foals near water sources in the summer months and likely need to switch to other prey in the winter. The BLM can make a list of areas that fit the criteria. Perhaps the bureau can come up with plans to get herds to move seasonally into the high ground where lions hunt.

Managing horses to migrate would have benefits beyond population control. It might offer a seasonal break to deer and bighorn sheep populations. It would improve the landscape. Studies have shown that a healthy predator population keeps plant-eaters on the move. Horses that might otherwise hang close to their favorite springs would be forced to get a quick drink and then leave. This protects riparian areas, which in Wild Horse Country harbor a stunning array of birds, bugs, snakes, and amphibians. This ripple effect of reintroducing predators is most famously seen in Yellowstone National Park. When the park brought back wolves in 1994, it didn't just cut the deer and elk populations, it led to more grass, which led to more small rodents, which led to better-aerated soil, which led to more abundant flowers and a suddenly robust community of butterflies.

The BLM is in the range management business and often spends a lot of time thinking about quality and variety of grass. But how much time does it spend wondering how that grass is tied to the lion's claws?

Letting mountain lions do what they do is not just about reducing horses or saving money. It is about truly restoring the "thriving ecological balance" that has been the mandate of the BLM for thirty years. It is about learning to let the wild be wild in all its complexity. Right now, wild horses are embattled as a symbol. Whatever they once were, they have become an enfeebled emblem of controversy, cultural divides, mismanagement, and waste. Good management—wild management—could bring them back. If the horse is once again independent, pursued, tough, and free, its original symbolism will be revived. The legend of the White Stallion could be resurrected. It is not too late for the idea that an animal can represent our ideals as a nation, but it will take a broad effort similar to the one that passed the 1971 Wild Free-Ranging Horses and Burros Act.

Restoring the White Stallion through predator management is not an impossible endeavor, but it is far from simple. The BLM does not manage the mountain lions on its land—that is the job of state wildlife divisions. But states often partner with the US Fish and Wildlife Service on projects, and perhaps could be swayed by federal funding incentives, so there is potential for cooperation.

Both BLM and USFWS are part of the Department of the Interior, so the right Secretary of the Interior could encourage them to work together on mountain lions. But it would take a sustained effort—so far, no one is even mentioning it.

From there, it gets trickier. Wildlife Services, which funds mountain lion killing, is part of a separate agency—the Department of
Agriculture. Each department has different bosses, different bud-
gets, and different missions. Getting them to work together would
take serious leadership. It would likely take a strong president and
a willing Congress. Both of them would need sustained public pressure to act.

Then there is political will. Mountain lions have their defenders,
for sure, but they also have plenty of foes. Almost everyone in the
livestock business is dead set against them, and understandably so.
If you think of a rancher's cattle as his bank account, every missing
calf is a robbery. Why would any rancher open himself up to such
theft? But data show the losses are fairly small. In Nevada, according
to a study by Wildlife Services, lions kill an average of 257 cows and
sheep a year. This may seem like a lot, but it is just a fraction of what
is killed by coyotes, and far less even than what is killed by ravens. A
program set up to compensate deserving ranchers might cost far less
than rounding up and storing horses.

Perhaps a bigger hurdle could be hunters. Deer and bighorn sheep
populations in many western states are not growing. The sportsman
lobby has a huge influence over state wildlife agencies that decide
predator control strategies. Their license fees fund most of the management, and they generally favor any policy that will lead to more
game. That means keeping predator numbers low. It is hard to see
how the agencies would favor more mountain lions if it would mean
fewer deer and sheep. I could more easily see ranchers signing off on
the idea. At least for them, mountain lions that might impact their
livestock business would be taking out horses that certainly do. For
sportsmen, it's harder to find the upside.

But maybe there is one: Maybe, as in Yellowstone, encouraging
predators in Wild Horse Country could have positive, unexpected

effects well beyond horses. Wild horses are hardly the only tough wildlife issue in the West. Deer and sheep have been dwindling, even with the predator control programs that have been in place for decades. The sage grouse is also close to endangered. Part of the problem is that the land is out of balance. The land has always had predators, and it can't function properly without them.

To begin exploring predator management, the BLM would need to start with a survey of suitable test sites, then create pilot management programs. It took generations to get rid of most of the predators in the West, so I don't expect welcoming them back would be easy. But, as Lao-tzu said, and the Academy of Sciences seconded: "A journey of a thousand miles begins with a single step."

What will it take? First, money—which the bureau does not have. To fund such an ambitious program, there seem to be two options: Sell the horses in the holding system to slaughter or get Congress to increase the budget. Neither of those are very palatable choices, but neither is the status quo. Second, the BLM must do everything possible to avoid falling into the budgetary trap of storing horses again. That means as it builds a predator program, it has to drastically increase adoptions, drastically increase PZP use, or start euthanizing horses. It might have to do all three.

This leads to a final problem with making the change: The structure of the BLM. The bureaucracy is built in a way that favors a corrosive status quo over bold fixes. The directors of both the Wild Horse and Burro Program and the BLM are always senior civil servants nearing retirement. They have repeatedly shown a tendency to avoid making waves, preferring the low risk of a deteriorating situation to the high risk of a solution that may be controversial or a failure. Many want to maximize their highest three-year average salary and get out. Making a long-term predator plan happen will take a greater commitment and a more courageous leader than the program has so far produced.

The day after we toured Montgomery Pass, Turner and I hiked up a mountain near his camp to get away from the heat. The summit was a bare block of stone ringed by emerald shrubs. From the top, we could see one range of mountains after another, like rows in an auditorium, eventually disappearing into the distant desert haze. Wild Horse Country was on all sides, as far as the eye could see. Herds were out there, foraging in the searing heat, just as they had been since who knows when. In Stone Cabin, Slate Range, High Rock, and Rocky Hills. In Sand Springs, Sand Valley, Sand Canyon. In Black Mountain, Bald Mountain, Dead Mountain. I couldn't see the herds out there, but I knew they were thriving. The eulogies for the mustang in the 1950s had been premature, but their future was far from certain.

As we sat looking out at the distance, I knew that the legend of the mustang—a story we have told and retold about ourselves—wasn't doing so well. We had come a long way from the days of pulp novels, or even Wild Horse Annie. The wild horse was a welfare horse, a contentious creature, a symbol of bureaucracy. But everything needed to revive the legend was still out there in the desert. The question was, What would we do with it?

On that summit, we talked about PZP. Turner had been working on it for thirty years. It worked, but trying to get the BLM to use it had discouraged him. The bureau had chosen instead to pursue a quixotic test that year—spaying mares in the field—and it had been abandoned after lawsuits. There was no real talk of increasing PZP use. "I don't know if it will ever happen," he said. "I thought we could show people it worked and that would be enough, but every year there seems to be new resistance."

As we spoke, the BLM's wild horse management program was

grinding to a halt under the strain of storing horses. The program's citizen advisory board was calling for a total killing of almost fifty thousand horses. The wild horse advocates were suing to stop the PZP program that could offer a solution. The program's leaders were offering little leadership.

As a nation, would we keep storing the horses or kill them? Store them and we'd have to live with the cost. Kill, and we'd have to live with ourselves. Sometimes during my journeys I was in favor of killing the horses. Sometimes I worried that it would just make a bad problem worse. In the end, I knew only one thing: Whatever we decided to do, neither would protect the legend or the wildness unless we found a way to stop relying on roundups. We had to move toward a sustainable future. We needed to reforge the relationship between mountain lions and horses.

A few days after I made the trek home from that summit, I found a yellowed 1906 newspaper clipping with an amazing version of the legend of the White Stallion that seemed to fit perfectly with what Wild Horse Country needed. It seemed to tie the past and present together, and to show the promise of the steep and uncertain path toward welcoming back the wildness in the West that we had spent generations battling. It gave me hope. The piece, published by the writers of *McClure's Magazine*, was an account called "King of the Drove."[5]

It was the story of a valley out in Wild Horse Country during the early days. As long as anyone there could remember, the hills had been run by "a drove of wild horses numbering thirty." The drove was led by a white stallion "whose beauty and fleetness had been the talk of prospectors, trappers and Indians for two years."

The stallion harassed domestic horses and cattle herds, and the stockmen of the area might have shot a lesser animal, but they admired his speed and beauty and wanted to make him theirs. All the ranchers in the valley came together with a plan to catch him.

At sunrise one day, they stationed sixty men on horseback along the valley and forty men on foot with rifles to frighten the stallion away from thickets where he might hide.

"How could a lone horse hope to escape the net to be drawn around him?" the story read.

The horsemen planned to chase the White Stallion in relays the length of the long valley until he was exhausted, then rope him. "As if the plans of men had been whispered in his ear and as if he bade defiance to them and was anxious for the struggle," the stallion appeared at the end of the valley at sunrise to challenge them, and the chase began.

The men chased him fifty miles, but he did not seem to tire. At one point, he grabbed a rider and dragged him in his teeth. The riders pushed after him into the night, but still he ran onward.

"Next morning, as the east was purpling, the horse came out of the dark ravine in which he had rested in safety and kicked up his heels as a challenge," the story went. "Without a nibble at the sweet grass or touching his nose to the waters of the many brooks, he galloped a distance of 120 miles. No pursuing rider came within pistol shot of him. At night he again disappeared, and the opening of the third day saw him as fresh as ever."

For the legend of the White Stallion to work, the horse can never be caught. He *must* never be caught. If he can, he is almost not worth having. He must remain free and independent. Roundups and PZP won't do. Even death is better. He is, in a very real way, the embodiment of that founding American ideal: Liberty.

"Man always kills the thing he loves," Aldo Leopold said, speaking of the West, "and so we the pioneers have killed our wilderness. Some say we had to. Be that as it may, I am glad I shall never be young without wild country to be young in. Of what avail are forty freedoms without a blank spot on the map?"[6]

We've made a mess of our attempt to preserve the mustang, but the wild horse is not dead yet, and doesn't need to be.

Eventually the White Stallion began to tire. The men were closing in on him. It looked hopeless. The narrator then took an unusual path in telling the legend of the White Stallion, by giving the perspective of the fleeing horse: "His enemies were too many for him. His drove had been killed off, and he was all alone to contend with the machinations of man. He might evade them for a few days and remain in the valley where he was born and where he knew every foot of the ground, but in the end he must be captured."

But then the Stallion realized there was another way. There was a pass that led through a narrow gap in the mountains. His herd had always avoided it because of the only thing he knew could catch him: a lion. But now he had to take a chance. A hundred men were right behind him. They had regrouped with their ropes and rifles.

The Stallion accelerated with "a burst of speed that elicited cheers of admiration from the men. They compared it to the flight of a cannon ball. He had ten miles to go to reach the pass, and a bird could hardly have made the distance sooner."

Soon he was at the foot of the mountains. He galloped up and up into the pass, higher and higher. The sides were steep and thick with trees. He could hear the men behind him. The close forest made him uneasy. "He heard the water dripping from the rocky sides. He heard the whine of coyotes and the growl of a wolf that had sneaked into the pass as day broke. He caught the odor of pine and cedar and tried to feel confidence in himself."

He did not like this terrain. He feared what was ahead, but what choice did he have?

What choice, at this point, do any of us have? After pursuing a way to preserve and manage this American legend, the money has been exhausted and the patience is running out, too. We are out of options. Even though we fear what is ahead, we must take the path toward lions.

The White Stallion stepped forward. He could see the land opening on the other side of the pass. He moved to run. Just then, a mountain lion landed on him from above.

"There was no snarling, no growling, no sound of claws against bark to warn the horse. A body suddenly descended on his back, a great paw, struck him a fatal blow to the head, and a fierce-eyed beast stood with his paws on the dead horse and growled defiance at the men who came up the pass. The life of the horse had gone out, but he had not submitted to the thralldom of man."

Acknowledgments

Like anyone who works on reporting in dusty and remote country, I relied on the graceful guidance of many locals who made my work easier, pointed out unmarked roads, warned of washed-out arroyos, and at one point helped me replace the bumper on a pickup. Many thanks to them. Just as important, the Ted Scripps Fellowship in Environmental Journalism at the University of Colorado in Boulder gave me the time, companionship, and first-rate research library to start my work. *Propublica*, *High Country News*, the *Gazette* of Colorado Springs, and the *New York Times* allowed me to continue the reporting that made this book possible. A number of very gracious wild-horse lovers were willing to guide me even though I didn't know a halter from a hat, including Ginger Kathrens, Laura Leigh, and T. J. Holmes. The scientists whose work I relied on, and who were patient and generous with their time, deserve great thanks: Gus Cothran at Texas A&M, Douglas Bamforth at the University of Colorado, and Ken Rose at Johns Hopkins University; and a special thanks to John Turner and his crew who not only showed me Montgomery Pass but also showed me that beer mixed with Gatorade can be a refreshing field ration when the thermometer in Wild Horse Country climbs above 100 degrees. Thanks also to Jay Kirkpatrick, who died during the time when I was writing but whose spirit lives in the growing number of people pursuing wildlife fertility control.

Thanks to Julie Litts Robst, who helped me track down information on her great uncle, Frank Litts, whom she described as a "rather strange man." Thanks to the many people from the Bureau of Land Management who helped in public and private ways to get the information and access I needed, even when it often meant opening the agency to criticism. Thanks to the many reporters whose work I relied on, especially Martha Mendoza of the Associated Press, who did phenomenal work and whose footsteps I followed years later. And a special thanks to my two sons and my wife, who showered me with patience and support, even when it meant long hours away in the desert or sequestered at a keyboard. You mean more to me than I can ever fully express.

Notes

CHAPTER 1. THE DAWN HORSE

1 George Simpson, *Attending Marvels* (New York: Time Inc, 1962), 82.
2 Thomas and Leonard Huxley, *Life and Letters of Thomas Henry Huxley* (London: Macmillan, 1913), 203.
3 Melanie Pruvost et al., "Genotypes of Predomestic Horses Match Phenotypes Painted in Paleolithic Works of Cave Art," *Proceedings of the National Academy of Sciences* (2011).
4 David Meltzer, "The Pleistocene Colonization of the New World," California Academy of Sciences (2003), 30.

CHAPTER 2. RETURN OF A NATIVE

1 Matthew Liebmann, *Revolt: An Archaeological History of Pueblo Resistance and Revitalization in 17th Century New Mexico* (Tucson: University of Arizona Press, 2012), 37.
2 John C. Duval, *Early Times in Texas* (Austin, TX: H. P. N. Gammel & Co., 1892), 12.
3 Mark Van Doren, *100 Poems* (New York: Hill and Wang, 1967), 38.
4 J. Frank Dobie, *The Mustangs* (New York: Bramhall House, 1952), 34.
5 *The Memorial of Fray Alonso de Benavides, 1630* (Albuquerque, NM: Horn & Wallace, 1965).
6 E. Douglas Branch, *Hunting of the Buffalo* (Lincoln: University of Nebraska Press, 1929), 24.
7 William W. Dunmire, *New Mexico's Spanish Livestock Heritage: Four Centuries of Animals, Land, and People* (Albuquerque: University of New Mexico Press, 2013), 43.
8 Ibid., 43.
9 John C. Kwelts, *The Horse in Blackfoot Indian Culture* (Washington, DC: Bureau of American Ethnology, 1955), 9.
10 *A Song for the Horse Nation* (Washington, DC: National Museum of the American Indian, 2011), xxii.

11 Richard K. Young, *The Ute Indians of Colorado in the Twentieth Century* (Norman: University of Oklahoma Press, 1997), 23.

12 Kenneth Kidd, *Blackfoot Ethnography* (Peterborough, ON: Trent University, 1937).

13 George Ruxton, *Adventures in Mexico and the Rocky Mountains* (London: John Murray, 1847), 101–2.

14 Régis de Trobriand, *The Life and Mémoirs of Comte Régis de Trobriand* (New York: E. P. Dutton & Co., 1910), 344.

15 Dobie, *The Mustangs*, 63.

16 George Catlin, *Illustrations of the Manners, Customs, and Conditions of the North American Indians* (London: H. G. Bohn, 1857), 66.

17 George Catlin, *Letters and Notes*, vol. 2, no. 42 (1841; reprint, New York: Dover, 1973).

18 John Ewers, *Horses in Blackfoot Culture* (Washington, DC: Smithsonian Institution Press, 1980).

19 Dobie, 100.

20 *The Journal of Jacob Fowler* (1898; reprint, Minneapolis: Ross & Haines, 1965).

21 Stephen Harding Hart and Archer Butler Hulbert, *The Southwestern Journals of Zebulon Pike* (Albuquerque: University of New Mexico Press, 2007), 236.

22 Ulysses S. Grant, *Personal Memoirs of Ulysses S. Grant* (New York: Charles L. Webster & Co, 1885), 28.

23 Agricultural, Stockraising, and Industrial Association of Western Texas, *A Brief Description of Western Texas* (San Antonio: Herald Steam Printing House & Bindery, 1872), 44.

24 Dobie, 108–9.

CHAPTER 3. THE DOG-FOOD DECADES

1 "Round-up, Ground-up," *Time*, June 17, 1929.

2 *Rockford: The Pet Food Story, 1923–1987* (Rockford Pet Foods Division, Quaker Oats Company), 3.

3 Robert W. Eigell, "Rounding Up Canners for the Corned Beef and Cabbage," *Montana*, vol. 36, no. 4 (Autumn, 1986).

4 Washington Irving, *A Tour of the Prairies* (New York: John W. Lovell Co., 1832).

5 Dobie, 219.

6 Zebulon Pike, *Exploratory Travels through the Western Territories of North America* (London: Longman, Hurst, Rees, Orme & Brown, 1811), 367.

7 Dobie, 141.

8 Vernon Louis Parrington, *Main Currents in American Thought*, vol. 3 (New York: Harcourt, Brace, 1954), 23.

9 Bernard DeVoto, *The Western Paradox* (New Haven: Yale University Press, 2001).

10 Dobie, 316.

11 *New York Times*, May 3, 1888.

12 *New York Times*, January 27, 1889.

13 Ibid.

14 Ibid.

15 *New York Times*, July 27, 1896

16 "A Recent Letter from Sargent, Kansas," *Saline County Journal*, March 5, 1879.

17 *Colorado Transcript*, May 26, 1897.

18 "War on Horses," *New York Times*, December 26, 1884.

19 *San Francisco Call*, December 26, 1903.

20 *Wallace's Monthly*, vol. 15 (1888), p. 39.

21 "To Hunt Wild Horses in Nevada," *San Francisco Examiner*, November 21, 1894.

22 Ibid.

23 *Breckenridge Bulletin*, Colorado, October 28, 1899.

24 Overton Johnston and William H. Winter, *Route across the Rocky Mountains with a Description of Oregon and California, etc., 1843* (1846; reprint, *Quarterly of the Oregon Historical Society*, vol. 7, no. 3 (September, 1906).

25 *Rocky Mountain Sun*, July 7, 1894.

26 "The Horse Hunters," *New York Times*, August 18, 1912.

27 Ibid.

28 *San Francisco Call*, March 30, 1902.

29 "Troops Refused Forestry Bureau," *Lompoc Journal*, November 21, 1908.

30 "Urge War Against Herds of Wild Horses," *Los Angeles Herald*, 1908.

31 *Eureka Sentinel*, 1927.

32 "New Game for Hunters," *New York Times*, July 18, 1920.

33 "Horse-meat," *New York Times*, July 25, 1895.

34 *New York Times*, September 23, 1928.

35 "Wild Horses of the West Are Vanishing," *New York Times*, February 10, 1935.

36 "Expect to Round Up 5,000 Wild Horses," *New York Times*, July 23, 1929.

37 "Buck High Old Paint," *New York Times*, June 3, 1994.

38 Russell Lord, "The Mustang Returns to Europe in Tin Cans," *The Cattleman*, October, 1928.

39 Ibid.

40 Ibid.

41 "In Serious Condition," *Rockford Republic*, December 5, 1925.

42 "World Famous Ken-L Ration Is Made Here," *Rockford Daily Republic*, April 7, 1930.

43 Dobie, 329.

CHAPTER 4. PRINT THE LEGEND

1 Washington Irving, *A Tour of the Prairies* (London: Bell & Daldy, 1866), 96.

2 Ibid., 73.

3 "Frontier Yarns" *Putnam's Monthly Magazine of American Literature, Science, and Art*, vol. 8, no. 47 (November, 1856).

4 Ibid.

5 Herman Melville, *Moby-Dick* (New York: Harper & Brothers, 1851), 181.

6 Dobie, 148.

7 James A. Henretta, Kevin J. Fernlund, and Melvin Yazawa, *Documents in American History*, vol. 2 (Macmillan, 2011), 161.

8 Letter quoted in display at Zane Grey Museum, Lackawaxen, PA.

9 Zane Grey, *The Last of the Plainsmen* (New York: Grosset & Dunlap, 1911), 105.

10 Dolly and Zane Grey, *Letters from a Marriage* (Reno: University of Nevada Press, 2008), 5.

11 "The Evolution of the CowPuncher," *Harper's New Monthly Magazine*, vol. 91 (1895).

12 Ibid.

13 Ibid.

14 Ibid.

15 Ibid.

16 Ibid.

17 Owen Wister, *The Virginian, a Horseman of the Plains* (Macmillan, 1902), 4.

CHAPTER 5. WILD HORSE ANNIE

1 *Popular Mechanics*, October, 1938.

2 "Wild West Showdown," *Sports Illustrated*, May 5, 1975.

3 Dobie, 331.

4 Hope Ryden, *America's Last Wild Horses* (New York: Lyons & Burford, 1990), 226.

5 David Cruise and Alison Griffiths, *Wild Horse Annie and the Last of the Mustangs* (New York: Simon & Schuster, 2010), 41.

6 "Wild West Showdown," *Sports Illustrated*, May 5, 1975.

7 Cruise and Griffiths, 66.

8 Ibid., 75.

9 *Territorial Enterprise*, June 13, 1952.

10 "A Devoted Few Fight to Save Wild Horses," *New York Times*, November 15, 1970.

11 *Nevada State Journal*, February 27, 1955.

12 "The Mustang's Last Stand," *Reader's Digest*, July 1957.

13 Walter Barring obituary, *Las Vegas Review-Journal*, February 7, 1999.

14 Judiciary Committee, House of Representatives, "Treatment of Wild Horse and Burros on Land Belonging to the United States," *Congressional Record*, July 15, 1959.

15 Cruise and Griffiths, 126.

16 "Treatment of Wild Horse and Burros on Land Belonging to the United States."

17 Ryden, 227.

18 Cruise and Griffiths, 238.

19 "One Man's Fight to Save the Mustangs," *True*, April, 1967.

20 Cruise and Griffiths, 239.

21 Aldo Leopold, *A Sand County Almanac* (New York: Oxford University Press, 1949).

22 J. Brooks Flippen, *Nixon and the Environment* (Albuquerque: University of New Mexico Press, 2000), 102.

23 Richard Nixon, *Special Message to Congress on Environmental Quality*, February 10, 1970.

24 *Nowhere to Run*, J/Max Films, 1976.

25 Transcript of hearing, "Protection of wild horses and burros on public lands," Senate Committee on Interior and Insular Affairs, April 20, 1971.

26 Senate Interior and Insular Affairs Committee, "Hearing on the Wild Free-Roaming Horse and Burros Act of 1971," *Congressional Record*, April 19, 1971.

27 Ibid.

28 "Wild West Showdown," *Sports Illustrated*, May 5, 1975.

CHAPTER 6. LIFE UNDER THE LAW

1 Ryden, 237.

2 *Kleppe v. New Mexico*, 1976.

3 "Debate Continues about Future of Wild Horses," *Reno Gazette-Journal*, November 3, 1981.

4 "Federal Government to Kill 6,000 Horses," *Santa Cruz Sentinel*, July 5, 1981.

5 "BLM Cutting Back Adopt-a-Horse Program Subsidy," *Reno Gazette-Journal*, June 25 1981.

6 *Improvements Needed in Federal Wild Horse Program*, Government Accountability Office, August 20, 1990.

7 Ibid.

8 Ibid.

9 "Ranchers, Protectionists War over Future of Wild Horses," *Los Angeles Times*, August 30, 1987.

10 "Report Acknowledges Wild Horses Are Being Slaughtered," *New York Times*, January 29, 1997.

11 "Whistleblowers Claim Abuses Run Rampant in Horse Policy," *Christian Science Monitor*, August 14, 1996.

12 "Report Acknowledges Wild Horses Are Being Slaughtered," *New York Times*, January 29, 1997.

13 "Probe of Wild Horse Slaughter Derailed," Associated Press, March 23, 1997.

14 Ibid.

15 Bureau of Land Management report: "Administration of the Wild Horse and Burro Program, Tenth Report to Congress, fiscal years 1992 to 1995," draft version.

16 *Bureau of Land Management: Effective Long-Term Options Needed to Manage Unadoptable Wild Horses* (Washington, DC: Government Accountability Office, November 10, 2008).

CHAPTER 7. RANGE WARS

1 Richard Symanski, *Wild Horses and Sacred Cows* (Outing, MN: Northland Press, 1985), 136.

2 "Nevada Horses, Victims of Man, Nature," *Los Angeles Times*, October 19, 1991.

3 "Nevada Justice," *Reno Gazette-Journal*, December 25, 1988.

4 "Data Show Few Convictions under Horse Law," Associated Press, August 11, 1997.

5 "BLM Program Questioned," *Reno Gazette*, August 7, 1979.

6 "Agency Padded Report of Convictions under Wild-Free Roaming Horse Act," Associated Press, November 27, 1997.

7 "George Parman on the Wild Horse Situation," www.scottraine.com/Parman.htm, retrieved February 3, 2016.

8   "Wild Horses Ensnared in People's Battles," *New York Times*, July 2, 1989.

9   "Public Lands Ranching: Welfare State in the West," *Watershed Messenger*, Spring 2002.

CHAPTER 8. ALL THE MISSING HORSES

1   "Trail's end for horses: slaughter," Associated Press, January 5, 1997.

2   Statement of Ken Salazar, budget hearing before the Senate Energy and Natural Resources Committee, March 30, 2010.

CHAPTER 9. DISAPPOINTMENT VALLEY

1   Symanski, 208.

CHAPTER 10. A WILD SOLUTION

1   P. D. Greger and E. M. Romney. "High Foal Mortality Limits Growth of a Desert Feral Horse Population in Nevada," *Great Basin Naturalist*, no. 59 (1999): 374–379.

2   "Scientists Tracking Mountain Lion to Find Out Impact on Wild Horses," *Reno Gazette-Journal*, January 8, 2007.

3   Kelley Stewart, "Characterizing Mountain Lion Distribution, Abundance, and Prey Selection in Nevada," University of Nevada, USDA report, 2014.

4   Rosalie Edge, "The United States Bureau of Destruction and Extermination: The Misnamed and Perverted 'Biological Survey,'" pamphlet (Emergency Conservation Committee, 1934).

5   "King of the Drove" (McClure and Phillips Co., December 31, 1905). Reprinted in *The Daily Times* of New Philadelphia, Ohio, January 24, 1907.

6   Leopold, 149.

Illustration Credits

Index

control of grazing on, 201–2, 217
    federal subsidies to ranchers on, 218–20
    number of wild horses vs. number of
        cattle on, 170
Pueblo people, 34–35
    first reaction to Spanish horses, 40
    Oñate's settlers among, 42
    Pueblo Revolt, 36–37, 45–46
    runaways from Spanish ranches, 42
    trade by, 42, 44
    treatment by Spanish conquistadors,
        35–36
Pueblo Revolt, 36–37, 45–46
PZP vaccine, 245–46, 249–64, 291

Quaker Oats Company, 102
Quaternary Extinction, 32

railroads, 71–72, 74
rain shadow, 1–2
ranchers
    after Wild Horse Annie Law, 153–54
    attitude toward BLM, 204, 208
    attitude toward wild horses, 61, 74, 80,
        177–78
    BLM lawsuits by, 177
    on citizen advisory board, 180–81
    destruction of wild horses by, 75–76,
        79–81, 206, 214–16
    early capture of horses by, 205–6
    federal subsidies to, 218–20
    and game of using public lands, 143
    and holding system, 187, 188, 191, 194
    manipulation of law on roundups by,
        147–48
    nuanced understanding of land among,
        199
    and ownership of wild animals, 158–59
    position of wild horse advocates vs., 199
    reactions to Wild Free-Roaming Horses
        and Burros Act, 156–57, 174

roundup strategies of, 79, 82, 147
    sustainable land management by, 204
    on wild horses as escaped livestock, 3
    on wild horses as invasive, 33
range wars, 197–221
    and early capture of horses by ranchers,
        205–6
    and federal subsidies to public land
        ranchers, 218–20
    and government mismanagement of land,
        214, 217–18
    impact of Wild Free-Roaming Horses and
        Burros Act in, 206–14
    importance of water in, 201–2, 209
    and mistrust of government, 207, 215
    and move to slaughter horses in holding
        system, 210–11
    and natural die-off of uncontrolled
        horses, 212–13
    and pre-protection-laws management of
        wild animals, 213–14
    ranchers' destruction of wild horses,
        214–16
    ranchers vs. wild horse advocates'
        positions, 199
reintroduction of wild horses, 34–59
    Americans' records of, 55–57
    from de Soto's expedition, 40–41
    factors in, 37–38
    from Horse Nations' horses, 54–55
    and native tribes' acquisition of horses,
        42–54
    from Oñate's expeditions, 41–42
    and Pueblo Revolt, 36–37, 45–46
    and Spanish conquest/settlement, 36–50,
        52–53
    spread of mustangs through the West,
        36–37
    and spread of war, 37–40
Rin Tin Tin, 84
Robbins, Frank, 132–33